PLAYING

WITH THE

BRIDGE

LEGENDS

BARNET SHENKIN

Master Point Press
331 Douglas Ave
Toronto, Ontario, Canada
M5M 1H2
(416) 781-0351   Internet www.masterpointpress.com

Distributed in the USA by Barricade Books
150 Fifth Avenue, Suite 700
New York, NY 10011
(800) 59-BOOKS

Canadian Cataloguing in Publication Data
Shenkin, Barnet, 1950-
Playing with the bridge legends

ISBN 1-894154-21-5

1. Shenkin, Barnet, 1950- I Title. Bridge players-Biography

GV1282.26 S53A3 2000   795. 41'.5 092   C00-931458-X

Cover design : Olena S. Sullivan
Editor: Ray Lee
Interior formatting and copyediting: Deanna Bourassa

Printed and bound in Canada

1 2 3 4 5 6 7   07 06 05 04 03 02 01 00

Contents

foreword by Zia Mahmood

'm not sure why, but fate has fixed it that I have spent more time discussing bridge with people from Glasgow, Scotland than any other place on earth!

High amongst them are my long-standing (he might say suffering) bridge partner, Michael Rosenberg, and equally long-standing friend, Barnet Shenkin.

I first met Barnet when he was a 'normal' person, a successful businessman with a bridge habit. I would like to think I could take part of the credit for helping him to see the light and convert to being a full-time bridge-bum who left the friendly pastures of Scotland for the savage fields of bridge at the top in America.

As famous for his deep reveries at the table at a crucial moment as for the thoroughness and accuracy of his post-hand analysis, what attracts me about Barnet (and will you here) is his undisguised enthusiasm and passion for the game.

As well as revealing a few of my secrets this book is packed with humorous stories and great hands from the world's best — all in all ideal entertainment for lovers of the expert game.

Zia Mahmood

Foreword by
Michael Rosenberg

I have hundreds of memories (mostly good ones) of my partnership with Barnet. Here are a few of them.

In 1974 we played in the Monte Carlo tournament, both pairs and teams. We played on a team with Rob Sheehan and Andrew Thompson. After working our way through a difficult round-robin, we reached the quarterfinals where we played a strong American team that included Al Roth and the late Johnny Crawford. We beat them and went on to play the Blue Team — Avarelli, Belladonna, Forquet and Garozzo. These men were legends to me, and to Barnet also, although he was more experienced than I. We were leading them at the half, but in the end they proved too good for us. Still, it was a thrill just to play them.

In 1975, we represented Great Britain in the Common Market Championships in Vittel. We played short matches (about ten boards) against each country. I remember playing against one of the strongest teams (I think France, but it may have been Italy). After about six hands we had yet to register a plus score, although we had done nothing wrong. Barnet opened a 12-14 notrump vulnerable, and I had a fair 11-count. I decided to pass to try and go plus. Unfortunately, the opponents took eight tricks for −200 (nothing Barnet could do about it). We still hadn't gone plus going into the last deal and we were dealt a hand in the slam zone. We bid gingerly to 6NT and Barnet made a tough hand (which, sadly, I don't recall). Incidentally, the boards were all flat except the slam and one partscore board, so we won the match.

In the Gold Cup final in about 1976 we were playing against the legendary John Collings. Going into the last eight-board segment we had a comfortable lead of more than 40 IMPs. On the first hand the bidding went pass, pass, 1♠ by Collings. Barnet held a strong hand with five spades and five diamonds. He passed, and it went 3♠ (invitational) pass, pass back to Barnet. Barnet gave Collings a glance. Obviously, if John, who was famous for his 'operations', passed an invitation at this stage in the match, he *must* be psyching. So Barnet doubled. But Collings had his bid — a four-card suit and a twelve-count. In a nail-biting hand, the contract hung in the balance and, at one point, could have been made. But in the end, Collings misguessed and went down one. The match was over.

We represented Great Britain in the European Championships in Copenhagen shortly after that. We were playing with bidding boxes, which were then unfamiliar to me. On one hand it went 'pass' on my right and I opened a 12-14 notrump. Then I looked up a little, and saw the bidding had actually gone 1◊, pass to me! Barnet bid 3♣, and I kept making forcing bids until we reached 6◊. After the auction, Barnet was shaking his head in bewilderment, but he did not allow the unusual circumstances to deflect his concentration. Instead, he played a great hand and made it on a trump coup (see page 26).

Finally, I'd like to say that if Barnet ever tells you 'Four spades is makable' or 'Three notrump can be defeated', I advise you not to argue. In all my years of encountering analysis by players, Barnet has by far the best track record. I pride myself on being an expert analyst, but I know of no-one more accurate than Barnet.

Michael Rosenberg

Author's Foreword

The game of bridge and its characters have proved to be a constant fascination to me for some thirty years or more. There has been nothing like the thrill of playing with or against the world's best players, amongst whom I include my wonderful wife Mags, as she and I have walked the tenuous tightrope of bridge partnership and lived to tell the tale.

As well as playing with Mags, I have also enjoyed playing the occasional tournament with my father, who played international bridge before I was born, and my eleven-year-old son Daniel.

The secret to good bridge results is having a good partner and I have been most fortunate to have played with an excellent group of partners on both sides of the Atlantic. This book tells the many stories of my most exciting or amusing bridge experiences; some of them are fond memories but many are disasters. As well, there are stories about the bridge elite of today, as well as the bridge characters of days gone by.

Try the problem hands, all of which actually occurred in tournaments, or if you're not feeling energetic, just read the accounts of the championships they come from. This is not an instructional bridge book, it is meant to be entertaining and occasionally amusing; I hope it works for you, as I certainly had a good time writing it.

I would like to thank those people who took the time to share their stories with me. I would also like to thank my wife and my family for their support and the friends who supported us in our move across the Atlantic.

Barnet Shenkin

Photo Credits

ACBL:	162
Barnet Shenkin:	16, 19, 39, 66, 106, 113, 115, 179, 182, 186, 226
Chris Cooper:	cover (Chemla) 100, 124, 135, 138, 143, 189
Ray Lee:	cover (Rosenberg, Meckstroth)78, 79, 154, 161, 174, 181, 187, 216, 233
Sheri Winestock	85
Shireen Mohandes:	21, 35, 43, 140, 217, 229

PLAYING WITH THE BRIDGE LEGENDS

The Pursuit of Happiness

C H A P T E R 1

Dreamland

was twenty-four years old. Across the table from me, studying his cards, sat Michael Rosenberg — himself barely twenty. On my left sat Italy's Pietro Forquet, fifteen times a world champion and the man many considered the best player of his era. On my right was Forquet's fellow-countryman Walter Avarelli, a mere twelve-time world champion. The room in which we sat was part of the palatial Monte Carlo casino, the favorite playground of the European aristocracy. Our teammates, London experts Rob Sheehan and Andrew Thomson faced perhaps an even more daunting challenge in their opponents: Giorgio Belladonna and Benito Garozzo. The former owned sixteen world titles, having played on every winning Italian team since the world began. Garozzo owned a mere thirteen, but some thought he might be the best player of all time.

This was the quarterfinal of a knockout teams tournament carrying a big money prize — more than $30,000 to the winners. The year was 1974 and at that time these four players were considered unbeatable — yet after eight boards we led by 31 to 0. A few partscore swings had gone our way and Belladonna-Garozzo had gone down in a slam. Could this be happening? Was it all a dream? Spectators began to gather as news filtered through that the 'invincibles' were in trouble.

Tension mounted as the room began to fill with kibitzers. The first few boards of the second set were even, and then on Board 12 Avarelli had to play this 3NT contract as South:

```
                 Forquet
                 ♠ K J 5 4
                 ♡ K 6
                 ◇ J 8 6 5
                 ♣ Q 10 6

Barnet                            Michael
♠ 9 8 6 3 2       N               ♠ A 7
♡ 7 5 2       W       E           ♡ J 10 8 4 3
◇ A K             S               ◇ 7 3
♣ K 7 2                           ♣ J 9 5 3

                 Avarelli
                 ♠ Q 10
                 ♡ A Q 9
                 ◇ Q 10 9 4 2
                 ♣ A 8 4
```

The ♡5 was led to the ten and ace, and Avarelli led a diamond to my king. Had I played a second heart at that point, he would have had to guess to knock out the ♠A before leading a second diamond. However, as I was uncertain about the position in the red suits, I decided to switch to clubs and tried the effect of the king. Declarer won in hand, and if he had played a second diamond at that point, a second club would have defeated the contract. However, Avarelli chose to play a spade, taking out Michael's entry, and that was that. Perhaps a low club switch by me instead of the king would have been more successful. Assuming declarer ducked, Michael's nine would have forced the ace; now a second low club after I had won the ◇K would have given declarer a nasty guess. As it was, Avarelli's decision to play spades ahead of diamonds put the Italians on the board, and by half-time the gap had narrowed to 34-27.

The World Champions now changed their lineup with Forquet-Garozzo playing against Sheehan-Thompson, while we faced Belladonna-Avarelli. On Board 17 it was Michael's turn to play 3NT on the hand on the right.

Avarelli led the ◇K. Michael won the second round of diamonds, and when he continued with five rounds of clubs, Avarelli threw three spades and a heart before he was squeezed into parting with a diamond. Declarer now simply conceded a spade for his contract. In the other room, Forquet went down on the same defense after misreading the diamond position. We gained 12 IMPs on this deal, and after Board 22 led the match by 53-28.

```
                ♠ Q 9 8 7 3
                ♡ 5 3
                ◇ 9 7
                ♣ A Q 8 5
  ♠ A 10 6 2         N          ♠ J 5
  ♡ Q 10 8 6                    ♡ 9 7 2
  ◇ K Q J 10 2   W       E      ◇ 8 6 4 3
  ♣ —                S          ♣ 6 4 3 2
                ♠ K 4
                ♡ A K J 4
                ◇ A 5
                ♣ K J 10 9 7
```

West	North	East	South
Avarelli	Barnet	Belladonna	Michael
			1♣
dbl	1♠	pass	2♡
pass	3♣	pass	3NT

However on Board 23 our bubble began to burst. Try this as a defensive problem. With both sides vulnerable, you hold

♠ K 9 6 3 2   ♡ 8 3   ◊ 5 4   ♣ K Q 10 8

Your partner opens 1◊ in fourth chair. It goes 2♡ on your right (showing both majors), you pass again and hear four hearts on your left. With this spade holding, you know declarer will be playing a ruffing game so it seems logical to start a trump. You see the layout on the left when the dummy hits the table.

Belladonna
♠ —
♡ Q J 6 4
◊ J 9 6 3 2
♣ A J 3 2

Barnet
♠ K 9 6 3 2
♡ 8 3
◊ 5 4
♣ K Q 10 8

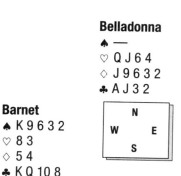

The World Champion on your right wins the first trick in hand, thinks for a few minutes, and then plays a club. You split your honors and he ducks in dummy as partner shows an odd number. You decide to play a diamond before it gets away on the club; partner wins the queen, declarer playing the ten, and partner now exits with a second trump. Declarer wins in hand, finesses the club jack and cashes the ace, throwing a spade from hand. He now ruffs a diamond to hand, and the position reached on the left.

Declarer has made five tricks and now leads the ♠7. What do you play and why?

Belladonna
♠ —
♡ Q J
◊ J 9 6
♣ 3

Barnet
♠ K 9 6 3 2
♡ —
◊ —
♣ K

If you played the ♠9 without understanding the reason, just because you have been presented with the position as a problem, you get no points. It's the right play, but you should understand why it is right. Here is the full hand:

To recap the play, a trump was led and Walter Avarelli took a long time before leading a club at Trick 2. I played the king, which was ducked by declarer. We now cashed our diamond before Michael returned a second trump. Avarelli won in hand, finessed in clubs, cashed the ♣A discarding a spade and ruffed a low diamond in hand, reaching this next position.

Declarer needed five more tricks and led the ♠7. I lazily followed low and declarer *pitched dummy's club* as partner won his ♠J. Michael could not lead a high diamond now, since declarer would ruff and make an extra trick by taking a ruffing finesse with dummy's ◊J9. So he returned the ♠A, which was ruffed in dummy. Another diamond ruff and a ruffing finesse in spades set up the tenth trick.

In making the play he did, declarer was hoping that East

Belladonna
♠ —
♡ Q J 6 4
◊ J 9 6 3 2
♣ A J 3 2

Barnet
♠ K 9 6 3 2
♡ 8 3
◊ 5 4
♣ K Q 10 8

```
      N
  W       E
      S
```

Michael
♠ A J 5
♡ 7 5
◊ A K Q 8 7
♣ 9 5 4

Avarelli
♠ Q 10 8 7 4
♡ A K 10 9 2
◊ 10
♣ 7 6

Belladonna
♠ —
♡ Q J
◊ J 9 6
♣ 2

Barnet
♠ K 9 6 3 2
♡ —
◊ —
♣ 8

```
      N
  W       E
      S
```

Michael
♠ A J 5
♡ —
◊ K Q 8
♣ —

Avarelli
♠ Q 10 8 7
♡ A 10
◊ —
♣ —

held the ♠AJ9 alone, in which case the contract would be unbreakable. On the actual hand, I could have beaten the contract by covering the ♠7 with the ♠9, which prevents the endplay on East. Covering the ♠7 really was a no-cost play... When I didn't cover, Avarelli's game contract slipped through while in the other room Forquet was allowed to play in 4♠ undoubled three down on our cards, for 10 IMPs away.

That was the key moment, perhaps, the beginning of the end for us. Over the last eight boards the tide turned for good, due to a good slam bid by Belladonna-Avarelli and two very thin games reached by Garozzo-Forquet. A further couple of partscore swings in their direction left them winners by 33 IMPs. We had given them a fright, but that was all; they had been so strong when the going got tough. We went back to our hotel most disconsolately. Michael and I were sharing a room and I remember him yelling at me "How could you let those four old men beat us?" I actually still think he had no idea who they were. Either that or he didn't care.

The Italians went on to win the big money prize, of course. On the way back to Scotland, I happened to run into Walter Avarelli at Nice airport. He walked over to me and said "You youngsters play good bridge. Keep practicing and you'll be like us one day."

Fat chance, I thought, despite the kind words of encouragement.

I first met Michael Rosenberg when we were both schoolboys in Glasgow. At the age of twelve he was outplaying the seniors on the chess team and therefore was not too popular with the older, established players. By the time he was twenty he had been playing bridge seriously for only a couple of years but was already on the Scottish international team. Young, ambitious and looking for adventure, we packed our bags and headed for the Teams event in Monte Carlo that I have just described. It proved to be the start of what was to be a most successful partnership.

A young Barnet

After winning the Harrison-Gray, a British tournament for players under twenty-six, we were selected to play for the senior Great Britain side in the Common Market Championships in Vittel, France. Actually, all the members of that team were under twenty-six, and Michael was a mere twenty-one. The hotel that had been booked for us was only average and we had to hunt around for good food. I remember visiting Sam Leckie, the captain of the British Junior team, who was feasting every night at the Club Mediterranée, the five-star hotel at which he was staying. He invited me to join him for a few meals — "Just pretend you are staying here," he whispered!

Most of the countries had their top teams out for this event, but we played well, and our team was still in the running for a medal when we played Italy. Here was our chance to get some revenge for Monte Carlo. In the second half, our captain played Michael and me against Belladonna and Garozzo, probably at the time the outstanding pair in the world. It's nice to recall that we actually got slightly the better of them and won the match 17-3 to secure third place. Michael made a nice defensive play on this hand.

Garozzo declared 3♠ and I led a trump. He won in hand and led a diamond to the king. When that held, he crossed back to hand with a second trump to lead the ◇J. Not sure of where the queen was, I won and shifted to the ♡5. Benito called for the nine and let

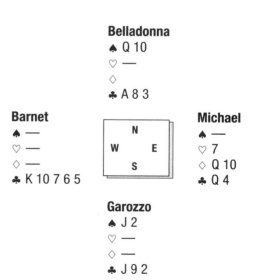

Belladonna
♠ Q 10 7 5 4
♡ J 9 4
◇ K 7
♣ A 8 3

Barnet
♠ 6 3
♡ K Q 5
◇ A 9 3
♣ K 10 7 6 5

Michael
♠ 9 8
♡ 10 8 7 2
◇ Q 10 6 5 4
♣ Q 4

Garozzo
♠ A K J 2
♡ A 6 3
◇ J 8 2
♣ J 9 2

Michael's ten hold the trick. A second heart was taken by declarer who now ruffed his last diamond before exiting with his last heart. I won and switched to a low club in the position just below.

When I shifted to the club, no sooner had Benito called for the ace than Michael dumped his queen, allowing me to win the last two club tricks. While Benito was thinking, he had seen immediately that he had to get rid of that queen to avoid the endplay.

The national newspapers reported our bronze medal performance, noting the outstanding play of the youngest player, Michael Rosenberg.

Belladonna
♠ Q 10
♡ —
◇
♣ A 8 3

Barnet
♠ —
♡ —
◇ —
♣ K 10 7 6 5

Michael
♠ —
♡ 7
◇ Q 10
♣ Q 4

Garozzo
♠ J 2
♡ —
◇ —
♣ J 9 2

Michael and I were selected for the Scottish team in 1976 and to our delight got one of the prized invitations to play in Britain's most famous pairs event — the *Sunday Times* Invitational (now the Macallan). This was an event where about two or three British pairs competed in an international field containing many of the world's best players. Film star Omar Sharif was also often invited. Naturally, Omar was a big box-office draw, but he was also an excellent player; that year he was playing with Christian Mari, one of France's truly great players, who has won both the Bermuda Bowl and the Olympiad. Also in the field were Sam Stayman and Matthew Granovetter (he and his wife Pamela were later to become close friends of mine), Gabriel Chagas and his partner Assumpçao, and many other fine pairs. The format involved head-to-head matches between pairs, scored across the field using IMPs, which were then converted to Victory Points for a match result.

Although most people wished us well, not a lot was expected of us and it was reported to me that one of the English women players had bet that we would finish last! I bought a new red smoking jacket from Gieves and Hawkes, a top tailor in Savile Row, London, and Michael wore a black tuxedo. The tournament started on Friday and ran through Sunday, at the prestigious Churchill Hotel in the West End of London. On the Friday night Harold Franklin, the chief tournament director not only of this event but of many World Bridge Federation events, introduced us to a packed crowd: "Shenkin-Rosenberg, at twenty-five and twenty-one the youngest pair ever to play in this event." I remember most of the other players giving us a cheer of encouragement.

Well, the tournament went well for us and we were always in contention. In Round 10 I held:

♠ **A K Q 6 5**   ♡ **K 6 3**   ◇ **Q 9**   ♣ **9 8 6**

With both sides vulnerable, the bidding started with 1NT (12-14) on my right. I said double, which was for penalties, and LHO ran to 2♠. Now Michael said double, which by agreement was for takeout and showed either one or two spades. We had learned this method from a touring USA team a year or so earlier and incorporated it in our system. Well, I certainly knew what to do now — I passed and collected a sweet 1100 against our partscore. How lucky we were to have that bid in our armory!

It turned out that the key match for us was against the top Israeli pair Frydrich-Shaufel, who later that year placed third in the Bermuda Bowl. Here is the hand which was to decide the championship:

I led the ♠2 and Julian Frydrich won the ♠5 in hand and studied for a short while before playing the ♡A. Immediately, I played the king under it! Having read about this kind of position (I think in one of Terence Reese's books), I was ready to make the actual play at the table. Well, poor Frydrich agonized over his next play for at least ten minutes. Nobody moved, nobody spoke, and finally and inexplicably, he went down. I don't remember the exact line he took but I think he led a club from his hand.

```
                  ♠ Q 9 6 3
                  ♡ Q 10 6 4 3
                  ◇ A Q 3
                  ♣ 7
♠ 10 8 7 2             N           ♠ 4
♡ K 7           W         E        ♡ J 9 5 2
◇ K 8 6               S            ◇ J 10 9 7
♣ Q J 4 3                          ♣ A 9 6 2
                  ♠ A K J 5
                  ♡ A 8
                  ◇ 5 4 2
                  ♣ K 10 8 5
```

West Barnet	North Shaufel	East Michael	South Frydrich
pass	pass	pass	1NT
pass	2♣	pass	2♠
pass	4♠	pass	pass
all pass			

I do remember Michael looking on in amazement as declarer could only garner nine tricks. If I had played a low heart instead of the

Michael Rosenberg (left) and Barnet during the 1976 Sunday Times *Pairs, playing against French stars Leon Tintner and Leon Yallouze*

king, and Frydrich had continued with another heart, he would have an easy three heart winners, along with two diamonds and five trumps (via a heart ruff in hand). He was the only declarer to go down in 4♠, and we picked up a game swing and won the match 15-5. As a result, we were now leading the tournament going into the last round and had to play Berah and Vernon from Venezuela.

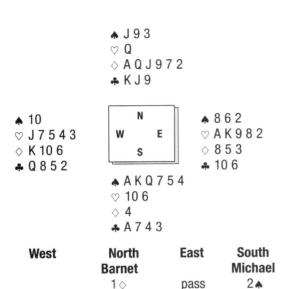

♠ J 9 3
♡ Q
◇ A Q J 9 7 2
♣ K J 9

♠ 10
♡ J 7 5 4 3
◇ K 10 6
♣ Q 8 5 2

♠ 8 6 2
♡ A K 9 8 2
◇ 8 5 3
♣ 10 6

♠ A K Q 7 5 4
♡ 10 6
◇ 4
♣ A 7 4 3

West	North Barnet	East	South Michael
	1◇	pass	2♠
pass	3♠	pass	4♣
pass	4◇	pass	5♠
pass	6♠	all pass	

The very last board of the match and the tournament was the one on the left.

We were always aggressive bidders. Here Michael forced in spades and then asked me to bid a slam with a heart control, and so I did. With the cards behaving kindly, Michael wrapped up twelve tricks. Not everyone had bid the slam, so we earned a swing which won us the match 13-7. We finished with 185 Victory Points, while Frydrich-Shaufel were second with 179, only six back. Had it not been for that one 4♠ hand, they would have won.

Like most young bridge players, we had started the event confident of our own abilities, but it had to be admitted that winning the *Sunday Times* was a success even we had not expected. Curiously, since my dad was chairman of the British Bridge League at the time, he got to present us with the trophy! Nowadays the Macallan Invitational Pairs carries a substantial cash prize but at that time there was no money, only the cup. We didn't care, though — we had won and that was what mattered. We got more good news, too, as Harold Franklin invited us to go to Philadelphia in the summer to play in a Great Britain-USA challenge match as part of the American Bicentennial celebrations.

On the Monday following the Sunday Times, I flew back to Glasgow still in a daze. My real job was working in my father's carpet business, and that week I had many clients to meet and greet at a major trade show. However, our bridge win got a big write-up in Scotland's main newspaper and after that a well-known sports journalist arrived at the carpet show to interview me for Scottish Television! What a weekend!

The rest of the year was not too bad either. As members of the Scottish team, we defeated our arch-rivals England and won the Camrose Trophy, the championship of the four home countries. We also teamed up with my friends Patrick Jourdain-Victor Goldberg and English stars Tony Priday–Claude Rodrigue to win the Gold Cup, Britain's major Teams Championship. It was not all roses though. After leading in our national team trials for the Olympiad we blew our lead and lost on the last board. We would not be going to Monte Carlo to play in that important event, and would have no chance to end the year by winning a world championship. As it turned out, the British Team finished third after having made a good challenge for the gold medal, which was won by Brazil. I often wonder what would have happened if Michael and I had made the team.

In July, 1976 we headed off to the USA for the special Bicentennial challenge match. Michael had been born in the States, despite growing up in Scotland, but it was my first trip. First I spent a few days in Springfield, Massachusetts with Bill August, with whom I had made friends a couple of years before in Monte Carlo. I was surprised that the surroundings were so green and fresh — like Scotland, in a way. I flew from Springfield to Philadelphia, where a special Regional coincided with the Bicentennial celebrations.

Playing for the Redcoats team in the big match along with Michael and myself were Priday and Rodrigue. The team from USA was Edgar Kaplan-Norman Kay and Bobby Goldman-Mark Blumenthal, along with Arthur Robinson-Robert Jordan, a pair who had retired from bridge but had been one of the strongest in USA. There were more than 300 spectators watching on VuGraph. We took an early lead in the match and led by five at the half. Alan Truscott's daily column in the *New York Times* featured the following two hands.

Tony Priday

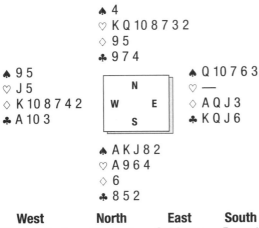

```
                    ♠ 4
                    ♥ K Q 10 8 7 3 2
                    ♦ 9 5
                    ♣ 9 7 4
♠ 9 5                               ♠ Q 10 7 6 3
♥ J 5            N                  ♥ —
♦ K 10 8 7 4 2   W     E            ♦ A Q J 3
♣ A 10 3            S               ♣ K Q J 6
                    ♠ A K J 8 2
                    ♥ A 9 6 4
                    ♦ 6
                    ♣ 8 5 2
```

West	North	East	South
Blumenthal	**Michael**	**Goldman**	**Barnet**
	2◇¹	pass	2NT²
pass	3♣³	3♡	4♡
pass	pass	dbl	all pass

1. A weak two in one of the majors or 17-24 HCP, 4-4-4-1.
2. Enquiring.
3. Weak two in hearts.

One of the great weapons in our bidding arsenal at that time was the Multi 2◇, which we played as either a weak two in a major or a strong (17-24 points) 4-4-4-1 hand. Contrary to what many Americans think, this convention did not originate in the USA but was invented by England's Jeremy Flint in the early 1970s. Its effectiveness had been demonstrated when Garozzo-Forquet went astray over it during the 1972 Olympiad and played in a 2-2 fit. At that time, Multi was a huge points winner mainly because pairs had no organized defense against it, and tended to wait to see what happened as the auction developed. This was entirely the wrong approach, because sometimes by then it was too late! In 1976, although Multi had been around for a few years, it was still brand new in the USA and defenses had not been properly discussed.

On this deal, we were always going to play in game even opposite the weak-two hand, but I checked in case Michael had the strong version. I don't know if Bobby Goldman and his partner had discussed a defense but his 3♡ bid was quite clear and Mark Blumenthal should surely have bid 5◇, which makes easily. In the other room, 5◇ was the contract for 600 to our team. As sometimes happens, Goldman, who knew the heart length was on his right, now led the ♣K out of turn against four hearts doubled! I was able to require Blumenthal to lead any suit but clubs, and unfortunately for his side he picked spades. Perhaps there was an ethical consideration, since he knew his partner did not hold the ♠AK from his opening lead out of turn, and therefore had a clue that diamonds would be right, but he did not take any advantage of this information. When Goldman later let go a spade, I made twelve tricks for 1190 and 17 IMPs.

The match was close throughout and the USA led by 11 IMPs going into the last hand.

Unfortunately for Tony, his partner held no defensive tricks and 5♡ doubled made in comfort. In our room on VuGraph I liked my hand and knew we were behind. If Michael had held the ♣10 the slam would have been almost a 50-50 shot. In fact, if the West and East clubs had been interchanged we would have made the slam and won the match, but unfortunately for us, they were not and I had to go one down for the loss of 14 IMPs. USA had won a hard-fought but very enjoyable match by 25 IMPs.

The hospitality had been excellent and Michael and I had had a great time. Perhaps too great a time — in retrospect, the seeds had been sown for Michael's

```
              ♠ A J 7 5
              ♡ Q 8 3
              ♦ 4
              ♣ Q 9 8 4 3
♠ 10 9 4 2                    ♠ K Q 8 6 3
♡ 9 5 4          N            ♡ 6
♦ A K 7 6     W     E         ♦ Q 9 5 3 2
♣ K 7            S            ♣ 10 5
              ♠ —
              ♡ A K J 10 7 2
              ♦ J 10 8
              ♣ A J 6 2
```

West Priday	North Kay	East Rodrigue	South Kaplan
			1♡
pass	3♡	3♠	4♣
4♠	dbl	pass	5♡
dbl	all pass		

West Blumenthal	North Michael	East Goldman	South Barnet
			1♡
pass	1NT[1]	pass	2♣
pass	3♦[2]	pass	3♠
pass	4♡	pass	4♠
pass	5♡	pass	6♡
all pass			

1. 1NT forcing.
2. 3♦ showed club support with a singleton diamond.

future move across the Atlantic, not to mention mine. I had made many new friends and went on to New York to spend a very pleasant few days at the home of Edgar and Betty Kaplan. I had a chance to sample Edgar's famous cocktails and at the same time see the bright lights of Manhattan.

In January of the following year, Michael and I played again in the Sunday Times. My son Jonathan had been born earlier in the week and I was in good spirits, but lightning was not fated to strike twice. Perhaps we were not quite as lucky as we had been the previous year and we probably made more mistakes. We were in contention most of the way, and ended up a disappointing sixth behind Svarc and Boulenger of France. I did get the opportunity to shine on one hand when I held:

♠ J 9 3　♡ Q 10 8 5　◇ A Q 9 4　♣ K 8

Tony Priday on my left opened 1♣, Michael passed, Rodrigue bid 1♠ and I passed. Now Priday raised to 4♠ and everyone passed. What would you lead?

Who knows what is right? It could be a heart, but I knew my partner had little on the bidding. I suspected good clubs on my left and so I hit on the lead of the ♣8.

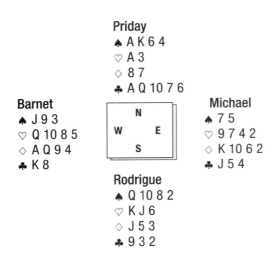

Priday
♠ A K 6 4
♡ A 3
◇ 8 7
♣ A Q 10 7 6

Barnet
♠ J 9 3
♡ Q 10 8 5
◇ A Q 9 4
♣ K 8

Michael
♠ 7 5
♡ 9 7 4 2
◇ K 10 6 2
♣ J 5 4

Rodrigue
♠ Q 10 8 2
♡ K J 6
◇ J 5 3
♣ 9 3 2

Rodrigue studied the hand awhile and called for the ♣A. He could visualize two club losers and decided to try for a diamond discard on the ♡K by cashing the ♡A and leading a heart to the jack. I was able to win the ♡Q and, of course, I should now have cashed the ◇A and the ♣K and led a diamond to Michael's king to get a ruff for down two. However, the diamond position was still not completely clear to me and I passively returned a trump. Declarer won in dummy and, still sure that the clubs were bad for him, took a diamond discard on the ♡K before leading a club. Now I was able to win my ♣K (noting the surprise on declarer's face) and underled my ◇A to Michael's king. When he returned a club, I got my ruff and declarer had gone down in a seemingly unbreakable contract!

Again that year, Scotland took the lead in the Camrose and we had to play three short matches against a strong English team in Newcastle. It was the only occasion in which a husband and wife played on an English team against me — Tony Priday was a European Champion and Jane Priday had won the Women's Olympiad Teams. We won the first match by 21 IMPs and we were in front in the second when Michael and I had a set from hell and dumped 50 IMPs to lose a blitz. Now everything depended on the Sunday match which was decided by this slam:

How would you play 6♠ on the lead of two top diamonds?

The trick is to combine the chances of both the heart suit and the club suit in case clubs do not break well. I ruffed the diamond in hand and played one high trump, all following. Then I cashed the ace and king of hearts, and ruffed a heart with the ten, again all fol-

♠ Q J 5 3
♡ A K 8 7 3
◇ 10 6
♣ A 3

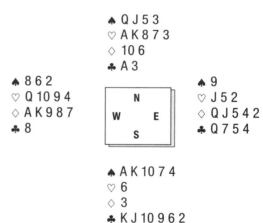

♠ A K 10 7 4
♡ 6
◇ 3
♣ K J 10 9 6 2

lowing suit. A club to dummy's ace and another heart ruff with the ♠K set up dummy's long heart. Now I led my ♠7 to dummy, drawing trumps to claim. This hand is a good example of taking an extra chance when you possibly can and also of not drawing trumps before you can see your contract home.

In the other room, declarer played the same contract from North's hand, and after the ◇A and a heart switch, strangely did not have the entries to ruff three red cards in dummy and had to put all his eggs in the club basket. When the hand with one club had three trumps, he was down.

As a result of this swing, we won the third match and although we

♠ Q J 5 3
♡ A K 8 7 3
◇ 10 6
♣ A 3

♠ 8 6 2
♡ Q 10 9 4
◇ A K 9 8 7
♣ 8

♠ 9
♡ J 5 2
◇ Q J 5 4 2
♣ Q 7 5 4

♠ A K 10 7 4
♡ 6
◇ 3
♣ K J 10 9 6 2

lost the three matches by a small amount in aggregate, we had done enough to win a second successive Camrose Trophy.

Michael and I did get our chance to play for Great Britain that summer in the European Championships in Denmark. Unfortunately none of our three pairs produced their best form and our team finished well down the field. There was one amusing incident when we were playing with bidding boxes for the first time. My hand was:

♠ K ♡ K Q ◇ A 10 9 4 3 2 ♣ A K 8 4

I opened 1◇, Michael bid 1NT and I bid 3♣. Michael then bid 3♡ showing values and I bid 4◇ which was raised to 6◇. West led the ♡7,

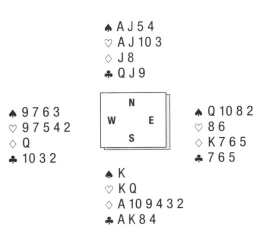

♠ A J 5 4
♡ A J 10 3
◇ J 8
♣ Q J 9

West
♠ 9 7 6 3
♡ 9 7 5 4 2
◇ Q
♣ 10 3 2

East
♠ Q 10 8 2
♡ 8 6
◇ K 7 6 5
♣ 7 6 5

South
♠ K
♡ K Q
◇ A 10 9 4 3 2
♣ A K 8 4

West	North Michael	East	South Barnet
		pass	1◇
pass	1NT (!)	pass	3♣
pass	3♡	pass	4◇
pass	6◇	all pass	

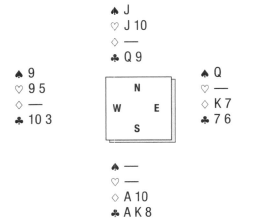

♠ J
♡ J 10
◇ —
♣ Q 9

West
♠ 9
♡ 9 5
◇ —
♣ 10 3

East
♠ Q
♡ —
◇ K 7
♣ 7 6

South
♠ —
♡ —
◇ A 10
♣ A K 8

and picture my surprise when Michael put down fourteen points for his non-forcing 1NT bid. He had not seen my opener and thought he was making an opening bid!

The opening lead was the ♡7, which I won in dummy in order to pass the ◇J. West won the ◇Q and switched to a spade. Still wanting to be in dummy, I rose with the ace (unusual for declarer to squander both the ace and king of a suit twice in the first three tricks) to pass the ◇8. When this exposed the 4-1 trump break, a spade was ruffed in hand, and a club to the jack was followed by another spade ruff. After cashing the ♡K, the position on the left had been reached.

Now came the *coup de grace* when two top hearts were played from dummy, pitching the ace and king of clubs from hand. If East ruffed it would be to no avail as my hand was high. We actually gained a rather lucky 15 IMPs on the board.

Michael departed Scotland for the USA shortly after the European Championships and I was left to find a new partner. However we did play one last event.

Early in 1978, I received an invitation to play in the Cavendish Invitational Pairs in New York. Naturally, I called Michael who was living there to see if he was interested and now here I was in the month of May strolling the streets of Manhattan. The sun was shining and I was walking down Fifth Avenue when I spotted a young man who was shuffling three cards on a small table. "Find the lady, find the lady," he chanted as people were throwing all sorts of bills on the table. I looked and I could see where the queen was — sure enough I would have won. So, the next time I took out a five-dollar bill and threw it on the table beside the queen. He looked down at me and said in a derisory voice, "Hey man, we don't take five-dollar bets on Fifth Avenue". So I put down a ten and surprise, surprise, I lost. I never did find out where that damned queen went.

The Cavendish (which these days is a multi-million dollar event held in Las Vegas) is a Calcutta, where players and onlookers bid auction-style to own a share in the success of competing pairs. After an elegant cocktail reception on the Thursday night, the forty participating pairs were auctioned. The highest bid of around $25,000 was for Eisenberg and Cayne, while Shenkin-Rosenberg were sold for $7000 to someone named Bob Hamman. There were players' pool prizes which came from the entry monies but the big prize pool of some $400,000 came from the prices paid in the auction. Whoever owned the winning pair would receive more than $100,000 while the second prize was to be around $50,000.

Michael and I took the lead early and were well ahead going into the last session. Again we were headliners in Alan Truscott's column in the *New York Times*, and I had visions of being met when I got back to Scotland by more television cameras! 'Young Scottish Pair Raid USA' — what a headline. But we had still one more session to play.

We went through a sticky patch in the middle of the last session but recovered well and were still in the lead going into the very last board. I looked at my cards and saw:

♠ K 8 4　♡ 6　◇ Q J 7 4　♣ K 8 7 6 5

It went 1♡ on my left, 1♠ on my right, 4♡ on my left. The young man on my right started to think, and as I noticed Edgar Kaplan walk behind me to watch, my brain was going 100 miles an hour. What was I going to do if he cuebid 5♣? We had worked on our lead-directional doubles. I knew my ♠K was a likely trick — should I try to keep them out of slam? But what if they bid it and Michael had the ◇K, and a club lead let them make it? I saw him pull out the 5♣ bid and I was there smoothly with my pass. If they bid it, let Michael find the lead.

The next bid was 6♡, and everyone passed. Some thought from Michael, and then the opening lead — the ◇5. My heart jumped. He had the king!

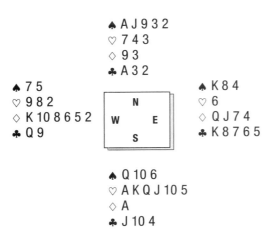

♠ A J 9 3 2
♡ 7 4 3
◇ 9 3
♣ A 3 2

♠ 7 5
♡ 9 8 2
◇ K 10 8 6 5 2
♣ Q 9

♠ K 8 4
♡ 6
◇ Q J 7 4
♣ K 8 7 6 5

♠ Q 10 6
♡ A K Q J 10 5
◇ A
♣ J 10 4

Declarer won my jack with his ace, drew trumps and ran the ♠Q to my king. I quickly returned a diamond and watched in horror as declarer ruffed and claimed. We got up silently from the table suspecting the worst. Shortly afterwards, it was confirmed that we had lost — we were second. If they had stayed out of the slam, or had gone down on a club lead, we would have won. I had blown the whole event with my deep thinking. Why could I not just have doubled 5♣ as 90% of all other bridge players would have?

Should Michael have found the $50,000 lead anyway? Maybe. A six-card suit was not attractive to lead from, but on the other hand, his partner had not doubled 5♣. He might just have saved us as he so often did, but not this time, and so there would be no television cameras waiting! When people ask me if there's anything I would like to change in my past life I always say "Please let me double 5♣!" However, the full story of this hand wasn't clear to me until more than twenty years had gone by. Recently I was at the Summer Nationals in Chicago and this guy came up to me and said, "Remember me? My partner and I bid 6♡ against you in the last round of the Cavendish in 1978." I looked at him as if I had just seen a ghost. "Yes," he carried on, "and you cost us a lot of money."

"*I* cost *you* a lot of money?" I spluttered.

"We owned 10% of you and we were young students and needed the money. You should have doubled 5♣," he said, "and then we would not have bid the slam. And you would have won. I calculated it out," he went on, "exactly how much it cost us."

He made my day.

CHAPTER 2

Back to the Beginning

I n Scotland when I was growing up, bridge tournaments were called 'congresses', and they used to be held in magnificent five-star hotels. My dad, who was himself an international player, took me along with him from when I was about six and that is probably when the bridge bug first bit. I had a good time and probably associated the idea of bridge with having a lot of fun — how times have changed!

At nine I bought my first bridge book, a copy of Howard Schenken's *Big Club* — perhaps I thought he was a distant uncle. It was difficult for a nine-year-old to play much in those days, so mostly I read and watched. By the time I was fourteen, I had convinced my cousins and a couple of school friends to play. We had an old set of boards and used to play a session of twenty-four hands. Two weeks later we would play the same hands but in opposite directions, so effectively we were our own teammates — something I discovered in later life to be the unfulfilled dream of many an expert bridge player.

I began to play in the local duplicate and on Sundays became a regular at rubber bridge for two shillings a hundred. That was about twenty cents (although perhaps rather more if you take inflation into account) and I actually did not know how much we were playing for until someone handed me some money — which was very useful for a fourteen-year-old. The local bridge club was run by Albert Benjamin and his wife Judy. Scotland's leading players used to have supper there between the rubber game and the duplicate tournament every Sunday. This group included the expert but volatile partnership of Sam Leckie and Victor Goldberg (Goldberg described his partner as 'a legend in his own mind') as well as Victor Silverstone and Willie Coyle. I learned a lot by watching these four play. They were young for bridge players by the standards of the time and used the methods played by Jeremy Flint and Peter Pender, who in 1966 had formed a brief partnership and successfully stormed the US tournament circuit. In 1969 my four friends became the first team from north of the border ever to win the Gold Cup, the major team championship of the UK.

At seventeen, I started a BA course at the University of Strathclyde in Glasgow, but fortunately or unfortunately, I found that the small format of *The Bridge World* magazine made it ideal for unobtrusive reading at the occasional lecture that I did attend. Every day, after perhaps going to one class, I would take the short bus ride over to the University of Glasgow and play rubber bridge. The standard was high and the players were sharp. The university A Team included alumni Coyle and Silverstone, and other pairs just under international standard. Glasgow had six divisions in its IMP league, and University of Glasgow A were always in the running for the championship. My first league partner was Cam McLatchie; we started off playing in the third division but soon graduated to the first.

In 1970 I went with a friend to Stockholm to watch the World Championships and was able to watch my heroes, the young Aces led by Eisenberg and Hamman, win their first world teams title. However, for some reason there was no *squadra azzurra* from Italy that year and so the Aces still had an important ghost to lay to rest before they could feel that they were the real champions. For much of the World Open Pairs, I followed another of my heroes, Benito Garozzo as he played brilliantly with a client, eventually missing first place only by a fraction. I also kibitzed my friends Coyle and Silverstone playing against Rubin and Westheimer from the USA. Ira Rubin, who was dressed in a black pinstripe suit, had a tremendous aura at the table and towered over everyone. He looked like a Chicago gangster, and his menacing presence seemed to unsettle his opponents in a similar fashion. When I sat down, he immediately ordered me to watch only one player's cards. Then disaster struck when Silverstone dropped a card on the floor and by the time he had picked it up, found that his partner had revoked! Later someone told me that Rubin was nicknamed 'The Beast'.

That was my first taste of international competition, and soon afterward, I got together with George Cuthbertson in the Scottish Junior team to win the Junior home internationals. George and I were then selected to the British team for the 1970 European Junior Championships in Delft, Holland. Junior bridge then was much like it is today, wild and exciting. Here are a few typical hands from the period, the first being from the Junior Europeans in Delft. Our captain for this event was the same Albert Benjamin mentioned earlier who, at that time, also captained the Scottish Open team. It was the first match in Holland, we were playing Germany and *el capitaine* Albert was watching. I held:

♠ K J 8 6 2   ♡ —   ◇ J 8 6 5 4 2   ♣ Q 9

Both sides were vulnerable and the guy on my right deposited the

6♡ card on the table. I blinked and passed and this was promptly raised to 7♡. Not having encountered an auction like this in my short bridge career and determined not to be left out, when it came back to me, I felt this strange force making me bid 7♠. Well, that was what I was planning to tell the captain if it all went horribly wrong. It went double on my left, and everyone passed. The opening lead was a low trump and George put down his beautiful dummy.

I lost one diamond, one trump and two clubs — down four for minus 1100. Our teammates (not mentioning any names but one was Phillip Alder, now a nationally syndicated bridge columnist) arrived at only 6♡ after a misunderstanding, but we still won 6 IMPs.

George
♠ Q 10 9 5 3
♡ J 4
◇ K Q 7
♣ J 8 7

♠ A 7 4
♡ 7
◇ A 10 9 3
♣ A 10 6 4 2

```
      N
  W       E
      S
```

♠ —
♡ A K Q 10 9 8 6 5 3 2
◇ —
♣ K 5 3

Barnet
♠ K J 8 6 2
♡ —
◇ J 8 6 5 4 2
♣ Q 9

Albert was pleased with the result and later wrote the hand up commenting on my having made a very brave bid. On looking back, I see it as a very lucky bid which would not bring much sympathy from today's teammates were it to misfire. But anyway, who opens 6♡ except a junior? Many of the young players from that tournament are today's stars — the French team included Michel Perron (now a world champion and one of the finest French players over the last twenty years) and Michel Abecassis (a European champion and good friend). The Israeli team included Sam Lev, a superb player who would later move to the USA and become a partner of mine.

Another wild hand came up in a Scotland-England match in the Junior home internationals. Scotland was 22 IMPs behind going into this hand, and about a hundred spectators were watching the VuGraph show.

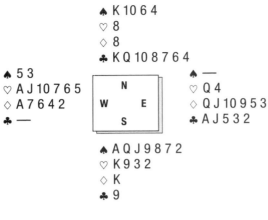

```
              ♠ K 10 6 4
              ♡ 8
              ◇ 8
              ♣ K Q 10 8 7 6 4
♠ 5 3                              ♠ —
♡ A J 10 7 6 5                     ♡ Q 4
◇ A 7 6 4 2                        ◇ Q J 10 9 5 3
♣ —                               ♣ A J 5 3 2
              ♠ A Q J 9 8 7 2
              ♡ K 9 3 2
              ◇ K
              ♣ 9
```

West	North Barnet	East	South George
		1◇	2♠
3♠	4NT	5♣	dbl
5◇	5♠	pass	pass
dbl	all pass		

VuGraph Auction

West	North	East	South
		pass	4♠
4NT	5♠	5NT	pass
6♡	pass	pass	6♠
pass	pass	6NT	pass
pass	dbl	7◇	dbl
all pass			

In Junior bridge, players usually make a bid every time it is their turn, at least in the early rounds, and so West found himself on lead and imaginatively tried a low diamond round to George's singleton king. Declarer then conceded the two remaining aces for plus 850.

Playing East-West for Scotland on VuGraph were my cousin David and Cam McLatchie. I cannot remember exactly which player sat West and which East.

West showed his two suits, East appeared to ask for his partner's minor by bidding 5NT and West picked hearts! East tried again for a minor with 6NT but West was somewhere else at the time and passed. However, North came to the rescue with a greedy double. Now East had a real stroke of wisdom — he didn't redouble in a final attempt to get partner to pick a minor but he didn't try his clubs either. He shot 7◇ and poor South, who had been looking forward to defending 6NT, doubled again in exasperation. After the ◇K dropped and the heart finesse worked declarer chalked up plus 2330. Added to our 850 that came to 3180 points which translated to 22 IMPs. After this huge result, the match finished in a dead tie and the two teams shared that year's championship! David and Cam are both now successful businessmen and Cam was eventually honored by the Queen for his services to industry.

Up to this point, I had not competed in the trials for the Scottish Open team, but after Delft, George and I were given a chance to play. The conservative group which ran Scottish bridge was probably not amused by this next hand, which also attracted our opponents' wrath.

East-West were in the running for selection and after a long and tortuous auction, I landed in 7◇. As was the rule, West led face down and then his partner was allowed to ask questions about the bidding. He quizzed me long and hard about each bid. I subsequent-

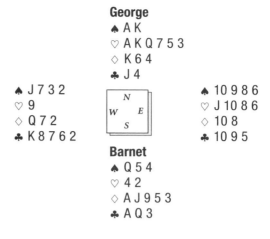

George
♠ A K
♡ A K Q 7 5 3
◇ K 6 4
♣ J 4

♠ J 7 3 2
♡ 9
◇ Q 7 2
♣ K 8 7 6 2

♠ 10 9 8 6
♡ J 10 8 6
◇ 10 8
♣ 10 9 5

Barnet
♠ Q 5 4
♡ 4 2
◇ A J 9 5 3
♣ A Q 3

ly tackled trumps by leading low to the ace and passing the jack, pinning the ten. I felt that if East had held the queen of trumps, he would not have been so inquisitive but would have been excited at the thought of scoring his queen! The opponents told me I had no right to play the hand like this and thereby damage their chances to qualify. Too bad, say I. Some bridge experts pay no attention to what is going on at the table and only play the percentages, whilst others like Zia or Sam Lev are masters of picking up the tiniest tell-tale sign from the opposition. There is a famous story from a high-stakes rubber bridge game when after a slam had been reached and the dummy had been laid down, one of the defenders reached across dummy's cards and moved the ♠A, which had been behind the ♣K, to the spade suit. When declarer misguessed who had the ♣A, Lev burst out laughing. Of course, it was the defender who held the ♣A who had noticed the misplaced card, and Sam would certainly have got it right!

Despite the distraction of bridge, I did graduate from university somehow, and I duly joined the family business, which was importing and distributing Oriental rugs. My father and my Uncle Lennie have played bridge together many times for Scotland and can perhaps boast of having the world's longest-running partnership, dating from the 1940s through to the 1990s. As a result, there were bridge hands to talk about every day at the office. I often acted as mediator on bidding problems — a tricky job, but the side benefit was that I had little difficulty getting as much time off as I needed to play in tournaments. It was a happy compromise that I enjoyed for many years.

C H A P T E R 3

Home and the Fat Lady

The most important tournament in the UK is the Gold Cup, a competition that dates back to 1932. It is an annual open knockout event for teams of four to six players. The early rounds are played zonally until there are sixteen teams left, after which the pairings are made by random draw. The last eight teams come together to play off over one weekend in 64-board matches. By 1982 I had been fortunate enough to have won the Gold Cup twice and to have lost the final once. My partner was Victor Goldberg, one of Scotland's all-time best players. As a pair, we performed creditably for two seasons, winning the Scottish National Championship each year as well as the Camrose International Trophy in 1979, before going on to play on the British team. This latter feat was not an easy accomplishment for a Scottish pair since the selection committee was mainly English!

In fact, the English were not at all pleased with the Scots at that time. The Camrose Trophy, which had been almost an exclusive English possession until the seventies, was lost to Scotland six times in that decade and ended in a tie two other years. These were Scotland's golden years. I remember the Scottish captain of these years, Charles Bowman — he was not a great player, but was an excellent administrator for the Scottish Bridge Union. He was a grain merchant in real life, and he smoked large cigars like Paul Chemla does today. We got on well together, and before he decided on his line-up for each session he would often sidle up to me and quietly ask me in which room I would like to play. He would then work out who would play in the other room. The 'auld enemy' were to get their revenge in the eighties but only after we had lost some of our best players to other countries — the brain drain!

However, 1981 saw a reversal in my partnership with Goldberg. We had a series of poor results, including finishing last in the Sunday Times — an event that we had won the previous year. We had been photographed by the press as the defending champions at the 1981 opening party and that had been enough to put a jinx on us from the start! A poor year and it was bon voyage to yet another partnership.

By this time, I was running out of partners in Scotland, since there were only a small number of top-class players. However, one of Scotland's best players, Willie Coyle, had not played serious competition for a few years. Although quiet and good-humored away from the table, Willie had very firm ideas on how the game should be played. He had enjoyed a long successful partnership with Victor Silverstone, but Victor now lived in London. I persuaded Willie to try playing with me, and we entered a team for the Gold Cup in 1982 consisting of Coyle, Goldberg, Cuthbertson, Haase and myself. Gerald Haase, a medical doctor and a good friend, had a reputation for being wild at the table and not very soft-spoken. Around 540 teams played in the Gold Cup that year, and after ten months of knockouts, the last three rounds were to be held in Birmingham, England. Out of the last eight teams, we were generally expected to get to the final against the top-seeded Zia Mahmood, Irving Rose, Jeremy Flint, Rob Sheehan, Victor Silverstone and Chris Dixon. We were then expected to lose.

Before the final, however, God has placed the semifinal, and in the semifinal we faced Jim Niblett, a team of good but not great players; this match we were expected to win comfortably due to our greater experience. Well, bridge just doesn't always happen that way and after fifty-six boards of a disastrous match we were 51 IMPs down with eight boards left to play. At this point, the opposing captain asked us if we would like to concede so that his team could get some extra sleep for the match the next day. It was bad enough losing to the English without being treated with contempt into the bargain! None of our team was happy but we decided to take a shot at the last eight boards. We sent Goldberg to the bar to drown his sorrows.

Now I knew that Gerald, the 'Mad Doc' as he was known, was a good man to have on your team when you're a lot down; he tends to create action. Coyle had a reputation for soundness but we knew we had to loosen our game to have any chance. Little did we know we were about to make history, and what followed must surely be the most amazing eight boards ever played at the end of a team match in a national championship. Bridge writers, like other journalists, have been known to embellish their stories from time to time, but this is a factual account of those last eight boards as we saw them.

Willie Coyle

Board 57
Both Vul.

♠ 9
♡ A Q J 8 6 5 2
♦ K 8 5
♣ J 9

♠ A Q 10 3 2
♡ 4
♦ J 9 6 3
♣ 8 3 2

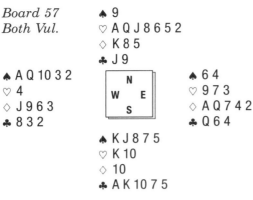

♠ 6 4
♡ 9 7 3
♦ A Q 7 4 2
♣ Q 6 4

♠ K J 8 7 5
♡ K 10
♦ 10
♣ A K 10 7 5

Although this looked like a flat board in our room, the Mad Doc opened the North hand 1♦ and was soon in 6♡. With diamonds bid on his right, East led a trump, the club suit ran for five tricks and Haase scored up his slam! The deficit was now 38 IMPs.

West Shenkin	North Cliff	East Coyle	South Burn
	1♡	pass	1NT
2♡	dbl	3♦	4♣
pass	4♡	all pass	

Niblett	Haase	Ellsworth	Cuthbertson
	1♦	pass	2♣
pass	2♡	pass	2♠
pass	4♡	pass	6♡
all pass			

Board 58
Neither Vul.

♠ A K Q 6
♡ K Q J 10 5
♦ 2
♣ Q 8 4

♠ J 7 5
♡ A 9 6 3
♦ K 10 6
♣ 10 9 2

♠ 8 2
♡ 8 2
♦ 8 5 4
♣ A K J 6 5 3

♠ 10 9 4 3
♡ 7 4
♦ A Q J 9 7 3
♣ 7

Coyle would probably have made 1NT redoubled but as it was the opposition had missed an easy game — a likely gain for us.

Haase knew he was off two aces again on this, the very next hand, and again bid a slam anyway, but this time his unsporting opponents cashed them. 5 IMPs away, down 43.

West Shenkin	North Cliff	East Coyle	South Burn
		1NT	pass
pass	dbl	pass	pass
redbl	pass	pass	3♦
all pass			

Niblett	Haase	Ellsworth	Cuthbertson
		pass	1♠
pass	4NT	3♠	4♣
4♠	dbl	pass	5♦
pass	6♠	all pass	

A much better auction by Haase-Cuthbertson as they reached their third straight slam off two aces! But with trumps 2-2, this one came home in spite of the bad diamond break. 13 IMPs our way, and we were only 30 down.

Board 59
N-S Vul.

```
              ♠ 10 7 4 2
              ♡ 9 8 6 4 2
              ◇ J
              ♣ A K 3
♠ Q 3                        ♠ J 8
♡ A K J 10 7      N          ♡ Q 5 3
◇ A 8          W     E       ◇ 9 5 4 3 2
♣ Q 9 7 5         S          ♣ J 8 4
              ♠ A K 9 6 5
              ♡ —
              ◇ K Q 10 7 6
              ♣ 10 6 2
```

West Shenkin	North Cliff	East Coyle	South Burn
			1♠
dbl	3♠	pass	4♠
all pass			

Niblett	Haase	Ellsworth	Cuthbertson
			1◇
dbl	redbl	pass	2♠
pass	4♣	pass	6♠
all pass			

Incredibly, the next board was yet another slam. At our table, South made twelve tricks in 3NT and we saw that a slam in clubs would fail due to the bad breaks. However, Cuthbertson played 6♡ on a diamond lead. He won the ace, played a heart to his ten and led the club queen. West covered, and the ace was ruffed by East. Now East played the ◇K and declarer ruffed with the six as West discarded! His only chance now was that West held the ♡32 doubleton, so he played ♠A, ♠K, ruffed his spade loser with the trump ace, finessed the trump again, drew the last trump and claimed six for 1210 and 12 more IMPs — down only 18 now.

Board 60
E-W Vul.

```
              ♠ 9 7
              ♡ A 8 4
              ◇ A 10 9 6
              ♣ A 7 4 2
♠ J 8 6 3 2                  ♠ 10 5
♡ 3 2             N          ♡ Q 9 7 5
◇ 8            W     E       ◇ K Q J 7 5 4 3
♣ K 8 6 5 3       S          ♣ —
              ♠ A K Q 4
              ♡ K J 10 6
              ◇ 2
              ♣ Q J 10 9
```

West Shenkin	North Cliff	East Coyle	South Burn
pass	1NT	2♣[1]	dbl
redbl[2]	pass	2◇	3NT
all pass			

1. Hearts and another suit. 2. Five clubs.

Niblett	Haase	Ellsworth	Cuthbertson
pass	1◇	pass	1♡
pass	2♡	pass	6♡
pass	pass	dbl	all pass

Board 61 was a flat game bid in both rooms — three to play. On Board 62, at both tables the defense started with the ◇K to the ace and a trump switch. Both declarers went down one so we gained a hundred or 3 IMPs — minus 15 with two boards to play.

Board 62
Both Vul.

```
            ♠ A 10 6 3 2
            ♡ 5 2
            ◇ 9 8 6 5 4
            ♣ 10
♠ 7 5                    ♠ K 9
♡ J 10 8 7 3      N      ♡ A 6
◇ A            W     E   ◇ K Q J 10 7 3
♣ K J 7 3 2       S      ♣ Q 9 4
            ♠ Q J 8 4
            ♡ K Q 9 4
            ◇ 2
            ♣ A 8 6 5
```

West Shenkin	North Cliff	East Coyle	South Burn
		1◇	dbl
1♡	2♠	3◇	4♠
dbl	all pass		

Niblett	Haase	Ellsworth	Cuthbertson
		1◇	dbl
1♡	1♠	3◇	4♠
dbl	all pass		

This was the penultimate board. After a heart lead we were plus 430 in the closed room. At the other table, George Cuthbertson slipped a club in with his spades and tried an offbeat Multi, which had the effect of helping the opposition to miss their game. The difference between 430 and 110 was an 8-IMP swing, and as we took our cards out from the board on the last deal, we were only 7 IMPs down. Of course, Willie and I did not know this as the swings were mostly in the other room. It was very late by this time, well after 1:00 a.m.

Board 63
N-S Vul.

```
            ♠ 9 2
            ♡ K J 9 7 5
            ◇ K 7 4
            ♣ Q 9 6
♠ K 10 7 5              ♠ J 8
♡ A Q 10 2        N      ♡ 6 3
◇ J 9 3       W     E    ◇ A 8 2
♣ A 10            S      ♣ K J 8 7 5 3
            ♠ A Q 6 4 3
            ♡ 8 4
            ◇ Q 10 6 5
            ♣ 4 2
```

West Shenkin	North Cliff	East Coyle	South Burn
			pass
1NT	pass	3♣	pass
3NT	all pass		

Niblett	Haase	Ellsworth	Cuthbertson
			2◇[1]
dbl	2♠[2]	3♣	all pass

1. Multi: 4-4-4-1 17-24 or a weak two in a major.
2. A heart fit .

I was sure that to have any chance we needed another big swing. My one notrump was supposed to have been 11-14, and Coyle raised me to game. South knew he was being fixed here and cautiously bid 4♠. However, his pass of 5◇ was astonishing. North let it go undoubled, and the defense took their ruffs for down four or 200. Meanwhile, Haase-Cuthbertson reached slam again without the use of any ace-asking conventions, and scored it up for 1430. We gained another 15 IMPs on this last deal and won the match by 8 IMPs.

Board 64
N-S Vul.

	♠ 10 6 3 2	
	♡ A 8 6 5	
	◇ 9 5 4	
	♣ 6 4	
♠ 9 7		♠ Q
♡ K Q 9 4	N	♡ J 10 3 2
◇ Q 10 8 3	W E	◇ A K J 7 2
♣ Q 9 8	S	♣ 10 5 3
	♠ A K J 8 5 4	
	♡ 7	
	◇ 6	
	♣ A K J 7 2	

West Shenkin	North Cliff	East Coyle	South Burn
1NT	pass	3NT	4♠
pass	pass	5◇	all pass

Niblett	Haase	Ellsworth	Cuthbertson
pass	pass	pass	2♣
pass	2◇	pass	2♠
pass	3♠	pass	6♠
all pass			

Of course, we had been incredibly lucky to have a set of boards like this when we needed it — our teammates had ventured five slams that were not bid in our room! So two of them were off a couple of aces — they had ridden their luck and played to win. When we came out to score the boards up, I said to our guys that I thought we might have a chance. The Mad Doc quickly replied "In that case we've won," and he was right. The opposition were understandably devastated by their experience.

The 'miracle' team from the 1982 Gold Cup — Left to right, Cuthbertson, Shenkin, Haase, Goldberg and Coyle.

So our all-Scottish team moved on to the final to take on two more Scotsmen, three Englishmen and a Pakistani. In fact, the opponents played very poorly for a team of their caliber and found themselves 60 IMPs down with eight to play. Although they did not concede either, a second miracle in two days was not to be — we won by over a hundred. The 1982 Gold Cup will always be remembered for a match which confirms the saying about the fat lady singing, or Yogi Berra's famous words, 'It's not over till it's over.'

However, on the home international front, things were not going so well. After Scotland's halcyon years in the seventies, the English dominated the Camrose Trophy, winning it every year through 1988. I am not sure that their team had improved that much but most of our top players had left the 'auld country' while a couple of our best had simply stopped playing completely. However, I persuaded Victor Silverstone (who now lived in London) to play in the trials and we played on the Scottish Camrose team from 1987-1989. After a string of losses, 1989 was going to be the last chance in the decade for Scotland. Victor and I finished fourth in the 1989 trials and were dropped by the selectors, but after a loss to Northern Ireland we were brought back to play against England at Nottingham. Perhaps Robin Hood country would be favorable to underdogs, we thought.

Interestingly, Mark Horton had arranged to prepare a video of this match for distribution in English schools to teach the game to youngsters. England was a heavy favorite, and was fielding a strong team — British internationals Kirby and Armstrong were playing and Tony Forrester was also on the team, but as his regular partner was unavailable he was paired with Sally Horton, then a women's world champion. The Scottish team arrived on the Friday evening before the match, and went to a reception held by the Lord Mayor of Nottingham. At the reception, Mark told us that in order to save time, all ninety-six hands had been predealt and that transparencies had already been prepared for the VuGraph. (Those days were long before computer-operated VuGraph shows.) Now the rules were that the captains were entitled to be present at any such predealing and the Scots, being traditionally cagey, decided to insist that all the hands be redealt! So the Scottish captain Sam Leckie stayed up till the small hours while all ninety-six boards were redealt.

Silverstone and I played every board of this match, and I can remember two hands very well. Playing on VuGraph I held

♠ 8 ♡ A J 10 ◇ K Q J 10 7 4 3 ♣ 6 3

I opened 1◇ and heard 2♣, and now my 2◇ rebid brought 2♠. When partner bid 3♠ over my 2NT, I jumped to 5◇, and over 5♡ signed off again in 6◇. Partner's hand was

♠ A K Q J 2 ♡ — ◇ 9 2 ♣ A K Q 9 8 2

Armstrong-Kirby had an accident and got to 7NT, which was not a success. That was a fast 17 IMPs and Scotland were well on their way to winning the first 32-board match by 39 IMPs.

The second hand that I can recall was another bidding hand, and came from Match 2.

♠ 10		♠ A K Q 5
♡ A Q 7 2	N	♡ J 5
◇ K 3	W E	◇ A Q 10 8 7 4 2
♣ A Q 9 7 5 2	S	♣ —

Open Room

West	East
1♣	1◇
1♡	1♠
3♣	3◇
4◇	4NT
5♣	7◇

Closed Room

West	East
Forrester	**Horton**
1◇	2♣
2◇	2♠
3♣	3◇
4♣	4◇
6◇	pass

You can see from Forrester and Horton's bidding that their system was somewhat unusual, but as top players they could be expected to know it. Horton held the long diamonds and I think Tony wanted her to bid one for the road. I am not sure what all their bids meant but I do know we won 13 IMPs and we went on to win the second match by 23 IMPs. By this time we knew it was going to be our weekend and we took the Sunday match by 19 IMPs. Scotland had won all three matches for the first time in Camrose history. And while I would never dream of accusing our opponents or the organizers of any kind of sharp practice, I sometimes wonder what would have happened had Sam Leckie not insisted on redealing all the hands!

We went on to win the Camrose trophy that year, and you may not be surprised to hear that the infamous educational video was never seen or heard of again. Rumor has it that a copy still lurks in a dark corner of Mark Horton's home.

CHAPTER 4

Traveling through Europe

I n addition to the time it afforded me to play bridge, another advantage of the family rug business was that I got the chance to travel a lot. For example, my business dealings took me to China and India. I have actually had lunch both at the Taj Mahal and on the Great Wall of China at Beijing — two of the world's wonders. One of my most remarkable memories is of sitting outside in the sunshine on the Great Wall with about fifty of my customers while the waiters we had brought with us from our hotel buzzed around our cloth-covered tables plying us with sumptuous food.

My bridge activities, on the other hand, took me to Europe, where international events included both the European Championship and the Common Market Championship, which was a mini version of the European. Until recent years, the European Championship was arguably the most difficult teams tournament in the world to win. Held over a full two weeks, this event attracts teams from twenty-five to thirty countries. You can usually count on about ten excellent teams, while at the other end of the field there are very few 'duffers', as we called them in Britain. The WBF Olympiad, held every four years, certainly has more good teams but also includes many more really poor ones. Today, the new-style Bermuda Bowl involves twenty teams including ten to twelve very strong ones, and perhaps now (as it should be) is the toughest to win.

Following my first debacle in Denmark in the 1977 European Championships, I had three further opportunities to play in the event, all with different partners. In 1979, I played in Lausanne, Switzerland with Victor Goldberg; in 1985, in Salsomaggiore, Italy with Willie Coyle, and in 1993 in Menton, France with Les Steel. On each occasion, our team performed reasonably, without finishing in the medals. Try these problems from my various European experiences.

Lausanne is one of Switzerland's prettiest cities. The 1979 winners there were Italy — Belladonna, Garozzo and their supporting cast. This hand came up playing against Giorgio Belladonna, who was not only one of the world's best bridge players but also one of the most charismatic with a great smile and laugh. He was partnered in this event by Lorenzo Lauria, who was making one of his earliest appearances for Italy. Lauria now visits the USA frequently for the Nationals, having won there as well as collecting a Rosenblum Cup gold medal for Italy some twenty years after the Lausanne tournament.

♠ Q 7 4
♡ A Q 6 5
◇ K Q 8
♣ K 10 2

♠ A J 3 2
♡ J 3
◇ A
♣ A Q J 7 5 3

West Barnet	North Belladonna	East Victor	South Lauria
	1NT	pass	2♣
pass	2♡	pass	3♣
pass	3♠	pass	4NT
pass	5◇	pass	7♣
all pass			

Lorenzo Lauria

The bidding seems a little strange, but in the Italian system South showed good clubs and a spade suit and North hearts. Giorgio confirmed all the aces and his partner tried 7♣. How did Lorenzo Lauria play to make 7♣ on the lead of the ♣4?

♠ A 3
♡ Q 8 7 5
◇ J 9 8 7 5 4
♣ 9

♠ K 10
♡ A J 6 4 3
◇ A 6
♣ Q 6 5 2

In the same match, both the Italian declarer and Tony Priday for Britain played in 4♥ after West had shown spades and at Priday's table had doubled the final contract. In both rooms the defense started with the ♣A and a spade switch. How did Priday make the contract and how did the Italian go down?

Salsomaggiore, Italy is a quaint little holiday village where I had the pleasure of playing in both the European and Common Market Championships, and where in 1985 Austria were the European winners. The next two hands were chances for me to shine and they were both subsequently included in a book by the great English player Jeremy Flint under the heading 'Spotting the Last Gasp Coup.'

Playing against Sweden, you hold

♠ A K J 8 2   ♡ 4 2   ◇ Q   ♣ K 8 6 5 2

♠ Q 9 4 3
♡ A K 8 6
◇ J 10 8 4 3
♣ —

♠ A K J 8 2
♡ 4 2
◇ Q
♣ K 8 6 5 2

You open 1♠ and hear two diamonds from partner. The next hand overcalls three clubs. You lick your chops and double this for penalties. Partner passes and you lead your ♠A. Dummy hits the table with the hand you see on the left.

Playing upside-down signals, partner plays the ♠7 (discouraging) and declarer Hans Göthe, a strong player, follows with the ♠10. Next you try the ◇Q, hoping partner may overtake, but he leaves you on lead playing the ◇5 while declarer follows with the ◇2. Hoping your partner started with a singleton spade, you try the ♠K only to see that ruffed by declarer. Declarer cashes the ♣A, partner following with the ten, before crossing to dummy with a heart, taking a heart pitch on the ♠Q and ruffing a spade. He then crosses to dummy with the remaining high heart arriving at this position:

♠ —
♡ 8 6
◇ J 10 8
♣ —

Declarer now ruffs a heart from dummy with his ♣Q. Do you overruff or pitch your last spade?

♠ J
♡ —
◇ —
♣ K 8 6 5

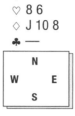

P R O B L E M 4

This hand is from our match against Austria. The opening lead against 4♠ was the ♣K; how would you play the hand? If you duck the first club, West continues with the ♣Q.

♠ A
♡ K Q 9 7
◇ Q 8 4 3
♣ 10 8 5 2

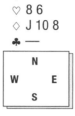

♠ 10 9 8 6 5 4 2
♡ A 8 5
◇ —
♣ A 7 3

West	North	East	South
1◇	1♡	pass	1♠
pass	pass	1NT	3♠
3NT	dbl	redbl	pass
4◇	pass	pass	4♡
pass	4♠	all pass	

The scene for the 1995 championships was Menton, a small town in the south of France. In mid-June we encountered ninety degrees of heat, sumptuous food and of course, plenty of French *vin*. The setting was right and the hands were interesting. This was to be my last chance to represent Britain in a Bermuda Bowl team. Our team needed to finish in the top three in Europe, but the reality of the situation was that the chance was all but gone before we began as Tony Forrester and Andrew Robson, easily our best pair, had withdrawn from the British team. Tony, for many years a stalwart on the British team, was to be seen a couple of years later trying his luck in the USA Team Trials. Not coincidentally, shortly after that, the ACBL made tighter rules to restrict their trials to bona-fide participants. Without Forrester-Robson, our team stayed in touch with the leaders until near the end but ended up about a match short. The winners were a very strong Polish team.

♠ 10 8
♡ Q J
♢ K Q 3
♣ K J 8 7 5 2

♠ A K 6 3
♡ A 10 9 8 7 2
♢ 2
♣ 4 3

West	North	East	South
pass	1♣	3♢	dbl
pass	3NT	pass	4♡
all pass			

You are playing against Hungary, and they lead the ♢10 against your 4♡ contract. Dummy's queen loses to the ace, and East returns the ♢4. How would you play from here?

P R O B L E M 6

On this deal you are up against France, the reigning Olympiad champions. At unfavorable vulnerability, you hold:

♠ Q 4 2   ♡ 7 4 3   ◇ K J 10 4 3 2   ♣ A

You are on VuGraph and you have to find the right lead with the eyes of the world upon you. What would you do? If you cash the ♣A, you are going to look like someone with a potential trump trick,

West Mouiel	North You	East Levy	South
1♠	2◇	dbl	pass
4♡	pass	4♠	pass
4NT	pass	5♡	pass
6♠	all pass		

but could the club go away? A diamond lead might be right — which one do you lead if so? If it helps, the illustrious Paul Chemla is in your chair in the other room.

P R O B L E M 7

Playing against Lauria and Versace, a new Italian pair in 1995, but World Champions today, you have to make 4♡ in Round 2 of the Championship with the VuGraph commentator watching your every move.

West leads the ◇2. East takes the king and then switches to the ♠8. You play low and West wins the king and returns the ◇6. Now you ruff in dummy and lead a low heart, East contributing the queen. How do you continue?

♠ Q J 7 3
♡ A 6 4 2
◇ J
♣ K Q 10 6

```
        N
   W         E
        S
```

♠ A 9 6
♡ K 10 9 7 3
◇ Q 5 4 3
♣ 2

West Lauria	North Steel	East Versace	South Barnet
	1♣	1◇[1]	1♡
pass	2♡	pass	3◇
pass	4♡	4♠	dbl
pass	5♡	all pass	

1. Minors.

Your team is still in contention, but you know this match against Spain is a must-win situation. Your hand is:

♠ 9 4   ♡ J 7 3   ◇ 9 7 3   ♣ A K 9 8 5

You hear 3◇ on your left at equal vulnerability, partner makes a takeout double, and it goes 3NT on your right. Since this could mean just about anything, you double to show some cards, and to your surprise, everyone passes.

You lead the ♣A, since your methods are that the lead of the ace asks for upside-down attitude, while the king asks for an unblock or upside-down count. The guy on your right calls for the queen from the dummy, partner contributes the ♣6, and declarer the ♣4. Can you keep the Spaniard from raining on your plain?

♠ 7
♡ 10 5 4
◇ K Q 10 8 6 5 4
♣ Q 10

♠ 9 4
♡ J 7 3
◇ 9 7 3
♣ A K 9 8 5

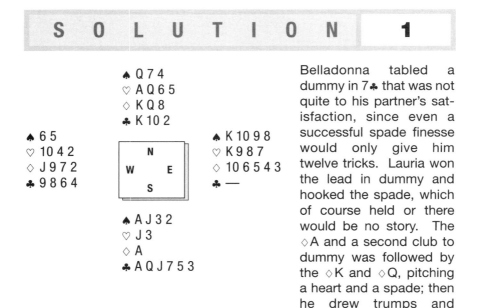

♠ Q 7 4
♡ A Q 6 5
◇ K Q 8
♣ K 10 2

♠ 6 5
♡ 10 4 2
◇ J 9 7 2
♣ 9 8 6 4

♠ K 10 9 8
♡ K 9 8 7
◇ 10 6 5 4 3
♣ —

♠ A J 3 2
♡ J 3
◇ A
♣ A Q J 7 5 3

Belladonna tabled a dummy in 7♣ that was not quite to his partner's satisfaction, since even a successful spade finesse would only give him twelve tricks. Lauria won the lead in dummy and hooked the spade, which of course held or there would be no story. The ◇A and a second club to dummy was followed by the ◇K and ◇Q, pitching a heart and a spade; then he drew trumps and cashed the ♠A. The position is shown in the right.

When declarer cashed his last two clubs, letting go a spade and a heart from dummy, poor Victor was squeezed into parting with two hearts and now the ♡A dropped his king. Not surprisingly, this was a 13-IMP swing to Italy, but we got the points back quickly.

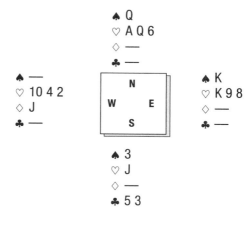

SOLUTION 2

After the ♣A lead, Tony Priday took the spade switch in hand and played ace and another heart. Now no defense could prevent him from setting up the diamonds for the loss of just one trick.

The Italian declarer won the spade switch in dummy and, without the information from West's penalty double at the other table, finessed the

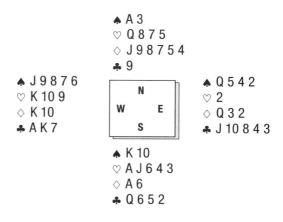

heart. Now a second spade put him in hand. After cashing the trump ace, he played ace and another diamond. Now I was able to play the ♣K, which had the effect of locking declarer in dummy and he had to lose a further trick — either a heart or a club.

The Italians went on to win the Championship but at least we had the pleasure of winning our match against them in spite of that cruel grand slam.

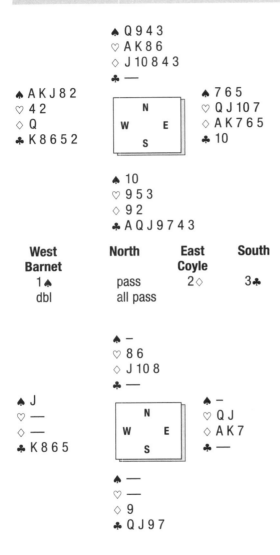

♠ Q 9 4 3
♡ A K 8 6
◇ J 10 8 4 3
♣ —

♠ A K J 8 2
♡ 4 2
◇ Q
♣ K 8 6 5 2

♠ 7 6 5
♡ Q J 10 7
◇ A K 7 6 5
♣ 10

♠ 10
♡ 9 5 3
◇ 9 2
♣ A Q J 9 7 4 3

West Barnet	North	East Coyle	South
1♠	pass	2◇	3♣
dbl	all pass		

♠ —
♡ 8 6
◇ J 10 8
♣ —

♠ J
♡ —
◇ —
♣ K 8 6 5

♠ —
♡ Q J
◇ A K 7
♣ —

♠ —
♡ —
◇ 9
♣ Q J 9 7

You led the ♠A and switched to the ◇Q which held the trick. The ♠K was ruffed by declarer who then scored his ♣A, the ♡A, the ♠Q and a spade ruff. Then the ♡K and a heart, declarer ruffing with the queen, left the position below on the left with you to play.

Did you overruff or pitch a spade? If you did either, you let the contract through! Sorry if I misled you, but the only defense is to underruff and when declarer plays his losing diamond, play that carefully preserved spade and let partner win the trick. Now when partner plays a card and declarer ruffs with the jack you can underruff for the second time (!) and score the K-8 of clubs as the setting tricks.

If you did that, well done — you did better than I did. I knew that I had compounded a soft defense with a poor play in the endgame and was annoyed. However I felt worse when my partner told the captain that the only reason I had missed the winning play was that I had had a glass of wine with dinner! It was true that I did have a single glass, but that was not the reason for my ineptitude.

We would have collected an easy 500 if partner had doubled 4◇, but then there would be no story. After the ♣K lead and continuation, I thought I needed West to be 3-3-5-2, so that I could throw my losing club on the long heart. I won the club and crossed to the spade ace noting the queen on my left. Now I ruffed a diamond back to hand and played a second spade. Unfortunately West had another club and cashed it for down one.

	♠ A		
	♡ K Q 9 7		
	◇ Q 8 4 3		
	♣ 10 8 5 2		
♠ K Q			♠ J 7 3
♡ J 6 3	N		♡ 10 4 2
◇ K 10 9 7 5	W E		◇ A J 6 2
♣ K Q J	S		♣ 9 6 4
	♠ 10 9 8 6 5 4 2		
	♡ A 8 5		
	◇ —		
	♣ A 7 3		

West	North	East	South
1◇	1♡	pass	1♠
pass	dbl	redbl	pass
4◇	pass	pass	4♡
pass	4♠	all pass	

I knew at once I could have done better by winning the first club and after cashing the ♠A running four rounds of hearts, pitching my club. What could the defense do? If West ruffs, it is with a trump trick and if East ruffs, I can crash the remaining trumps in one round.

I had blown it again. I can remember very clearly the final line in Flint's write-up: 'In France they call this the *coup d'agonie*; I wonder what they call it in Glasgow?' Problems 3 and 4 are the kind that I would expect to get right if someone showed them to me on a slip of paper or a napkin but they are not quite so easy at the table. I just hoped that if a similar position came up again, I would remember it.

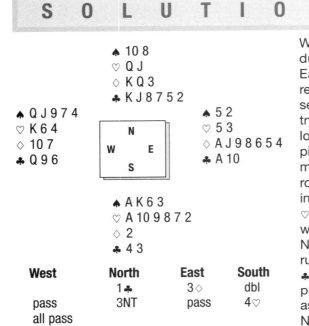

```
                 ♠ 10 8
                 ♡ Q J
                 ◇ K Q 3
                 ♣ K J 8 7 5 2
♠ Q J 9 7 4                        ♠ 5 2
♡ K 6 4          N                 ♡ 5 3
◇ 10 7       W       E             ◇ A J 9 8 6 5 4
♣ Q 9 6          S                 ♣ A 10
                 ♠ A K 6 3
                 ♡ A 10 9 8 7 2
                 ◇ 2
                 ♣ 4 3
```

West	North	East	South
	1♣	3◇	dbl
pass	3NT	pass	4♡
all pass			

West led the ◇10 to dummy's queen and East's ace, and East returned the ◇4. Let's see what happens if you try to ruff your spade losers in dummy and pitch a club on the diamond. You play three rounds of spades, ruffing in dummy with the ♡J and ruff a diamond with the trump ace. Now a second spade ruff is followed by the ♣K. East wins this to play another diamond as you ruff with the ♡10. Now when you lead the ♡9 West wins this to play a spade which East ruffs with the ♡5, and as a result West's mighty ♡6 takes the setting trick. Seems strange to lose a trick to the six when you hold all the spots down to the seven, but play it through.

Anticipating this problem I paid careful attention to the ◇4. When East played it he thought that his partner might be ruffing, so perhaps he was telling him to play clubs after he ruffed. I therefore pitched a spade on the diamond, and played three rounds of spades, ruffing in dummy. Now I played the ♡A and the ♡10. I could deal with 4-1 heart breaks and backed my judgement by leading a club to the jack to make the game. In other matches, many declarers had in fact gone down in 4♡ after the trump promotion. In our match, the opposition tried 3NT at the other table without success.

I thought declarer might well be 5-5-1-2 for this auction, so leading the ♣A would lose when declarer had the king or when he thought that I was leading my ace because I had a possible trump trick. It's also very unlikely on the auction that declarer has the ♠AK. So instead, I led a careful ◇K in case declarer had the bare ◇Q (if partner had it, it did not matter which diamond I led). However, as you can see from the above layout, this was not an overpowering success as declarer was able to dispose of his club loser imme-

```
              ♠ K 9 7
              ♡ 10 6
              ◇ A Q 8 5
              ♣ K 7 6 5
♠ Q 4 2                        ♠ 7
♡ 7 4 3          N             ♡ J 8 2
◇ K J 10 4 3 2  W   E          ◇ 9 6
♣ A                S           ♣ Q J 10 9 8 4 3
              ♠ A J 10 8 6 3
              ♡ A K Q 9 5
              ◇ 7
              ♣ 2
```

West You	North Levy	East partner	South Mouiel
			1♠
2◇	dbl	pass	4♡
pass	4♠	pass	4NT
pass	4♡	pass	6♠
all pass			

diately, and simply played two high trumps.

In the other room, Paul Chemla of France showed no imagination at all in leading the ♣A, which was in fact the only possible card to give him any chance to beat the contract! My teammate Graham Kirby, however, quickly laid down ♠A and ran the jack to tie the board — great play! If you decided to lead the ◇K, you should know that some teammates said you were unlucky and others were not quite so nice about it.

♠ Q J 7 3
♡ A 6 4 2
◇ J
♣ K Q 10 6

♠ K 10 2
♡ J 8 5
◇ 10 6 2
♣ J 9 8 7

	N	
W		E
	S	

♠ 8 5 4
♡ Q
◇ A K 9 8 7
♣ A 5 4 3

♠ A 9 6
♡ K 10 9 7 3
◇ Q 5 4 3
♣ 2

West Lauria	North Steel	East Versace	South Barnet
	1♣	1◇¹	1♡
pass	2♡	pass	3◇
pass	4♡	4♠	dbl
pass	5♡	all pass	

1. Minors.

Lauria led a diamond to Versace's king, and he returned the ♠8 to Lauria's king. A second diamond was ruffed in dummy and a low heart to the king fetched the queen from East. The problem here is that if you run a heart through West, he does not cover. Now, when you play spades to throw your club, West can ruff and return a diamond to leave you with a diamond loser. If you play a club, East can win and tap dummy, promoting partners ♡J.

The only way to make the hand is to delay your entry to dummy — leave both trumps outstanding and play three spades throwing your club. Now if East ruffs in to play a diamond, you can ruff, ruff out the ♣A, draw the last trump and throw your last diamond on the high club. It does not help East not to ruff as you just ruff out the ♣A and then draw West's last trump before cashing the high club for a diamond pitch. This one I did get right. Maybe there is a small similarity to Problem 4 in that the key to the hand is to play winners while the defense has a trump position outstanding.

	♠ 7	
	♡ 10 5 4	
	◇ K Q 10 8 6 5 4	
	♣ Q 10	
♠ 9 4		♠ A Q 10 5 2
♡ J 7 3	N	♡ K 8 6 2
◇ 9 7 3	W　　E	◇ —
♣ A K 9 8 5	S	♣ J 7 6 3
	♠ K J 8 6 3	
	♡ A Q 9	
	◇ A J 2	
	♣ 4 2	

You led the ♣A, asking for upside down attitude, declarer played the queen from dummy, and partner contributed the ♣6 while declarer followed with the ♣4. What did you do next?

What is happening here? In these situations, where there is much scope for falsecarding by declarer, it is partner's duty to play a clear card. After leading the ♣A, I studied partner's ♣6 and declarer's ♣4. Where were the ♣2 and the ♣3? Partner might have started with ♣J76, but then he would probably have played the jack under my ace. Alternatively, his ♣6 was discouraging, in which case he started with exactly ♣632. There was no holding where he would play the ♣6 to discourage if he also held the ♣7.

West	North	East	South
	3◇	dbl	3NT
dbl	all pass		

The more I thought about it, the more likely it seemed that declarer had the ♣J. Could it cost to cash the ♣K and see which spot partner played on that? Yes — if declarer held the ♠K and ♡A along with the ♣J, I had to switch to a heart immediately to set up our tricks before he established the club as his ninth trick. The cute poker play of the ♣Q did not affect my view — everything followed logically from my partner's signal. In order to make the position clear to partner I placed the ♡J on the table, which at least speeded the pace to a quick minus 950.

From partner's angle, the double followed by the lead suggested a decent suit. In that case, his correct card at Trick 1 was the ♣3; even the ♣J could only cost when declarer held ♣9xx. In any event, our loss to Spain put us out of contention to qualify to play in the Bermuda Bowl. At the same time, as a direct consequence of this same hand, my partnership with Les Steel broke up amidst much acrimony. As it turned out, we were the last Scottish pair ever to play in a European championship for Britain; from 2000 onward, each home country is entering its own team. Sans partner, my international bridge playing was suspended.

We defended the Scottish Cup with my wife Mags as my partner instead of Steel, and had the satisfaction of winning handily in the final against my three former Gold Cup teammates. However, I did not have and could not find another suitable regular partner. As a result, I stopped playing in many tournaments and started to visit the USA for their Nationals. In partnership with the Mad Doc — Gerald Haase — I joined a Spingold team with Eddie Kantar, Alan Sontag and Kyle Larsen. I remember one time we reached the round of sixteen in the Spingold and came up against Martel-Stansby, and Zia-Rosenberg. On one hand, the Mad Doc opened one club and over my one heart response rebid 3NT. I had a sixteen-count with a stiff club and bid 5NT which I meant as 'Pick a slam'. The Doc picked *seven* clubs — a level higher than I had intended — and Martel led the ace of spades which took the first trick. It transpired that the Doc had a singleton spade. In the corridor outside, while comparing our results (which were, alas, without distinction), Sontag went apoplectic after hearing our bidding sequence. His voice reaching an even higher register, he turned to the Doc and screamed, "You bid 3NT with a singleton spade? *In Scotland is a singleton a stopper?*"

I enjoyed the Nationals; they were certainly the most competitive bridge I could get. There just was no player in the UK that I could consider suitable as a partner. In fact, British bridge was sinking to a low ebb. Britain had won the European Championship in 1991, a great achievement, but had then squandered their chance in the Bermuda Bowl in Yokohama. With no strong USA team that year, the Bowl was up for grabs and in fact, extraordinarily, Iceland had grabbed it. From that point on, the quality of the British team started to sink. They lost their best pair when Forrester and Robson, a pair of world class, declined to play for Britain and in fact, never played in partnership internationally after 1992. The old stars of British bridge were there no longer. The days of Harrison-Gray, Konstam, Meredith, Reese, Flint, Cansino and Tarlo were long past. Amazingly, John Collings had resurfaced to make his mark again on bridge in Britain after a long absence — a genius returned to the fray.

Armstrong and Kirby were still continuing their long partnership.

Here was a pair who had played on many British teams, and had taken part in the 1987 Bermuda Bowl final in Jamaica when they lost to USA. However, their bridge was very inconsistent; like the girl in the nursery rhyme, when they were good, they were very, very good. Their style was wild, with five-card preempts a normal occurrence. This may sound like sour grapes, as I did lose three Gold Cup finals against their teams in about a seven-year period — they usually had the best team! But even this longstanding partnership was wavering, as Kirby had recently married and was playing a lot less.

Playing sponsors were also now beginning to appear in the UK and while this was good for the few professionals, it really ended Britain's chances of doing well in international competition. There was no team that included two pairs good enough to carry the third pair. One year a sponsored team won what was considered an unofficial trials for the European Championships, and when the selectors tried to send the team without the sponsor, the other two pairs withdrew. Finally a sponsor did manage to qualify for the Olympiad in 1996, but the rest of the team was just not strong enough to carry the load. The three Hacketts, father and sons, were seen over the next few years playing all over the world on various professional teams and achieving some surprisingly good results — an enjoyable lifestyle, but they could not seem to make the same impact on a British team. Forrester and Robson were plying their skills with increasing success as part of the newly formed Shugart team and seemed to have little interest in playing on a British team. Perhaps they felt that they would have no realistic chance of success as part of one. Today this is all inconsequential, as the home unions have broken up. There will not be any more British teams. The countries will play as England, Scotland, Ireland, and Wales. England will have best chance to do well, especially if they can find a way to re-entice their wayward stars. For the other three countries, finishing in the top half of the field may exceed initial expectations.

Meanwhile on the business side, I had grown tired of all the travel involved in the rug business; going to China four times a year for a two-week visit was taking its toll. After I arrived, it was a hard grind with hours of driving around the country. It was also harder to get over the jet lag for that particular trip. Although I was still enjoying the research for new product lines, there were numerous aspects of the business that were no longer fun. Two of the critical areas of my life, bridge and business, were therefore at a standstill. I had worked happily alongside my dad since 1970. He still enjoyed what he was doing at the age of eighty and worked every day. Of my three sons, Raymond (the oldest) was working as a sales representative with the rug company, Jonathan (the middle one) was in Israel and Daniel was in his last couple of months of high school before going to college.

I decided to try to bring about a major change in my life. The other family members in the company agreed to an arrangement that would allow me to exit and with the help of my wife Mags, I made plans early in 1997 to move to the USA in 1998. The plan was to combine playing bridge with writing and teaching and with luck, not go hungry while attempting it. I wanted to compete at the highest level in US bridge and make my mark by winning a national championship or, at least, coming close. At that time few British players had enjoyed any real success in the US Nationals, with only Michael Rosenberg being a consistent winner. Of course, not having a partner added a small complication but I was not to be daunted, and as the song goes, 'with a little help from my friends', we arrived in sunny Miami in March, 1998. After half an hour in an office at Miami airport we successfully passed through US Immigration.

Life in the USA had begun.

C H A P T E R 5

A Late Invitation

After our disappointments in the European Championships in 1993, I headed off to Israel for the Maccabiah Games, the 'Jewish Olympics'. My intended partner, Irving Rose, had had to drop out of the team at a late stage for health reasons and I played with Irving Gordon instead. Despite having lived in England most of his life, Irving was from Scotland originally and was known as 'Haggis' to his friends. We played reasonably well, and our team ended up getting the silver medal — we lost to a young but strong Israeli team in the final after being a few IMPs ahead going into the last quarter.

After this, Haggis was supposed to play in the Macallan Invitational (the renamed Sunday Times Invitational) with Boris Schapiro, but now Schapiro had taken ill and so I was invited to partner Haggis, some dozen years after I had last played the event. Play took place over three days and the players wore evening dress at all sessions, including the morning ones. All the players were interviewed by tournament organizer Irving Rose, both for television and video. Omar Sharif was there in his favorite role of bridge player partnering Paul Chemla, the French world champion whose cigars were second only to those of Ronnie Rubin. The grand old man of European bridge, Jean Besse, still a great player, provided VuGraph commentary. There were sixteen pairs and we finished in eighth place, 102 points behind the winners, Balicki and Zmudzinski from Poland (or B-Z as we called them for simplicity). I will give you some of the problems I faced — if you solve them all, you would have won the tournament and a nice pot of cash. Your methods are natural and partner's bidding can be considered fairly solid.

You hold the following collection, both sides vulnerable, and your opponents are B-Z.

♠ A K Q 8   ♡ A 8 7   ◇ A J 2   ♣ 9 8 6

You open 1♣ and then B-Z go into their dance:

West	North	East	South
You	**Z**	**partner**	**B**
1♣	1NT[1]	pass	2NT[2]
dbl	3◇[3]	3♠	pass
?			

1. Majors or minors.
2. Four-card support for one suit.
3. Six diamonds and four clubs.

What do you bid now?

You hold:

♠ —   ♡ K J 7 3   ◇ A Q 6 2   ♣ K J 8 5 2

West	North	East	South
You		**partner**	
		1♠	pass
2♣	pass	2♡	pass
3◇[1]	pass	3♡	pass
?			

1. Forced by your methods.

What is your next bid?

Both vulnerable, you hold:

♠ Q   ♡ K 9 8 6 5 4   ◇ 9 7 6 2   ♣ K Q

You hear 1♠ on your right, pass by you, 2♠ on your left, pass by your partner and pass on your right. There is a hungry young American on your left with a Florida suntan. Do you put your head on the chopping block?

| P | R | O | B | L | E | M | 4 |

You hold:

♠ Q 10   ♡ 7 5 2   ◇ K J 7 6 4   ♣ 8 6 3

Playing against the Olympiad champs from France, Levy and Mouiel, partner opens 1♣, righty bids 1♡, and you pass. Lefty bids *quatre coeurs* and partner doubles. Do you sit it out or pull to 4NT or 5◇?

| P | R | O | B | L | E | M | 5 |

Playing against the new but so far unlucky partnership of Bob Hamman and Zia, you hold:

♠ K 7 6   ♡ 7   ◇ A K Q J 6 2   ♣ K J 10

You open 1◇ and partner responds 1♡. You bid 3NT and partner raises to 4NT. Do you bid a slam, try for slam, or pass 4NT?

| P | R | O | B | L | E | M | 6 |

Playing against Meckwell you hold:

♠ 6   ♡ J 10 7 6 2   ◇ 6 2   ♣ K 10 8 5 4

West	North	East	South
	Rodwell	You	Meckstroth
	2◇[1]	pass	2NT
pass	3♡[2]	pass	4♠
all pass			

1. Weak two in one of the majors.
2. Poor weak-two in spades.

Partner leads the ◇K. You follow with the ◇2. Meckstroth takes the ace and plays the ♠2 to the queen followed by a spade to the ten and partner's jack. Partner cashes the ♠A, drawing declarer's king. You discarded the ♡2 on the second trump; what do you throw on the third round?

♠ Q 8 7 5 4 3
♡ 4
◇ 7 5
♣ Q J 9 6

◇ K led

```
        N
   W         E
        S
```

♠ 6
♡ J 10 7 6 2
◇ 6 2
♣ K 10 8 5 4

P R O B L E M   7

Last problem. You are on defense against a slam as West and hold

♠ 10 5   ♡ K 9 8 4   ◇ J 10 8 5   ♣ 9 8 2

West	North	East	South
			2NT
pass	3♣	pass	3♡[1]
pass	4NT	pass	5♣[2]
pass	6♡	all pass	

    1. Five hearts.
    2. 0 or 3 keycards.

```
        ♠ K J
        ♡ Q 7 3
        ◇ A Q 6 4 3
        ♣ J 5 4
♠ 10 5
♡ K 9 8 4       N
◇ J 10 8 5   W     E
♣ 9 8 2         S
```

You decide to lead a sneaky ◇10. Dummy plays the deuce and South the king. Declarer leads a spade to the king on which partner plays the ♠7. Next, a low heart is led from the table, partner plays the ♡5 and South the ♡10. How do you defend from here?

S O L U T I O N   1

```
        ♠ J 6 5 4 3 2
        ♡ K J 10 4
        ◇ 10 8
        ♣ 5
♠ 9 7                    ♠ 10
♡ Q           N          ♡ 9 6 5 3 2
◇ K Q 9 7 4 3   W   E    ◇ 6 5
♣ A K Q 2         S      ♣ J 10 7 4 3
        ♠ A K Q 8
        ♡ A 8 7
        ◇ A J 2
        ♣ 9 8 6
```

Four spades by you saves 12 IMPs. Partner could have bid more, earlier.

```
                           ♠ J 9 7 5 4
                           ♡ A Q 10 9 2
                           ◊ K 5
                           ♣ A
```

Bidding only four hearts
loses 12 IMPs, as every
other pair reaches six. If
you bid anything other
than game, award your-
self 12 IMPs.

```
        ♠ A Q 10              ┌──────────┐      ♠ K 8 6 3 2
        ♡ 6 5                 │    N     │      ♡ 8 4
        ◊ J 10 9 7 4          │ W     E  │      ◊ 8 3
        ♣ Q 6 3              │    S     │      ♣ 10 9 7 4
                             └──────────┘
```

```
                           ♠ —
                           ♡ K J 7 3
                           ◊ A Q 6 2
                           ♣ K J 8 5 2
```

```
                           ♠ 10 8 2
                           ♡ A J 10 2
                           ◊ Q J
                           ♣ 8 4 3 2
```

If you play chicken and
pass, award yourself 13
IMPs. If you bid 3♡,
Bobby Levin doubles
and partner sits it out.
There were better spots,
but if you can err so can
he.

```
        ♠ Q                   ┌──────────┐      ♠ J 9 4 3
        ♡ K 9 8 6 5 4         │    N     │      ♡ —
        ◊ 9 7 6 2             │ W     E  │      ◊ A K 8 3
        ♣ K Q                │    S     │      ♣ J 10 7 6 5
                             └──────────┘
```

```
                           ♠ A K 7 6 5
                           ♡ Q 7 3
                           ◊ 10 5 4
                           ♣ A 9
```

                    ♠ Q 10
                    ♡ 7 5 2
                    ◇ K J 7 6 4
                    ♣ 8 6 3

♠ K J 9 3   ♠ 8 5 4
♡ K J 10 9 4   ┌─────────┐   ♡ A Q 8 6 3
◇ —   │   N   │   ◇ Q 8 3 2
♣ K 10 7 2   │ W   E │   ♣ 9
                │   S   │
                └─────────┘
                    ♠ A 7 6 2
                    ♡ —
                    ◇ A 10 9 5
                    ♣ A Q J 5 4

If you pass, you lose 990. I did, but I was in good company — Hamman passed also and lost 18 IMPs along with me.

                    ♠ A J 9
                    ♡ Q J 8 5
                    ◇ 9 8 3
                    ♣ 9 5 4

♠ K 7 6   ♠ Q 8 5 2
♡ 7   ┌─────────┐   ♡ A K 9 6 3
◇ A K Q J 6 2   │   N   │   ◇ 7 5
♣ K J 10   │ W   E │   ♣ A 7
                │   S   │
                └─────────┘
                    ♠ 10 4 3
                    ♡ 10 4 2
                    ◇ 10 4
                    ♣ Q 8 6 3 2

If you bid you will save 12 IMPs. Six diamonds is cold, but if you try 6NT you better guess the ♣Q.

You had better throw an encouraging club to stop partner doing anything foolish (like playing a red card). If you worked this out, you win 15 IMPs (you gain nine instead of losing six).

```
                     ♠ Q 8 7 5 4 3
                     ♡ 4
                     ◇ 7 5
                     ♣ Q J 9 6
  ♠ A J 9                              ♠ 6
  ♡ K 8 5          N                   ♡ J 10 7 6 2
  ◇ K Q 9 8 3    W     E               ◇ 6 2
  ♣ 3 2              S                 ♣ K 10 8 5 4
                     ♠ K 10 2
                     ♡ A Q 9 3
                     ◇ A J 10 4
                     ♣ A 7
```

You must win the ♡K and return the ♡8 or ♡9 — only by leading a second trump do you stop him from ruffing a spade in dummy. It's a marvelous position. Now to make the hand, declarer will have to play double-dummy. He will have to draw all the trumps without attempting a spade ruff and then

```
                     ♠ K J
                     ♡ Q 7 3
                     ◇ A Q 6 4 3
                     ♣ J 7 5
  ♠ 10 5                              ♠ Q 8 7 4 3 2
  ♡ K 9 8 4        N                  ♡ 5
  ◇ J 10 8 5     W     E              ◇ 9 2
  ♣ 9 8 2            S                ♣ Q 10 6 4
                     ♠ A 9 6
                     ♡ A J 10 6 2
                     ◇ K 7
                     ♣ A K 3
```

discard two diamonds on the fourth and fifth round of trumps. Next he must cash the ♣AK and lead a diamond to dummy to squeeze East in the black suits. I wish I had put him to that test! Unfortunately, I stupidly ducked the ♡10 and declarer could now play the ♠A and ruff a spade with no problem. When he led the ♡Q to my king I could not stop him from shedding his club loser on dummy's high diamonds.

If you won the ♡K and returned the ♡8 or ♡9, take 13 IMPs.

If you answered all eight questions correctly, you have won one of the world's most prestigious tournament. Well done! If not, just add your score to ours and see what top pairs you would have beaten and how much cash you would have won.

1	A. Zmudzinski - C. Balicki	543	$10,000
2	R. Levin - G. Kasle	520	$ 5000
3	T. Forrester - A. Robson	514	$ 2500
4	E. Rodwell - J. Meckstroth	493	$ 2100
5	G. Helgemo - T. Helness	478	$ 1800
6	P. Forquet - G. Belladonna	474	$ 1500
7	M. Becker - R. Rubin	444	$ 1250
8	B. Shenkin - I. Gordon	441	Unlucky!!!! No cash

Ninth through sixteenth places included ten world champions but I have accepted a small inducement not to mention their names.

Barnet contemplating his hand

The closing banquet was a fine and humorous affair. Bob Hamman, who finished only thirteenth with Zia, told the audience that if he had to play for his life Zia would be his second choice of partner. Everyone else would be first! Zia, whose results here were not up to his usual high standard, was not to be outdone, and said that with hard practice they could come twelfth next year. Omar Sharif concluded the speeches by telling everyone that if someone had told him before the event that he would finish only four places higher than Zia and Hamman, he would not have bothered to come! Yes, bridge is a strange and funny game. Great champions lose in every tournament, but it takes an extra something to do so gracefully and then come back even more determined to win the next one.

Last Chance Saloon

I t is 1998, and after an enjoyable but expensive summer during which we had participated in the *joie de vivre* of Paris, the World Championships in Lille, and a splendid family wedding in Edinburgh, the only possibility of recouping some of the cost lies at the bridge club in London. After ten sessions I am dead even (of course I have been dealt a run of terrible cards) and this is my last chance. The afternoon session is nearly over, and these are to be my final four hands. We are, as usual, playing Chicago, a form of scoring where each player plays four hands at different vulnerabilities with the same partner before cutting again. My current partner is Maurice, the accountant, and we are playing against Bob, the professional bridge player, and Peter, the barrister.

On the first hand I pick up:

♠ 10 7 6 2   ♡ K 10 9 8 4   ◇ Q   ♣ A 6 4

Bob, my left-hand opponent, opens 3♡ (neither side is vulnerable), partner is there with 3♠ and it goes 4♡ on my right. To double or to bid? I choose 4♠ and when it goes 'double' on my right, I redouble. RHO leads the ◇A and the full hand is as you see it here.

West switches to a club at Trick 2, and declarer wins in hand, ruffs a diamond and leads a trump. Nothing can prevent him from scoring his game. I write 830 points on my side of the scoresheet.

Barnet
♠ 10 7 6 2
♡ K 10 9 8 4
◇ Q
♣ A 6 4

Peter
♠ A J 8
♡ J 6
◇ A K J 9 7
♣ J 7 3

Bob
♠ 3
♡ A Q 7 5 3 2
◇ 10 8 4 2
♣ 10 2

Maurice
♠ K Q 9 5 4
♡ —
◇ 6 5 3
♣ K Q 9 8 5

On the next deal we are not vulnerable against vulnerable, and I pick up:

♠ **A K 9 7**   ♡ **4**   ◇ **Q 7 4 3**   ♣ **9 6 4 3**

This time Maurice opens 1♡, and I hear a takeout double on my right. I redouble, hopeful of a possible juicy penalty. To my astonishment I hear 4♠ on my left, followed by two passes. Now Maurice does not psyche, so I confidently place a red card on the table. It now goes 'redouble' from lefty, and everyone passes! What is going on? I know I have my bid, and Maurice surely does, so who doesn't? Partner leads the ♠10 — nice to see he has one — and the full hand is as you see it to the left (rotated for convenience).

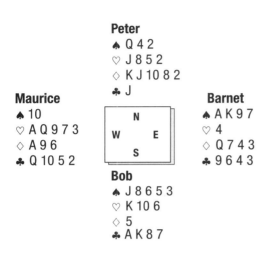

Peter
♠ Q 4 2
♡ J 8 5 2
◇ K J 10 8 2
♣ J

Maurice
♠ 10
♡ A Q 9 7 3
◇ A 9 6
♣ Q 10 5 2

Barnet
♠ A K 9 7
♡ 4
◇ Q 7 4 3
♣ 9 6 4 3

Bob
♠ J 8 6 5 3
♡ K 10 6
◇ 5
♣ A K 8 7

Declarer plays the queen, I win and shift to my heart. Partner wins this and cashes the ♡A but I stupidly pitch a club. I ruff the next heart, cash the other high trump and play my last trump. Declarer wins and tries a diamond but partner takes his ace to lead the ♣Q. Declarer wins this, cashes the ♣A and gets out with the ♣8. As a result of my previous careless play, I now have to jettison my ♣9 or be endplayed and partner now can only score his ♣10. Four down is 2200, but had I been more careful it would have been 2800. I suppose you shouldn't worry too much over that kind of mistake.

It turns out Peter had pulled the wrong card from the bidding box, so had doubled when he meant to pass originally. Peter apologizes to his partner who calmly tells him not to worry, it could happen to anyone!

However, the game has gone very silent as I pick up my hand on the third deal:

♠ **K Q 9 2**   ♡ **Q 7 4 2**   ◇ **6**   ♣ **J 8 4 3**

Pass on my right, pass from me, 1♡ from lefty, 3◇ from my man, double on my right (which is penalties in this game), all pass. We are vulnerable, and I have some bits and pieces despite my lack of diamond help. Peter leads the ♡5.

Bob wins the ♡K and switches to a club. Maurice wins the ace, cashes the ◊A and plays four rounds of spades pitching his losing club. Now he concedes three trump tricks, making three for another 670.

With 830, 2200, and 670 in the bag, I pick up the last hand:

Maurice
♠ A 8 4
♡ 8
◊ A J 10 8 7 5 2
♣ A 5

Bob
♠ J 7 5
♡ A K 10 9 3
◊ 3
♣ 10 7 6 2

Peter
♠ 10 6 3
♡ J 6 5
◊ K Q 9 4
♣ K Q 9

```
      N
  W       E
      S
```

Barnet
♠ K Q 9 2
♡ Q 7 4 2
◊ 6
♣ J 8 4 3

♠ Q   ♡ A K 9 5   ◊ Q 7   ♣ A Q J 9 5 2

This time both sides are vulnerable. I open 1♣ and hear 1◊ on my left, pass from partner, 1♡ on my right. I bid 2♣, it goes double on my left, and again everyone passes. Now in this game almost all doubles are for penalties, but this can't be that terrible, surely.

Bob leads the ◊A and switches to his heart. I win, draw trumps ending in dummy, and lead a heart to establish a third heart trick. Two clubs doubled making three, and as this was the last hand we score

Maurice
♠ 9 7 6 3
♡ 8 6 4
◊ 6 3 2
♣ K 10 3

Bob
♠ A J 10 4
♡ 2
◊ A K J 9 8
♣ 8 7 6

Peter
♠ K 8 5 2
♡ Q J 10 7 3
◊ 10 5 4
♣ 4

```
      N
  W       E
      S
```

Barnet
♠ Q
♡ A K 9 5
◊ Q 7
♣ A Q J 9 5 2

130 plus 100 for the partscore and 200 for the overtrick — a total of 430. This combined with the other three deals makes 4130 for a rubber of 41 points. Strange, when we only actually bid one game contract! 'Hard luck, boys,' I say, trying to appear sympathetic as we all quit the table.

To add to my good fortune I bump into Zia, who wants to discuss some hands from his game and invites me for dinner. As I enjoy some excellent grilled peppered tuna, he tells me about the day's adventures and I start to tell him about mine. I tell him about our 830 for four spades redoubled and immediately he says "Don't be stupid, Barnet, it's not 830 anymore, it's 880 — a very common score for me, I can assure you." I have forgotten that these days, the score is 100 'for the insult' in a redoubled contract, not 50. That would have made my total score 4180, enough for a 42-point rubber. Needless to say, I am not very worried about it and decide not to go into the club the next day to claim one more point!

CHAPTER 7

A Scottish Transfer

aving finally exhausted the supply of suitable partners in the UK by the middle 1990s, I was in the position of being forced to play with my wife Mags. Although we did enjoy some success (winning the Scottish Cup one year) I realized that the way things were going I would have to find either a new bridge partner or a new wife, and having no wish for the latter, I decided on the former. I had always wanted to play golf in sunshine instead of wind and rain, and thought that by moving to the USA (and Florida specifically) I would have my chance to do that, as well as being able to play bridge in the Nationals. There are three North American National Championships each year, tournaments of the highest standard that, mainly for geographic reasons, I had previously visited only on rare occasions. Many of the world's best players can be found at these events, and indeed, the Nationals have been assuming an increasing international flavor in recent years — to the chagrin of some of the USA's professional players, more and more foreign stars are attending. Many of these are Europeans with whom I am on friendly terms.

Of course, having played in the USA previously, I was aware that there are substantial differences between European tournaments and those in the USA. In the UK, for instance, the key national championships (which compare to the Spingold, Reisinger or Vanderbilt in importance and quality of field) are run on a knockout basis. Perhaps because there is less travel involved than would be the case in the USA, teams meet locally for head-to-head matches in the early rounds of both the Gold Cup and the Scottish Cup. Sometimes if there is a large distance involved, teams agree to meet at a halfway house as it were. The Gold Cup final rounds for the last eight teams are held at a central venue over a weekend. In England, the other prestigious teams event is the Crockfords Cup, where the original entry play knockout matches and the final eight teams play a Round Robin, also over one weekend, for the title. Another popular event is the Spring Foursomes; in this event, no team is eliminated until they have lost two matches. There is a lot of comfort for the participants knowing they can lose a knockout match and still be in the main event! A team that reaches the final with no losses has the right to play an extra eight boards should they find themselves behind at the end of the regulation number of boards.

In England, large numbers gather for the Spring Foursomes and also for the Brighton Teams and Pairs, which are traditionally held in August. These events would be similar to a US Nationals with many tables in play in large hotel ballrooms and exhibition halls. In Scotland, it was more common to hold local Bridge Congresses, sometimes in the very best hotels, albeit with smaller numbers of people attending. My favorite spots were Turnberry, Gleneagles and more recently, Peebles Hydro. These were all magnificent venues in the Scottish countryside. The five-star hotels dramatically reduced their rates in order to fill all their rooms for the weekend. All meals would be included in the price and the standard was generally excellent. In the past it was also customary to wear evening dress for dinner; today this is optional, but it makes such a pleasant contrast to the usual dress code of bridge players, with the women in beautiful gowns and the men in tuxedos. As many of the same people went to each of these events, we all knew one another and the weekends turned into one long party which went on long after the bridge had finished.

During play, waiters constantly visited the card tables to provide refreshments to the players, and the occasional scotch, glass of wine or pint of beer generally made it possible to take a more charitable view of partner's dubious plays. That's not to say that the bridge wasn't extremely serious. I remember playing in a qualifying session for a match-pointed pairs event when the fire alarm went off late in the evening. At the table next to me a very assertive woman, who was in the middle of playing a slam, took the arm of her right-hand opponent. "Nobody leaves this table until the hand is finished!" she said in a loud voice. Play was terminated very shortly after, with declarer scoring her contract. Bridge players and guests alike stood outside the hotel while the fire brigade checked the premises out. Fortunately it was a warm summer's night, otherwise the few hotel guests that were not bridge players and had retired to bed early would certainly have caught their deaths of cold standing in various states of disarray in front of the hotel for nearly an hour as the fire brigade determined that the hotel was not in fact burning down.

In Europe the tournaments were varied and catered to bridge players with different tastes. There were week-long Festivals of Bridge in France — Juan les Pins, Deauville, and Biarritz. Juan les Pins is a favorite venue for many players, situated in the unique Côte d'Azur. The Festival was often held at the same time as the Cannes Film Festival just a few miles away. The format (one long session of play in the afternoon) left plenty of time for the beach in the morning.

Likewise, after the session you could take your pick from any number of fine restaurants in the area to sample the delights of French cuisine or you could nip along to Cannes and rub shoulders with the glitterati.

One significant feature of this and the other French tournaments was the large number of cash prizes. Often the list would go down many places and there would be special awards for the leading women's pair and the leading mixed pair as well as one for the juniors. The organizers would give a large amount of the entry money back in prizes — indeed, sometimes with the aid of a sponsor more money could be given back than was taken in. I remember playing in the Coupe D'Or Cino del Duca which used to be played annually in or near Paris. A number of times it was played in the quite magnificent Palais de Chaillot in Paris — a magnificent setting in wonderful gardens. The first time I played there was in 1971 with my friend, Victor 'Stoney' Silverstone. I was just twenty years old and the first pair we had to play against was Garozzo and Forquet. As we arranged the unfamiliar French playing cards, I noticed about a dozen kibitzers positioning themselves behind our opponents. I can't in all honesty say I remember the hands but I do know we finished in twentieth position and I happily received my cash prize of 500 francs, the first cash I had ever won in a serious event. I still have a letter signed by Madame del Duca to remind me of the occasion.

In the United States, of course, events are run very differently and some of the ideas still seem quite strange to me. First, if you pay the entry fee for an event and qualify for the next day, you keep paying more entry money. So the successful players keep paying more money and the losers pay less. Why not let everybody pay one entry fee at the beginning and reward the winners by not having to pay the next day? Even at the recent International Team Trials, entry fees were hefty and we saw the peculiar scenario of a Junior team, who had proceeded much further than they had expected, trying to gather together enough funds to pay yet another entry fee. Where is their reward for exceeding expectations? Let there be one entry fee only — this would have the added benefit of perhaps discouraging teams that are in fact holidaymakers with no chance of making even a good showing.

But even stranger than the attitude to entry fees is the lack of prizes of any kind. The ACBL takes in many thousands of dollars in entry fees at its tournaments, yet gives the successful players back nothing. Perhaps this is because many of the winners in national competitions are professional players and it is felt that they should not be rewarded, but what of all the other players? Those who travel all over the country to play and win an event in any flight should receive some kind of reward or memento. I played in a large Charity pairs event with Mags on the first evening of a recent Nationals. There were more than three hundred pairs participating at an entry fee of $40 a pair and we won. Our prize — 25 master points each! Not exactly a memento of the occasion. Of course, the object of this particular event was to raise money for charity, but surely a commemorative pen, for example, would not have broken the bank! Incidentally, I now have played in seven Nationals, picking up bundles of master points, but I still haven't made Life Master. There is a peculiar rule that to do this, a certain number of 'silver' points are required. Now silver points are only obtained by playing in the small sectional tournaments, and I don't play in them so maybe I will never make Life Master. That is just too bad but it does perhaps point out that the ACBL currency of master points seems to be undergoing devaluation.

As for the standard of play, I would judge that the top teams in today's Nationals are at a level above that of most events in Europe, with the exception of perhaps only a few special tournaments which bring together some of the best European teams. France, Italy, Poland, Norway, the Netherlands, and Sweden all have the ability to be strong contenders in the Bermuda Bowl, and can field teams that will be in contention in any event they enter. European players will usually play more complex systems, however, and are often prepared to work hard on them. Bidding style in general was more complex in UK, with many players playing the Multi two diamonds as far back as the early seventies while Precision Club also had a large group of followers.

Mags and I had in fact played our first game in USA at the Boston Nationals in 1990, where we played in the Mixed Teams with Peter Nagy and Donna Hay. After the first qualifying session, we started to score up. The first few results were called out and and Donna, who was scoring, would call out, 'That's 1. That's 1.' Then came a board where we had plus 420 and Donna and Peter had plus 50. When Donna said, 'Another 1,' Mags exclaimed, 'Come on, I know that's not 1!' We had both thought we were playing IMPs and that they were using a very strange IMP scale in the USA! It turned out the event was Board-a Match, and in spite of never having played this kind of scoring before, we finished a creditable fourth. We also encountered other new terms and expressions that seem to be peculiar to the States. I remember in Albuquerque after the first quarter of an early Spingold match, Mags passed Paul Soloway heading back to the hotel.

"How are you doing, Paul?" she asked.

"We're stuck sixty," was the response.

Having no idea what that meant, she nodded knowledgeably. "That's good," she said, as Paul shrugged his shoulders and disappeared. Michael Polowan was at hand to explain this strange terminology — for non-Americans, it means he was *down* sixty IMPs!

In the beginning Maggie was very nervous in playing at the Nationals. One year, since Peter Nagy was involved in a late round of the Spingold, we played the Mixed Teams with Donna and Tony Forrester as teammates. Mags dressed to give herself confidence — black silk dress pants and a low-cut glittering top. In an early round she was playing a 4♠ contract against a well-known American bridge dignitary (at the time we had no idea who he was). She had to strip the hand and then play ace, king and another in a side suit, hoping that the dignitary would win and be endplayed. Holding Qxx in the key side suit, he thought a while about unblocking and started bantering with Mags, trying to find out whether she had the jack and therefore if he would give up a vital overtrick by unblocking. Finally he asked her directly if she was going to make the contract and she promptly replied, "Yes." He did not unblock and was duly thrown in to give her the contract. As we walked to the next table, he was talking vehemently with the director, accusing Mags of misleading him by telling him she was going to make the contract. Although he was completely in the wrong (after all, he had started the coffeehousing) it wasn't that which really attracted my wife's attention — he was pointing her out to the director and describing her as 'the woman with the big boobs'. I think she was secretly quite flattered — in Europe, she was not accustomed to such eloquence from her opponents!

My first Nationals after moving across the ocean was the 1998 Fall Nationals, which were held at the Peabody Hotel in Orlando, Florida. This was an excellent venue, highlighted by watching the famous Peabody ducks descend in the elevator daily and walk in procession across the hotel lobby to the fountain. Our team for the Reisinger was Wolff-Morse, Ross-Nagy, Mike Becker and myself. All three pairs had played together before but none were regular partnerships. I had played with Mike in his weekly IMP game in Boca and also in a couple of Regionals.

The Reisinger is Board-a-Match format, and attracts fewer weak teams in its entry list than do the Spingold or the Vanderbilt; it therefore has the reputation of being the toughest of the three to win. After qualifying for the final two sessions, our team scored 16 out of 27 in the afternoon set, moving into second place behind Shugart, Robson, Helgemo and Forrester. In the evening I sat out, and had the dubious pleasure of watching the progress of my team on VuGraph. Although we had the lead near the end, we slipped in the final furlong and finished 1.1 boards behind the winners, Shugart, and 0.3 of a board behind the second-place team (Jacobs, with his Italian World Champions Versace-Lauria). So there were actually European players on each of the first three teams.

Here are two deals where I could have won extra points for the team; try them and see how you do.

You lead the ♡A and partner plays the ♡9 (discouraging); it's not clear that switching to a diamond is right at this point, so you cash the ♠A and play a second heart, partner playing the ♡5. Declarer wins and plays three rounds of clubs, ruffing the third in hand. Now he ruffs a spade, plays a diamond to the ace and cashes his last two trumps. On the last trump, you have to keep either two diamonds and the ♠Q or two diamonds and the ♠10. What do you keep?

```
                ♠ K
                ♡ 10 6 5
                ◇ 7 5 4 2
                ♣ K J 8 5 4
♠ A Q 10 7 6 2      ┌──────────┐
♡ A 3               │    N     │
◇ Q 10 3            │  W   E   │
♣ 7 2               │    S     │
                    └──────────┘
```

West	North	East	South
1♠	pass	pass	dbl
pass	2♣	pass	2♡
pass	3♡	pass	4♡
all pass			

You hold:

♠ 7 4 3   ♡ K 4 2   ◇ 10 6   ♣ A Q 9 8 5

Neither side is vulnerable; on your left Alan Sontag passes and partner opens 1◇. You hear a pass from Peter Weichsel and you bid 1NT. Now Sonty emerges with 2◇ (for majors) and partner says 'double' to show a good hand. It goes 3♡ on your right — what would you bid now?

West Sontag	North Becker	East Weichsel	South Barnet
pass	1◇	pass	1NT
2◇	dbl	3♡	?

If you pitched your ♠Q so as not to be thrown in, bad luck — declarer's ♠J is the tenth trick. It is impossible to know for sure what is right, but if you kept your ♠Q you win the board and an extra half-point.

♠ K
♡ 10 6 5
◇ 7 5 4 2
♣ K J 8 5 4

♠ A Q 10 7 6 2
♡ A 3
◇ Q 10 3
♣ 7 2

	N	
W		E
	S	

♠ 9 5 4
♡ 9 4 2
◇ J 8 6
♣ Q 9 6 3

♠ J 8 3
♡ K Q J 8 7
◇ A K 9
♣ A 10

It looked to me as though partner had heart shortness and strength in the minors, so I tried 3NT and when that went round to East, who doubled, I ran to 4♣. The defense took their two diamonds, a ruff and the ♠A for down one. In the replay 3NT also went down a trick so we ended up with a tie. To win the board you have to pass or double 3♡ — since you can have at most three hearts, perhaps double is correct.

♠ K 5
♡ A 8 7
◇ K J 9 8 7 2
♣ K 3

♠ A Q 8 6 2
♡ J 10 5 3
◇ 5
♣ 10 7 6

	N	
W		E
	S	

♠ J 10 9
♡ Q 9 6
◇ A Q 4 3
♣ J 4 2

♠ 7 4 3
♡ K 4 2
◇ 10 6
♣ A Q 9 8 5

West Sontag	North Becker	East Weichsel	South Barnet
pass	1◇	pass	1NT
2◇	dbl	3♡	?

If you came up with both winning answers, the Reisinger is yours, but every member of our team had the opportunity to win it, of course. A little bit of luck can also go a long way. Against the winners near the end, one of our team had to decide what to open with:

♠ A 10 5   ♡ A Q 8 7 2   ♢ 7 6   ♣ A J 10

In first chair he opened 1♡, ending up in a heart partscore for a loss, as the opponents bid to 4♡ and made ten tricks. Had he chosen to open 1NT, however, he would certainly have reached 3NT and collected the same ten tricks to win the board — and the event. As is often the case in bridge, there is no right answer. The result merchant advocates 1NT while the purist opens 1♡, and in the end perhaps fate lends a hand.

Undaunted, it was on to Vancouver in the spring of 1999 and I partnered Sam Lev with Jaggy Shivdasani playing with Rav Murthy and Michael Polowan making up our team. We had a fair run before losing by 3 IMPs (ouch!) in the quarterfinals of the Vanderbilt. While we were drowning our sorrows in the bar, Brian Glubok came up to us and asked Sam who his winning team should be in the two-day National Swiss event starting the next day. As the start was only a few hours away, we hurriedly put together a team consisting of Sam and Brian, Polly, John Mohan and myself, with Jaggy and Rav deserting to join Zia. Sam was captain and handed out instructions to each of us: 'You will have four partners,' he said, 'you three,' and so on. The qualifying sessions were on Saturday and I played with Sam, with Brian for the first time, and with Polly. We won seven of our eight matches and qualified eighth behind Chemla, who was leading, and Shugart who was second.

In the final I started with Sam, moved on to Brian, and completed the full set by playing with John before finishing the tournament with Sam — a bit like musical chairs really. Sam Lev, by the way, is a really great player. Some think he's hard on his partners but that's certainly not true if you play perfectly. For the first match I had a kibitzer, and she came up to me afterwards and asked me if we had lost that match.

'We won 20-0,' I told her.

'From listening to your partner, I thought you had lost 20-0!' was her reply.

Here are two critical deals from this event.

Jaggy Shivdasani

After hearing Sam open 1♣ at favorable vulnerability, Chip Martel overcalled 1♡ and I had to choose how many diamonds to bid. I opted for 4◇ and when Zia bid 4♡, Sam doubled. Obviously I was very nervous, but I decided to let it go — pulling one of Sam's penalty doubles would be our last board together if I was wrong. I led a club and Chip won the ace, unblocking his jack. He now played a heart, ducking when Sam played the king. Sam cashed the ◇A and continued with the ♡10. Chip won, played a spade to dummy's ace and finessed the ♠J. He now threw Sam in with a spade, and was able to shake his diamond loser for down one. Close — if Sam had held one fewer spade and one more club, he would have made it. In the other room Michael Rosenberg leapt to 5◇ on my cards and went down 300 when that was doubled. We won this key match 17-3.

Another fun deal came up when we played Berkowitz and Cohen in the sixth match.

```
              ♠ A 9 6 3
              ♡ 9 5 4 3
              ◇ 4 3
              ♣ A K 10
♠ 8                        ♠ Q 10 7 2
♡ —          N            ♡ K Q 10 8
◇ K J 9 8 7 6 5 2  W  E   ◇ A
♣ 6 4 3 2       S        ♣ Q 9 7 5
              ♠ K J 5 4
              ♡ A J 7 6 2
              ◇ Q 10
              ♣ J 8
```

West Barnet	North Zia	East Sam	South Chip
		1♣	1♡
4◇	4♡	dbl	all pass

Sam Lev

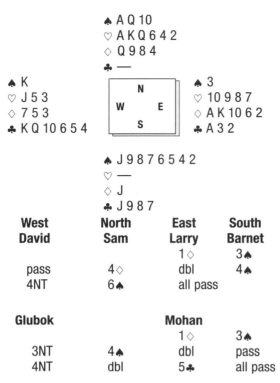

```
              ♠ A Q 10
              ♡ A K Q 6 4 2
              ♦ Q 9 8 4
              ♣ —
♠ K                        ♠ 3
♡ J 5 3          N         ♡ 10 9 8 7
♦ 7 5 3      W     E       ♦ A K 10 6 2
♣ K Q 10 6 5 4    S        ♣ A 3 2
              ♠ J 9 8 7 6 5 4 2
              ♡ —
              ♦ J
              ♣ J 9 8 7
```

West	North	East	South
David	Sam	Larry	Barnet
		1♦	3♠
pass	4♦	dbl	4♠
4NT	6♠	all pass	

Glubok		Mohan	
		1♦	3♠
3NT	4♠	dbl	pass
4NT	dbl	5♣	all pass

Larry Cohen, my golfing buddy, opened 1♦ and I took a deep breath and bid 3♠ (vulnerable against not!). We were soon in 6♠ and before his final pass David asked Sam if he would promise to bid 7♠ if David bid 6NT. That wouldn't have been bad for us, as after a club lead I made all the tricks!

At the other table, Glubok introduced a diversion when he bid 3NT over 3♠ and North-South ended up having a misunderstanding when they let 5♣ go by them. Three down and a mere minus 150 against our slam. As a result of this board, we won the match by a small margin.

It was to be our day — we won our first seven matches and were assured of victory before we played the strong Polish team in the last match. Yes, we had our share of luck but the revolving partnerships had worked well and I enjoyed two firsts — a National Championship in the USA and congratulations from Meckstroth and Rodwell, who seldom give anything away.

The Summer Nationals that year were in San Antonio. Our hotel was right beside the Alamo, and I had to go take a look at a part of American history. Then in the evening, I watched the ACBL Hall of Fame awards. My old friend Don Krauss, who I had first met in 1974, presented Bob Hamman with his Hall of Fame award and told some good stories. Don had been one of Bob's early partners and they had represented USA in the Bermuda Bowl. One day they were having coffee with a friend when Hamman said to Krauss (who had a reputation in his earlier years for being a playboy) "Don, your problem is that you can't concentrate properly. When a pretty girl passes the table, I can see you're not focused. When you should be thinking of bridge, you're thinking of sex." Krauss was temporarily lost for words when his friend chirped up, "You're just as bad, Bob — when you're having sex, you're thinking about bridge!"

Our team had come up with a new formula for the Spingold, the premier KO event. We fielded two trios — Lev, Mohan and myself, and Jaggy, Murthy and Polowan. I was talking to Lev when Richie Schwartz came over. 'I like your way of playing,' he said, with a big smile on his face. 'Two threes, I mean; maybe it will catch on and everyone will play like this.' As fate would have it, in the round of sixteen we would play Schwartz's team (including Zia-Rosenberg and Levin-Weinstein, one of the tournament favorites) but the match was pretty well decided by the end of the third quarter when we established a lead of more than 60 IMPs. Perhaps he *will* try it some time!

In the quarterfinals we played a tough match against my friend Matt Granovetter from Israel, who was playing with Lipsitz, Rich Pavlicek and his son Richie, along with Norman Kay and Eddie Kantar. In a tight match I held this hand:

♠ A K J 5 ♡ A K 9 8 6 ◇ K 7 5 ♣ 6

In fourth position with neither vulnerable, I heard 2♠ from Pavlicek junior, pass, pass. I said 'double' and now it went 3◇ on my left, 4♡ from Lev, and 5◇ on my right. What do you bid now — 5♡ or 6♡? It's close, I think, but I decided to be conservative and bid 5♡. Now a surprising development occurred — Pavlicek senior doubled!

As I had been thinking of bidding six, I showed the blue card. The odds had to be with me as we were most unlikely to go down at all and if so it would surely only be by one trick.

Sam won the spade lead in dummy and led a club to the king. East won and shifted to a low trump which Sam ran to his ten. He now had the entries to set up clubs and make twelve tricks for a score of plus 1200. This helped us post a small lead which stood until we blew the match open in the third quarter. In the final quarter there was an echo from that earlier deal. Young Pavlicek doubled Sam again in a game and then

```
              ♠ 8 3
              ♡ 10 7 5 3 2
              ◇ —
              ♣ K Q 10 7 4 3
♠ Q 10 9 7 4 2          ♠ 6
♡ —           N         ♡ Q J 4
◇ Q J 9 8 6  W     E    ◇ A 10 4 3 2
♣ 9 5           S       ♣ A J 8 2
              ♠ A K J 5
              ♡ A K 9 8 6
              ◇ K 7 5
              ♣ 6
```

| West | North | East | South |
Pavlicek Jr.	Lev	Pavlicek	Barnet
2♠	pass	pass	dbl
3◇	4♡	5◇	5♡
pass	pass	dbl	redbl
all pass			

looked at me in mock surprise when I passed. "No redouble?" he asked, smiling. As soon as he said that, I knew Lev was booked for minus 500!

So we had reached the semifinal and faced Nickell — for sure one of the world's best teams. Almost anyone would start as underdogs against Meckstroth-Rodwell, Hamman-Soloway and Nickell-Freeman. Four Spingolds in five years was their goal; could we stop the juggernaut? I knew we were favorites to lose but in the shadow of the Alamo, we vowed it would not be without a fight. We looked forward to a tough match, with not many IMPs changing hands.

I started with Lev against Nickell-Freeman while Polly and Rav played Hamman-Soloway. The match started with a bloodbath and unfortunately, it was my blood. On the very first board I picked up

♠ A Q 8 4 3 2   ♡ K 10 6 5 3   ◇ 3   ♣ 4

This was perfect for a Polish 2♠ opener, showing either five spades with a five-card minor or six spades and five hearts. It went 'double' on my left, 3♣ from Sam, 'double'. I bid 3♡, and it went 'double', all pass.

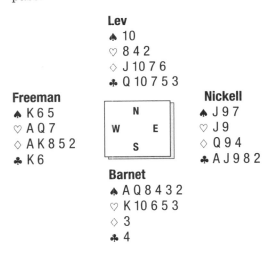

Lev
♠ 10
♡ 8 4 2
◇ J 10 7 6
♣ Q 10 7 5 3

Freeman
♠ K 6 5
♡ A Q 7
◇ A K 8 5 2
♣ K 6

Nickell
♠ J 9 7
♡ J 9
◇ Q 9 4
♣ A J 9 8 2

Barnet
♠ A Q 8 4 3 2
♡ K 10 6 5 3
◇ 3
♣ 4

Freeman led the ◇A and switched to a low club. Nickell won the ♣8 to play the ♡9; would you cover with the ♡10? It seemed the hearts were 4-1 so I played low, trying to retain some control in the trump suit. However, since if hearts were 4-1 I was booked for a disaster anyway, I should probably have covered and hoped for the best.

Nickell had made a great play, making me think he held a singleton heart, and when I played low, he continued hearts. Now they could draw trumps, tap me and eventually get me for 1100 — down five! If I had covered the ♡9 and they had continued trumps, I could have set up the spades and got out for down two. What a way to start the match. I had blown 15 IMPs — teammates made 3NT in other room, so down two for minus 300 would actually have gained us 3 IMPs. Of course, even if I covered the ♡9 they could have got more than two down by not drawing my trumps (taking just one more trump and then tapping me) but that was not a likely defense.

Still shaky from this debacle, on Board 2, I picked up:

♠ A K 7   ♡ K 8 7   ◇ 5 4   ♣ 10 6 5 4 3

Sam opened 1♡ in third chair and and I bid 2♣ (Drury, a good pass with at least three hearts). He bid 2♠ and I raised to three with my great spade values. The next bid I heard was 5♣ which meant 'How many aces do you have excluding clubs?' I had the ♠A and the ♡K, and I also had the ♠K. Although hearts had been set as trumps, there was a danger that Lev might jump to 7♠ if I showed him three. Taking a precaution I bid 5♠ (that showed two) and when Lev tried again with 5NT I jumped to 7♡. I expected him to have something like

♠ Q J x x x   ♡ A Q x x x x   ◇ A K   ♣ —

Here is the hand (rotated for convenience):

We needed the trumps 2-2 or the hand with three hearts to have four spades — slightly more than 40 percent. Well, fortunately hearts obliged — had they not, we could probably have packed up and gone home right there and then.

Barnet
♠ A K 7
♡ K 8 7
◇ 5 4
♣ 10 6 5 4 3

Nickell
♠ 5 3
♡ 6 4
◇ K 8 6 3
♣ K Q J 9 8

Freeman
♠ 10 6 2
♡ 10 3
◇ Q J 10 9 2
♣ A 7 2

Lev
♠ Q J 9 8 4
♡ A Q J 9 5 2
◇ A 7
♣ —

In the other room the bidding went as shown on the right.

So a little luck for us and we regained 11 IMPs to be right back in the match — and we knew it.

On Board 5 Nickell-Freeman bid a close but good slam that was missed by Polly and Rav for 13 IMPs away. But we got some back on Board 6.

West Polly	North Hamman	East Rav	South Soloway
		pass	pass	1♡
pass	2♣	pass	2♠
pass	2NT	pass	3♠
pass	5♡	pass	6♡
all pass			

N-S Vul.

```
              ♠ K Q 4 3
              ♡ K J 8
              ◇ Q 8 4 3
              ♣ K 3
♠ —                              ♠ A 9 8 6 2
♡ 6              N               ♡ 9 5 4
◇ K J 10 9 6 5 2  W   E          ◇ A 7
♣ A J 10 9 7      S              ♣ 8 5 4
              ♠ J 10 7 5
              ♡ A Q 10 7 3 2
              ◇ —
              ♣ Q 6 2
```

West Freeman	North Sam	East Nickell	South Barnet
			pass
pass	1◇	1♠	2♡
3♣	3♡	pass	4♡
all pass			

Rav	Soloway	Polly	Hamman
			2♡
3◇	4♡	dbl	pass
4NT	dbl	5◇	pass
pass	dbl	all pass	

In our room I passed in first chair and Freeman also passed with his twelve minor-suit cards, expecting to be able to back in later. However, Sam stole his suit by opening 1◇ in third chair. Now when Nickell bid spades, Freeman could no longer bid diamonds naturally at a convenient level, so they lost the diamond suit and we made an easy eleven tricks in hearts. When Hamman opened my hand, Rav was able to get in at a low level and there then followed a delicate auction to 5◇ doubled. Rav went down two, which was a good save and worth 8 IMPs.

The score was 19-26 after six boards, but on Board 7 Lev found a worse lead than Soloway, allowing Freeman to bring home 3NT for another 12 IMPs. There was no let-up. On Board 8 I held this hand:

♠ 9 ♡ Q J 9 7 5 2 ◇ K J 9 5 ♣ K J

I heard 3♠ on my right, I passed, and it went 6♠ on my left. What would you have led?

If, like Hamman and myself, you decided to lead a diamond you better not have chosen the five. This was the whole hand:

If you lead the ◇5, partner has to put up his queen when declarer plays low from dummy. Even with a diamond return now, when declarer runs his spades you get squeezed in the red suits and one of the ◇8 or the ♡4 takes the twelfth trick. However, in order to execute the squeeze

```
                     ♠ 6 4
                     ♡ 10 3
                     ◇ Q 6 3 2
                     ♣ Q 10 6 5 2
     ♠ A J 3                        ♠ K Q 10 8 7 5 2
     ♡ A K 4          N             ♡ 8 6
     ◇ A 8 4       W     E          ◇ 10 7
     ♣ A 7 4 3        S             ♣ 9 8

                     Barnet
                     ♠ 9
                     ♡ Q J 9 7 5 2
                     ◇ K J 9 5
                     ♣ K J
```

declarer must cash the ♣A before running trumps to remove South's idle card; Polly did this and Nickell did not and that was a juicy 14-IMP slam swing for us.

Every year there are special Press awards for the best-bid hand, and the best-played and best-defended hands. Hands are sent in from all round the world. The next board would be my submission for the worst-defended hand.

Let's start with the opening lead. You hold:

♠ A J 6 ♡ K J 10 5 ◇ Q 10 ♣ A J 7 2

You open 1NT with both vulnerable, and, after two passes, righty bids 2♡ showing hearts and a minor. You double, full of testosterone, and it goes all pass. What would you lead ?

The Nickell team at the 1995 Bermuda Bowl medal ceremony.
Left to right: Hamman, Nickell, Rodwell, Meckstroth, Wolff, Freeman.

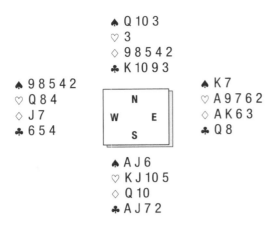

```
                ♠ Q 10 3
                ♡ 3
                ◇ 9 8 5 4 2
                ♣ K 10 9 3
  ♠ 9 8 5 4 2                    ♠ K 7
  ♡ Q 8 4        ┌──────┐        ♡ A 9 7 6 2
  ◇ J 7          │  N   │        ◇ A K 6 3
  ♣ 6 5 4      W │      │ E      ♣ Q 8
                 │  S   │
                └──────┘
                ♠ A J 6
                ♡ K J 10 5
                ◇ Q 10
                ♣ A J 7 2
```

Declarer seemed likely to have hearts and diamonds, but just in case he had hearts and clubs, I led the ♠A. A bad choice — he is more likely to hold diamonds, so the correct lead is the ♣A. Had I led the ♣A Sam would have encouraged, then won the second club, and a trump switch would have resulted in down two. Now back to the real world. When I led the ♠A, Sam played the ♠10 — encouraging. This was an error as we played king from A-K against doubled contracts. When I continued spades I played the jack and Sam played the queen! Declarer won the king and now had the good ♠98 in dummy. He played the ◇A and ◇K, ruffed a diamond and played the good ♠9 throwing a club. When the smoke had cleared, he had made an overtrick for 870. It is interesting to note that if partner retains his ♠Q we might still beat the hand, although even with perfect defense the contract can always be made from there.

And so we gave back the 14 IMPs earned on the previous hand, and the score now stood at 33-52. On the next few hands we gained 3 IMPs for an extra undertrick and Sam and I bid two non-vulnerable games that were not bid by Hamman-Soloway. One was a lucky one but the other was not:

Sam had no problem making 3NT on this board, while at the other table Hamman led the ♠9 against 2♡ doubled. If Polly had finessed this we would have won a double game swing, but it is not clear that it is the right play, and instead, he played ace and queen throwing a club — nice lead, Bob. This was still worth 7 IMPs for us, though.

On the last hand of the set, we picked up a swing for beating 4♠ a trick while our teammates stopped in 2♠. So we had scored twenty-one unanswered IMPs to lead by two after the first quarter. After all that spilling

```
                ♠ 10 8 7 6 4
                ♡ K 5 3
                ◇ K 10 3
                ♣ J 8
♠ A Q J 5 2                      ♠ 3
♡ 6 4 2          N              ♡ Q J 10 9 8 7
◇ 4 2        W       E          ◇ Q 9 8 5
♣ K 7 6          S              ♣ 10 5
                ♠ K 9
                ♡ A
                ◇ A J 7 6
                ♣ A Q 9 4 3 2
```

Freeman	Sam	Nickell	Barnet
			1♣
1♠	1NT	2♡	3NT
all pass			

Rav	Soloway	Polowan	Hamman
			1♣[1]
1♠	pass	2♡	dbl
all pass			

1. Strong, artificial.

of blood and guts, the match stood at 54-52. Bob Hamman later said to me that if someone had told him his teammates would bring in three large swings and that they would still finish the quarter behind, he would not have believed it.

The next set Lev played with John Mohan, and Polly played with Jaggy. Lev-Mohan had a very soft set but the loss was held to 24 IMPs as a result of a reasonable session by their teammates. So we were down by twenty-two at the half — not a huge amount but from here on we were only going to face their big four, Hamman-Soloway and Meckwell. Nobody gets rich playing these guys for money.

In the next quarter, I played with Mohan. John and I had played a few sessions together without problem. This set was much tighter than the first had been, but we were no better than most of Meckwell's opponents in letting chances slip away. For example, I held

♠ 8 3   ♡ 6 3 2   ◇ A Q 10 9 6   ♣ A Q 7

At unfavorable vulnerability I heard a strong club on my right from Meckstroth. I overcalled 1◇, Rodwell passed and John bid 1♡. Now Meckers bid 1♠, I passed and Rodwell bid 4♠. It's your lead.

Rodwell
♠ K 10 7 6
♡ 4
♢ K 5 4 3 2
♣ J 3 2

Barnet
♠ 8 3
♡ 6 3 2
♢ A Q 10 9 6
♣ A Q 7

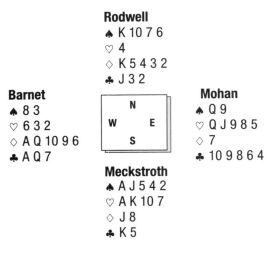

Mohan
♠ Q 9
♡ Q J 9 8 5
♢ 7
♣ 10 9 8 6 4

Meckstroth
♠ A J 5 4 2
♡ A K 10 7
♢ J 8
♣ K 5

I led a heart — wrong! If I had hit on the ◇A we would have defeated the hand. At Trick 2 I could then have continued with a low diamond, forcing partner to ruff and return a club. It would not have been unreasonable to try this lead as it was possible that Rodwell had a penalty pass of diamonds. Jaggy unfortunately went down when, after an uncontested auction and a trump lead, he played a diamond up to the king. Soloway won and switched to a heart but Jaggy tried another diamond before drawing another trump and the defense finally got their ruff.

And another chance: holding

♠ **K J 9 4 3**   ♡ **A 9 8 7**   ◇ **—**   ♣ **J 7 3 2**

as West, you hear:

West	North	East	South
		pass	1♣[1]
1♠	pass	pass	2NT
pass	3NT	all pass	

1. 16+.

♠ 10 8 7 6 5
♡ 10 3
♢ Q 10 6
♣ 10 9 4

♠ K J 9 4 3
♡ A 9 8 7
◇ —
♣ J 7 3 2

You decide to lead the ♠K in order to deny dummy an entry.

Rodwell wins the ♠A (partner following with the ♠2) and now plays the ♡J. What do you play? If you take the ace, what do you play next?

Here's the whole deal. You will see that unless you pounce on the heart and play a club, declarer has nine tricks. Also after your fine play, partner must be careful to follow up his club trick by playing the ♣A not the ♣6. I was not put to the test in clubs, as the ♡J was allowed to score. In the other room Hamman led hearts and continued them when declarer

Meckstroth
♠ 10 8 7 6 5
♡ 10 3
◇ Q 10 6
♣ 10 9 4

Mohan
♠ K J 9 4 3
♡ A 9 8 7
◇ —
♣ J 7 3 2

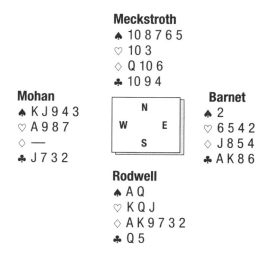

Barnet
♠ 2
♡ 6 5 4 2
◇ J 8 5 4
♣ A K 8 6

Rodwell
♠ A Q
♡ K Q J
◇ A K 9 7 3 2
♣ Q 5

played a second heart, so nine tricks came home there too. Well, at least if you got it wrong you can't be in much better company than these two players.

Not much happened in this set and the score was 13-25. If we had got the above two right we would have been down only 12 IMPs but now we were down thirty-four with only a small chance left. The small chance disappeared in the last set when the number one seeds played tough in both rooms against Jaggy-Rav and Lev-Mohan. They ran out easy winners in spite of a catastrophic bidding misunderstanding by Meckwell that resulted in their playing a slam in a cuebid. They were easily able to afford it, and their team went on to win in the final and take their fourth Spingold in five years.

And so my first cycle of Nationals as a US resident had come to an end. Close in them all, but no cigar yet in the three big ones. Just have to keep trying.

C H A P T E R   8

A Vintage Year

By 1999, I was firmly settled in my new home in Florida, making new friends, and participating fully in the active bridge life of the area. Florida seems to have attracted a fair number of world-class bridge players over the last few years, and it isn't hard to get a pretty good game together, even if it's at someone's home rather than at a tournament. Looking back on 1999, I recall a few hands that were especially memorable, just like glasses of a fine vintage wine.

First, here's a fascinating deal from the money IMP game at Mike Becker's house in Boca Raton. North-South were vulnerable, and in one room East passed as the dealer and 'Broadway Billy' Eisenberg also passed as South — maybe he is getting old! West was our host Michael Becker, who is usually a very sound player, but this time he opened 2◇ in

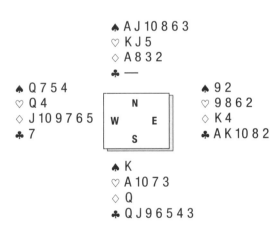

♠ A J 10 8 6 3
♡ K J 5
◇ A 8 3 2
♣ —

♠ Q 7 5 4
♡ Q 4
◇ J 10 9 7 6 5
♣ 7

♠ 9 2
♡ 9 8 6 2
◇ K 4
♣ A K 10 8 2

♠ K
♡ A 10 7 3
◇ Q
♣ Q J 9 6 5 4 3

third chair and the next hand said double. East bid 3♣ and Eisenberg passed again. West bid 3◇ and North doubled again, showing a good hand. This went round to Eisenberg who bid 4◇ and North, Bernie Miller, bid 4♠. Against this contract, East led the ♣A. Declarer ruffed, led a spade to the king and then played the ♣Q. West pitched a diamond as North ruffed, cashed the ♠A and exited with the ♠J to the queen. A diamond went to the king and another diamond to the nine, which was ducked. Declarer now won the ◇A and cashed his trumps. He knew that since East did not have an opening bid, West held the ♡Q. He also knew that East was 2-4-2-5. So declarer knew that the ♡Q was falling on the second round and that poor East would then get squeezed in hearts and clubs, which is what happened.

In the other room South declared 4♡ with no opposition bidding. West led a club and declarer ruffed. He laid down the ♠K and played a diamond to the ace in order to cash the ♠A, on which he pitched a club. Next, the ◇A and a diamond ruff was followed by a second club ruff, West pitching a spade. When declarer led a third diamond, trying to secure a trick with the ♡7, I was able to ruff in with the ♡8 from the East hand. South overruffed and ruffed his last club in dummy while West pitched the ♠Q. When he led the last diamond from dummy I ruffed with the ♡9. Now the best he could do was discard and a trump lead from me through the ♡A7 left him with no choice but to finesse and go down one. Double dummy, declarer can make the hand by ruffing only two clubs in dummy and cashing the ♡K before taking a diamond ruff in hand and then crashing the ♡Q which is doubleton. A tenth trick comes when East has to give declarer a club trick. However, declarer took the normal play given the bidding at his table. A very interesting hand at both tables.

This next hand came up in the Reisinger Board-A-Match teams, in November of 1999.

Playing on the eventual winning team, Andy Robson played in 3◇ doubled as West on the lead of the ♣Q. He won and played three rounds of hearts, ruffing with the ◇8. Now South *should* pitch his second club. If declarer plays a trump North can win and give South a ruff, and South can then clear trumps to let North take the setting trick with a heart. If declarer tries ♠A, spade ruff, heart ruff, South can overruff with the ◇6 and play a third spade, which North can ruff with the ace and then give South a club

	♠ K 4	
	♡ Q 10 8 2	
	◇ A	
	♣ Q J 10 7 5 3	

♠ Q		♠ A 8 5 3 2
♡ K 9 7 6 3	N	♡ A 5
◇ J 10 9 4 2	W E	◇ 8 5 3
♣ K 6	S	♣ A 9 4

	♠ J 10 9 7 6	
	♡ J 4	
	◇ K Q 7 6	
	♣ 8 2	

West Robson	North	East Shugart	South Barnet
	1♣	1♠	pass
pass	2♣	pass	pass
2♡	pass	pass	3♣
3◇	pass	pass	dbl
all pass			

ruff for down one. If declarer, after ruffing a heart, plays a club at Trick 5, the defense can ruff and play a trump to the blank ace. Now North can play a third club which South ruffs with his queen and draws dummy's last trump, leaving declarer with a losing heart in hand.

Do you see how declarer can make his contract? He must cash his ♣K before leading the third round of hearts. Now when South discards, he can either safely ruff a low club back to hand or even play a trump off dummy before ruffing a second heart in dummy. He only loses four trump tricks — a neat hand. Unfortunately I, as South, blew the defense and the winners received yet another gift in their procession to victory.

Here is a hand from a 1999 Regional teams event held in Marco Island, a beautiful resort on Florida's Gulf Coast.

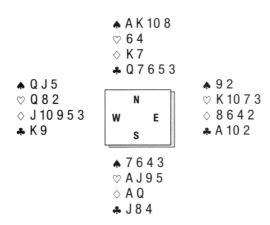

♠ A K 10 8
♡ 6 4
◇ K 7
♣ Q 7 6 5 3

♠ Q J 5
♡ Q 8 2
◇ J 10 9 5 3
♣ K 9

♠ 9 2
♡ K 10 7 3
◇ 8 6 4 2
♣ A 10 2

♠ 7 6 4 3
♡ A J 9 5
◇ A Q
♣ J 8 4

South declared 4♠ on the lead of the ◇J, East playing the six. At Trick 2, he led a spade to the ten, which held. Now he drew two more trumps and led a heart to the nine. West won the queen and led a diamond. South won in hand and led a club to East's ace. East played a third diamond as South ruffed in to lead a club. West won the club and returned a fourth diamond which declarer won in dummy with the last trump. South finessed the ♡J and made five trump tricks, two heart tricks, two diamond tricks and one club trick for a total of ten.

In the other room the defender in the West chair split his Q-J of trumps at Trick 2. Declarer was forced to cross back to his second diamond to lead another trump to dummy's ten. This was now the position as declarer cashed the ace of trumps in dummy:

What should East throw on the third round of trumps? If he throws a club, declarer can play clubs to set them up. If he throws a heart declarer leads a heart toward his nine, and if this runs to West's queen and he returns a diamond, declarer wins in dummy to play hearts and makes three heart tricks. If East rises with the ♡K

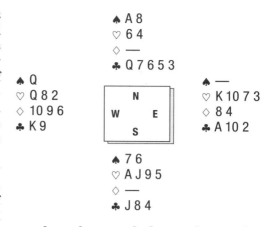

♠ A 8
♡ 6 4
♢ —
♣ Q 7 6 5 3

♠ Q
♡ Q 8 2
♢ 10 9 6
♣ K 9

♠ —
♡ K 10 7 3
♢ 8 4
♣ A 10 2

♠ 7 6
♡ A J 9 5
♢ —
♣ J 8 4

when declarer leads a low one from dummy, declarer wins to play a club towards the queen. He can't be prevented from scoring either the clubs in dummy or the hearts in hand. Back to the diagram then. What if East throws a diamond? Declarer leads a heart to the nine and queen. When West returns a diamond, he ruffs in hand to lead a club to the queen and king. Now East has no more diamonds and so declarer makes one club winner and two hearts. The only possible defense is for East to rise with the ♡K on the heart lead from dummy, which in effect breaks declarer's communications. East can now win the first club to play a diamond. At this point, West still has two diamonds along with the ♣K and ♡Q and can defeat the contract by playing another diamond to establish the fifth diamond as the setting trick.

On rare occasions, the defenders' tricks seem to disappear into thin air as their winners fall together, to their anguish and the declarer's delight. The hand on the right was a nice example from the 1999 Summer Nationals.

♠ K J 10 5
♡ A Q 10 6 5
♢ 7
♣ A 5 4

♠ —
♡ J 8 7 4 3
♢ A J 9 6 3
♣ J 9 6

West	North	East	South
		1NT[1]	pass
2♡[2]	dbl	3♠[3]	4♡
4♠	dbl	pass	5♡
all pass			

1. 15-17 HCP.   3. Four-card spade support.
2. Transfer.

Playing third and fifth leads, the ♣3 is led to the queen and the ♣2 comes back. Wanting to clear up the club situation, you play the ♣J, which fetches the king from West, and you win dummy's ace. What is your plan (a) if diamonds split, or (b) if they don't?

It looks as though hearts and diamonds are splitting and you can set up the fifth diamond for a club pitch, so you play a diamond to the king and ace, ruff a diamond, lead the ♠K and ruff out East's ace. Now you lead a third diamond, West ruffs with the ♡9, and you over-ruff in dummy. You know a lot about the hand at this stage — since the one notrump opening places East with the two missing hearts. If you stop to think about the distribution, it's easy to determine that West started with a 5-1-2-5 hand. However, stupidly, instead I counted East's points for his 1NT bid — the ♠A, ♡K, ◇KQ and ♣Q add up only to fourteen. Needing a pitch for my club, I therefore took the 'marked' ruffing finesse in spades and got my just desserts as West won the queen for down one.

The right line seems too easy — after you ruff the third diamond, you cash the ♡A, and crossruff spades and diamonds. If East ruffs in with his ♡K at any stage, you just pitch your losing club; if he clings to his ♡K throughout, he gets to make it at Trick 13, this time ruffing his partner's club winner!

Missing this straightforward play was especially annoying, as just before I left Scotland a hand with a similar theme had turned up across the street from Edinburgh Castle.

West led a heart to the jack, queen and king. It looked right to try and keep East off lead so I tried the ♠K, which went to the ace, and a second heart came back. Now a spade ruff, the ◇A pitching a heart, a diamond ruff, a spade ruff, and another diamond ruff came to seven tricks.

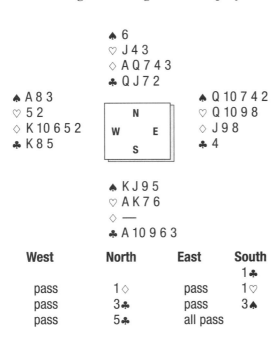

```
              ♠ 6
              ♡ J 4 3
              ◇ A Q 7 4 3
              ♣ Q J 7 2
♠ A 8 3                        ♠ Q 10 7 4 2
♡ 5 2           N              ♡ Q 10 9 8
◇ K 10 6 5 2  W   E            ◇ J 9 8
♣ K 8 5          S             ♣ 4
              ♠ K J 9 5
              ♡ A K 7 6
              ◇ —
              ♣ A 10 9 6 3
```

West	North	East	South
			1♣
pass	1◇	pass	1♡
pass	3♣	pass	3♠
pass	5♣	all pass	

This was now the position. When I played the ♠J, West lazily threw the ♦10 and dummy ruffed. Another diamond ruff in hand and then the ♡7 was played. West had to ruff his partner's trick and then lead away from his ♣K. Neat, but West could have defeated the contract by ruffing the losing ♠J low; on the critical heart play at Trick 11,

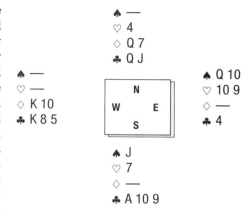

```
                    ♠ —
                    ♡ 4
                    ◇ Q 7
                    ♣ Q J
♠ —                            ♠ Q 10
♡ —           N                ♡ 10 9
◇ K 10     W       E           ◇ —
♣ K 8 5        S               ♣ 4
                    ♠ J
                    ♡ 7
                    ◇ —
                    ♣ A 10 9
```

he would pitch his last diamond and still score the ♣K.

To end the century on a happy note, here's a hand from the very high stakes rubber bridge game at TGR's club in London; the theme is 'protecting your partner'. First in hand, playing with a good player against two top professional players you hold:

♠ K 10 9 8 7 5   ♡ —   ◇ Q 7 6   ♣ K J 9 6

Not playing weak twos, you open 1♠, and partner makes a forcing jump shift to 3♡. You rebid 3♠ and partner now bids 4NT — the 'Old Black.' Not finding any aces, you bid 5♣ but partner bids 6♠ anyway. Righty promptly doubles this and you ponder. What would you do?

Your hand is certainly weak, but you have two big assets. Your trumps are good for the bidding and so righty must have doubled for a heart lead. If that is the case, most of partner's cards are outside hearts and the contract must have a great chance. But partner may be very worried about a heart lead, and the correct action therefore is to redouble just to make sure partner does not remove to 6NT.

Warned by the redouble, partner stood his ground, and I lost only a diamond trick to score up my slam for 1620. After I claimed, my partner quickly said that he *had* been intending to run to 6NT without my redouble! 6NT doubled would have gone at least two down for a difference of 1920 points — more than enough to buy a case of fine 1999 vintage wine!

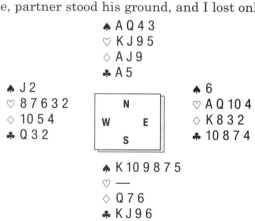

```
                    ♠ A Q 4 3
                    ♡ K J 9 5
                    ◇ A J 9
                    ♣ A 5
♠ J 2                          ♠ 6
♡ 8 7 6 3 2       N            ♡ A Q 10 4
◇ 10 5 4      W       E        ◇ K 8 3 2
♣ Q 3 2           S            ♣ 10 8 7 4
                    ♠ K 10 9 8 7 5
                    ♡ —
                    ◇ Q 7 6
                    ♣ K J 9 6
```

The

Bridge

Legends

CHAPTER 9

An Irreplaceable Rose

Anyone who has played this game knows that one of its charms is its ability to introduce you to people who in the ordinary course of life you might never encounter; lifelong bridge friendships can and do arise independent of a player's social background or occupation. One of my very best bridge friends was the late Irving Rose, who died of a heart attack in 1996 at the early age of fifty-eight.

The son of Scottish bridge international Louis Rose, Irving briefly studied accounting in his home town of Glasgow before moving to London, where he became one of the first bridge players in the country to make his living from the game. He was a wonderful rubber bridge player who played with a great deal of table feel; he was also able to play very quickly, something which often induced mistakes from his opponents. Unfortunately, his winnings at bridge usually did not make up for his substantial losses at other forms of gambling. Eventually, he sought and received help from Gamblers Anonymous before settling down for many years with his wife Annette and later their son. For a time he worked for an insurance company with some success, but for most of his life he managed the country's most prestigious bridge clubs. Eventually, two of his closest friends established a new club for him, called TGR — this, of course, stood for 'The Great Rose'. Today TGR is London's top rubber bridge club.

I first met Irving Rose in the early seventies when I was just starting my bridge career and he was already an established star, but we quickly became good friends. Rose had a personality which was both extraordinary and fascinating. He was a master of Cockney rhyming slang and his sharp wit and outrageous remarks made people laugh — indeed, no one else could have got away with his style of humor. At the bridge table, Rose was an intuitive player. He seemed to know what cards the other players held, and he often used his particular brand of table presence to bring home the most difficult of contracts. Although he was a master with figures and knew the mathematics of the game as well as anyone, he preferred to rely on his own judgement, being confident enough to back it and take the consequences should he be wrong. In Rose's case this did not happen often.

Here are a few hands that show Rose in action.

Rose declared 4♡ from the South chair on this hand in a European Championship match against Norway. West led the ♡5 which went to the ♡4, ♡Q and ♡J, and East returned the ◊10 to declarer's ace. Rose now led the ♡2 and when West played the ♡3 decided to play East for the ♡KQ and played

```
              ♠ 10 9 3
              ♡ A 10 9 8 6 4
              ◊ 8 5
              ♣ 7 2
         ┌─────────────┐
         │      N      │
         │  W       E  │
         │      S      │
         └─────────────┘
              ♠ K Q 6 2
              ♡ J 2
              ◊ A K 4
              ♣ A Q 10 8
```

dummy's ♡A, East following low. Now came a spade from dummy to his king, which held, then the ◊K and a diamond ruff. When Rose led a second spade from dummy, East won the ace and played a club through. Irving guessed to play the ace and when spades split 3-3 he was home.

This is a perfect example of his table feel, which told him that East had misdefended by not switching to a club immediately. How many times have you heard the line, 'I know I took the wrong line, but they could always have beaten me if they had defended accurately'? Rose would never assume accurate defense — he was too practical, and seemed to be able to smell out the defenders' errors.

On this hand from a British team trials, Rose was South and declared 3NT after the auction   1◊-2♣, 2◊-3NT. West led the ♣A and shifted to the ♡10. Rose won and played a spade to the queen then a diamond to the ten.

```
              ♠ A Q 7
              ♡ Q 5 4
              ◊ Q 8 7 6 4 3 2
              ♣ —
 ♠ 10 5 4     ┌─────────────┐   ♠ J 8 6 3
 ♡ 10 9 8 6   │      N      │   ♡ J 7 3 2
 ◊ 5          │  W       E  │   ◊ A J 9
 ♣ A K Q 9 7  │      S      │   ♣ 6 4
              └─────────────┘
              ♠ K 9 2
              ♡ A K
              ◊ K 10
              ♣ J 10 8 5 3 2
```

He felt that as West was likely to be long in clubs he might be short in diamonds, and he also took the inference that if East had held a doubleton ◊A, he might have hopped up with it to play a second club. On the next trick, Rose's ◊K was allowed to hold so he now played the ♣J to cut the defensive communications. West could not cash his third club without giving South nine winners, so he exited with a second heart. Declarer now cashed his spade tricks ending in dummy and played a diamond to East, who could take his long spade but then had to give dummy the last two tricks. Very stylish play.

Irving Rose

In 1975 I played in my first UK team trials with a very young Michael Rosenberg. We were trying to qualify for the WBF Olympiad the following year in Monte Carlo, and our team had a small lead going into the last match. On one critical deal, Michael chose to balance vulnerable as a passed hand; Rose eventually doubled him in 2♣ despite holding only three trumps and we went for 800. We lost the match and the trip. However, I decided to go to Monte Carlo anyway, and before the championship began I drove Irving to dinner at his favorite restaurant, which was at a farm in the hills some way down the coast. After dinner (and a liberal amount of fine red wine) I remember that at one point on the return journey along the winding roads by the seashore, my small Lancia car descended a number of steps before reaching a pebbled road at the edge of the sea! Subsequently, Rose loved to tell the story of how he nearly never made it to the championship at all. However, the experience did not affect him and he played brilliantly. Britain held the lead for a long time and was in contention right to the end, eventually finishing third.

Terence Reese, the British captain, nominated the following hand from Monte Carlo for a brilliancy prize; Rose was sitting South against the Israeli team.

Sam Lev, who had just taken Israel to third place in the Bermuda Bowl, led the ♠A and continued spades. Rose needed two ruffs in hand to come to twelve tricks. He won the spade, played diamond to the ace and took a diamond ruff. Romik gave this a brief look before he followed low. Rose then cashed the ♡Q, played a club to the king, and ruffed another diamond with the ♡9. The position was now as shown.

Rose led the ♣A and Lev did his best by pitching his diamond. Declarer then discarded dummy's last diamond and, confident that he knew all West's cards, led a heart to the ten, making six and scoring a big swing for Britain. It wouldn't have helped West to ruff in as Rose would have overruffed and then ruffed his last diamond.

Henri Svarc and Jean Michel

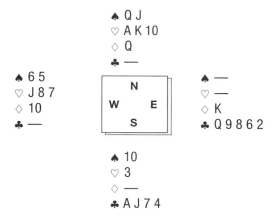

	♠ Q J 7 2		
	♡ A K 10 6		
	◇ A Q 9 4		
	♣ K		
♠ A 6 5 4			♠ 9 3
♡ J 8 7 2			♡ 5
◇ 10 8 5 2			◇ K 7 6 3
♣ 10			♣ Q 9 8 6 5 2
	♠ K 10 8		
	♡ Q 9 4 3		
	◇ J		
	♣ A J 7 4 3		

West	North	East	South
Lev	Flint	Romik	Rose
	2◇[1]	pass	2NT[2]
pass	4◇[3]	pass	6♡
all pass			

1. Multi — either a 17-24 4-4-4-1 hand, or a weak two in one of the majors.
2. Enquiring.
3. Strong hand with singleton club.

	♠ Q J		
	♡ A K 10		
	◇ Q		
	♣ —		
♠ 6 5			♠ —
♡ J 8 7			♡ —
◇ 10			◇ K
♣ —			♣ Q 9 8 6 2
	♠ 10		
	♡ 3		
	◇ —		
	♣ A J 7 4		

Boulenger were for many years one of France's best pairs. Svarc is now nearly seventy, but he still often plays on the French team, and indeed recently won a world championship. He is usually seen smiling, regardless of results, and has never been one to get involved in the internal team squabbling that, for many years, prevented the French from obtaining results that matched their ability. Jean Michel Boulenger was tall and looked like a French film star. Always dressed stylishly, he was one of the few bridge players who combined his excellent play with good looks and charm. Unfortunately, like Rose, he too died at an early age.

Here is another hand from Monte Carlo in 1975, this time showing Rose in action against the French.

```
              ♠ J 6
              ♡ 10 9 7 5
              ◇ A 10 8 3
              ♣ A 7 4
♠ A 4                        ♠ Q 9 7 3
♡ A K J 4 3      N           ♡ Q 2
◇ Q 7 4      W     E         ◇ 6
♣ Q 10 8         S           ♣ K J 9 5 3 2
              ♠ K 10 8 5 2
              ♡ 8 6
              ◇ K J 9 5 2
              ♣ 6
```

Rose liked to bid at favorable vulnerability and on this deal he opened a hand many would not. However, when Flint doubled 3NT he thought he should run to his second suit, although they could actually have beaten 3NT had he passed. After leading the ♡A against 4◇ doubled, West cashed the ♡K and switched to a club. Rose won the ♣A and led the ♠J, which was covered by the queen, king and ace. Boulenger now returned the ♡J but Rose ruffed, cashed the ♠10 and cross-ruffed for ten tricks and plus 510 — a gain

West Boulenger	North Flint	East Svarc	South Rose
			1♠
dbl	pass	3♣	pass
3♡	pass	3NT	pass
pass	dbl	pass	4◇
dbl	all pass		

of 7 IMPs when the British East-West were down two (undoubled) in 3NT in the replay.

Everything seemed to happen to Rose. In 1974 he led the qualifying rounds for the World Open Pairs by miles, but at that time there was no carryover to the final — everyone started again from scratch. During the final session he and his partner, Rob Sheehan, moved to the wrong line of tables by mistake; the director had to leave them there to avoid destroying the movement, and so they ended up playing another three boards against a number of strong pairs they had previously encountered, including Garozzo and Belladonna. Despite this handicap, they finished only just out of the money.

Irving was full of great stories of his exploits. He told me that just after he was married, he went to play in a pairs tournament in Dubai. He and Sheehan won and first prize turned out to be an electric mixer — just what his wife Annette needed for the kitchen. In addition, however, they each won a gold ingot. Rose volunteered to carry his partner's ingot through Customs at Heathrow — after all, he had his mixer in a big box to declare, so there was no way they would stop him! Reaching the Customs official, he was asked if he had anything to declare and proudly presented his box. The Customs official looked at him sternly and asked, 'Anything else, sir?' Rose, who was taken by surprise, stammered, 'Er, I have one gold ingot.' A brief examination revealed the other one, too. Shaking his head, he said 'They must have been breeding.'

In 1985, I persuaded Rose to play with me in the Maccabiah Games in Israel — this 'Jewish Olympics' always includes bridge among its events. There were about 40,000 spectators for the opening ceremony at the Ramat Gan Stadium, and the athletes had to assemble a full two hours beforehand in a nearby field. The ceremony itself then lasted for three hours, the athletes first marching round the stadium carrying their national flags and then watching the rest of the extravaganza from the center of the track. At around nine o'clock in the evening, having been there since five to make our march around the stadium, Rose turned to me and said "All this fresh air is killing me; I've had more here than the rest of my life put together." Our team won the Round Robin, which in previous years would have won us the gold medal, but now only qualified us for the knockout playoff round. Eventually we finished third.

We had another try four years later, and this time Rose took his wife Annette and his son, Adam, then aged five. Again our team won the round robin but finished with the bronze after the playoffs. Rose, who usually went alone to tournaments, was delighted to have his family there and put his medal round his son's neck before holding him aloft.

Irving was an extremely popular player, and he used to get invitations to all the top tournaments around the world. I remember one time we went to Tokyo with Jeremy Flint, Martin Hoffman and a sponsoring non-playing captain. We were playing Poker Two-bids: 2♡ showed five of either major and five of either minor. So there was this one hand when Rose opened 2♡ and I had two hearts and six spades. With the captain looking on, I said 'pass' — of course, Rose held spades, and we went down three in 2♡, with 4♠ cold.

In the pairs event, Rose played with our captain's wife and I played with Flint. The prize for winning was a solid gold bar and two return tickets to Hong Kong, and at the half-way stage Jeremy and I were leading the field by three boards. During the final session I took a particularly long time on one hand and, when we were finally ready to move, there was only one table open. We sat down, took out our cards and had started to bid when another pair who had apparently been even slower appeared at the table — we were in the wrong place!

The American tournament director did not take kindly to our mistake and penalized us a full board. We lost the tournament by half a board and as a result, only took home a wristwatch. Jeremy was not amused. 'Look on the bright side,' I told him. 'At least we don't have to take the gold bars through Customs.'

In 1987 Irving and I played together in the Staten Bank Pairs (now renamed the Cap Gemini) in Holland. On one memorable deal, the Dutch player Leufkens opened 2◊, which showed an unspecified weak hand. Rose passed, the Dutchman's partner bid 2♠ and the next minute we were in 6♡! Rose had passed over 2◊ in a flash with an eleven-trick hand. We finished third in the event behind Fucik-Terraneo of Austria and Helness-Aabye of Norway. This was a fair performance and we won several thousand Dutch florins. As well as being well looked after by the sponsors, as Rose's partner I was invited on two occasions to dine after the game with Omar Sharif and some of the other players. The food, served around midnight, was delicious and was accompanied by the absolute best of wines. Of course, the restaurant had been kept open for us at Omar's request. All that was missing was a bevy of beautiful young starlets, but Omar said he would arrange that for next year — as long we would guarantee that his bridge results improved!

Two years later, Rose was invited to take a British team to play in a tournament sponsored by Proton in Taiwan. Our team was Sheehan and Tony Forrester, both very fine technical players who combined well although they were not at the time a regular partnership, and Rose and myself — both of us a little more cavalier in our bridge approach. Actually Rose and Sheehan were at opposite ends of the bridge spectrum, and perhaps that was why they did so well as a pair. We got to the semifinal and played a strong USA team which included Meckstroth-Rodwell and Soloway playing with a sponsor. On the first board, Rose doubled the sponsor in 3NT after I had overcalled one spade. The contract should have been made but wasn't, perhaps because, as intended, the double had put extra pressure on the sponsor. After that, everything our team did was right and everything they did was wrong, and we went on to the final to play Patrick Huang's Taiwan team.

Towards the end of that final match, Rose got paler and paler and played faster and faster. Despite my being a fairly slow player, Rose and I were always finished before our other pair, but this time we lapped our teammates by eight boards! Rose, who looked very sick, went to his room to lie down and I went up with him to make sure he was okay. More than an hour later we learned we had won, although Forrester and Sheehan were somewhat perturbed at having to compare scores with each other.

Later that year I played with Rose in the Cavendish Invitational in New York. As usual, a lot of money was involved and we were going well when we encountered Meckstroth-Rodwell.

I held:

♠ J 9 7　♡ Q 10 6　♦ 3　♣ A K J 10 4 3

Rodwell on my right opened 1♦ and I overcalled 2♣. Meckstroth and Rose both passed and Rodwell reopened with a double. I redoubled to see what would happen and it went pass on my left (alerted as penalty), 2♠ by Rose, and the bidding proceeded from there.

I had to lead against this normal, run-of-the-mill auction. What would you choose? Logically, Rose must have either no clubs or a surprise. Rodwell should have second-round club control and I believe that is what his redouble showed. I stupidly led the ♣A. Here is the whole deal, so you can see what happened.

If you worked it out logically, you would realize that your best chance would be for partner to hold three diamonds along with his club void. After my lead Rodwell scored two spades, two hearts and eight diamonds. I needed to lead a trump, and then duck when declarer led his singleton club to force Rose to ruff, after

| West | North | East | South |
Me	Meckstroth	Rose	Rodwell
			1♦
2♣	pass	pass	dbl
redbl	pass	2♠	pass
pass	3♣	pass	3♡
pass	4♦	pass	4♠
pass	4NT	pass	5♡
pass	6♦	dbl	redbl
all pass			

Meckstroth
♠ K
♡ A 7
♦ K Q 10 6
♣ Q 9 8 7 6 5

Barnet
♠ J 9 7
♡ Q 10 6
♦ 3
♣ A K J 10 4 3

N
W　E
S

Rose
♠ Q 10 8 4 3 2
♡ J 9 4 3
♦ 7 5 2
♣ —

Rodwell
♠ A 6 5
♡ K 8 5 2
♦ A J 9 8 4
♣ 2

which he could play a second round of trumps; on that defense, the slam would fail by a trick.

The next hand Rose hit back by bidding a thin slam that made, and we were back in business. In fact, only a strange ruling kept us out of the money. We were the only pair to stay out of a non-making slam on one deal, and we were therefore due to gain 250 IMPs scored across the field. However, although I was supposed to be dealer, at our table my right-hand opponent dealt and passed, after which I opened and the opposition never bid. Somehow, the hands had been rotated, and although our auction and play were not affected, technically the board had been fouled, since there was now a different dealer. We lost our potential 250 IMPs, which proved costly to us but not to the ultimate winners. Who says you don't need luck to win a tournament?

Rose, living life his way

The last time I was scheduled to play with Rose was in the 1993 Maccabiah Games, but he had to drop off the team due to a sudden heart attack. He appeared to make a full recovery, but, typically, insisted on living his own lifestyle to the end, which came three years later. Irving Rose was up there with Chemla, Zia and Chagas as one of the few genuine characters in top-level bridge and he was so genuinely warmhearted that everyone loved him. His *joie de vivre* will always be remembered.

CHAPTER 10

Playing with the Wizard

I first met Zia in the early 1970s in London. At that time, he did not play much tournament bridge but was to be seen most of the time at Stefan's club in London, playing rubber bridge. There were many fine players in the big game and Zia had to work hard and rely on his own peculiar skills to earn a crust. Among his better-known opponents were Irving Rose and John Collings, both players of great flair. Collings has been a British international for more than forty years, and is a unique character about whom many stories are told. Once in the European Championships he psyched a preemptive opening, ending up at the seven-level when his partner could not take a joke. For some years he was part of a formidable partnership with Jonathan Cansino, in which Cansino played the straight man.

In these early years, bidding was not Zia's forte. He was already a fine card player but in addition he had several other weapons which over the years he has honed to a lethal edge. The first, and most important, was psychology. Zia liked to create problems for the opposition and then take advantage of the situation he had created. When an opponent was thinking, Zia seemed to know what the problem was, and when he was not thinking then that, too, would give something away. Zia would then play accordingly, always going for the play he felt was right rather than the best percentage chance. Invariably this worked, as he knew his customers and could depend on them. He also varied his game depending on whom he played with; he liked to bid slams with good players when he could rely on their bidding, but was more cautious with the poorer players. Similarly on defense, his strategy would vary with the strength of his partner.

He would make his dinner money by doubling the overbidders and underplayers. This was his second trademark — the Zia double. He would double a limited auction. He would double without looking at his cards if he didn't like the sound of an auction. He would double a slow tempo auction when the bidders seemed to be uncomfortable. He would double five of a minor frequently, but his favorite of all was to double a limited auction when he had short trumps (a singleton or void) and often he extended this to unlimited auctions if he had the feeling that the opponents were actually stretching. Most declarers would then play him for the long trumps and be sadly disappointed, losing an extra couple of tricks along the way. He still uses this tactic with much success even today, although the better players know about it and look to his hand for the trump *shortness*. So now he varies this strategy and occasionally doubles them with the trump length — a doublecross for those guys.

A third practice which he still uses today is an unusual or extraordinary opening lead. After listening closely to the bidding, he would select a card which would often put declarer on the wrong track. Sometimes he would lead an unsupported honor card, perhaps to hold the lead or to try to mislead declarer about the placement of the other honors or length in the suit, or to pin a possible singleton in dummy. He would underlead aces, just as his partner today, Michael Rosenberg, often does; indeed, together they underlead aces more often than most pairs. Of course, these extraordinary leads would often go wrong and in these cases he had to suffer both the setback of declarer making his contract and the jeers of his opponents who at the rubber bridge table were especially pleased when he slipped up. To Zia these were minor setbacks. He knew that in the long run he came out ahead with these plays.

There was another factor behind all this, too. As well as winning, he wanted to have fun. He enjoyed the opportunity to make a memorable play and if it worked, the success was worth more to him than the money. A couple of years ago, I was playing with Zia and defending a hand where declarer had Q10x of a suit in dummy opposite Axxxxx. She cashed the ace, Zia played low, and with K-J doubleton sitting over dummy, I followed with the jack. He chastised me for not dropping my king and scoring my jack later when declarer finessed the ten. Although there are many players who would never think of this (or even if they did wouldn't do it anyway), I agree with him that it is good to make some fun plays. And perhaps even Zia might not try this play in the final of a world championship, just in case declarer had a seven-card suit!

In the seventies he would talk a lot at the rubber bridge table. He would laugh and joke incessantly, and as he could concentrate much better than his opponents, this had the effect of increasing his winnings. Sometimes, too, his opponents simply got upset with his repartee and their play suffered because of that. There is nothing worse than losing your money to someone who is obviously having a good time at your expense. Today, although still a flamboyant player, Zia is older and wiser and much more conscious of not upsetting his customers; although he is still a lot of fun to play with, he will never say anything during a hand.

If there were a world rating for rubber bridge players, Zia would certainly be number one on the list of people you would want to play with if you were playing for your life. At tournament bridge, though, he was not well known until he led the Pakistani team to a surprising silver medal in the 1981 Bermuda Bowl. After that, he began to develop his partnership with Michael Rosenberg; they became one of the best pairs in the USA and now rank in the top few in the world. As Zia plays a lot and Michael does not, Zia plays with many other good players and does surprisingly well in top pairs competitions given the casual nature of these partnerships. A prime example is the Cap Gemini, now probably the world's most prestigious pairs event. He has won it with both halves of the old partnership of Andrew Robson and Tony Forrester, as well as having won it with Michael Rosenberg.

Zia does have his bidding idiosyncrasies, too. The weak notrump to Zia is what the lob wedge is to Phil Mickelson on the golf course — an invaluable tool for generating an advantage over the uneducated who disdain to use it. In the old days of simple systems, Zia liked to play weak notrumps except third in hand — a method often referred to at the table as the 'worker's notrump'. It got that name because Zia used it as one of the main tools of his trade — and of course, he did not always have to have the advertised 12-14. Recently, at the 2000 USA Team Trials in an attempt to generate a swing in a match he was losing he opened a first in hand nine-point notrump! He was down by 68 IMPs with fifteen boards to go and this was the whole hand:

The ♡4 was led. Looking at the dummy, Zia had two sure diamond tricks, two sure heart tricks and the ♠A — five tricks. He played low from dummy, and when the ♡Q appeared, he was up to six. Now a club went to the king which held, and he had seven. Another club went to East who played a second heart. Zia took this in dummy, led a third club, and when the clubs split he had eight. Now when West played a third heart, Zia won in dummy as East pitched a diamond. At this stage, he cashed dummy's long club.

	♠ A 8 5 4	
	♡ A J 3	
	◇ Q 2	
	♣ K 9 8 7	
♠ K 9 6		♠ Q 7 2
♡ 10 7 6 4 2	N	♡ Q 5
◇ 10 7	W E	◇ K 9 8 5 3
♣ A J 4	S	♣ Q 3 2
	♠ J 10 3	
	♡ K 9 8	
	◇ A J 6 4	
	♣ 10 6 5	

West	North	East	South
			Zia
			1NT
pass	3NT	all pass	

East could not believe that Zia did not hold the ♠K for his opening bid and let go a second diamond. This proved to be fatal for the defense as Zia led the ◇Q and let the ◇K hold the trick. Now the lowly ◇6 proved to be the ninth trick.

This whole thing produced a game swing when in the other room, the bidding made North declarer in the same ambitious contract. Even though he made three diamond tricks on the lead, he naturally misguessed hearts to go down a trick. This was the start of a comeback — a small slam was bid on the very next hand that succeeded off a cashing ace-king in a suit when Rosenberg boldly led that very suit himself at Trick 2 and then found a squeeze. However, the flat nature of the remainder of the hands made victory impossible, and the valiant effort fell short.

Getting back to Zia's bidding, in the mid-eighties I played on a Gold Cup team with him. We played nothing special but we did use the Multi 2◇. With Michael Rosenberg, I had played 2◇ to be either a weak two in a major or a strong 17-24 hand with a 4-4-4-1 pattern. This was a point winner with the weak hands and a good way to bid those very difficult strong hands. With Zia, I played only the weak version but when faced with a 2◇ opener he liked the responder to bid 4♣ which said, 'Please bid the suit below your six-card suit so I can play the hand.' This was an attempt to have the lead come up to the hand with some scattered values. How did I make out that year in the Gold Cup? Well, we qualified for the final weekend and actually reached the final with our 'surviving' four players, losing in the last eight boards to Tony Forrester and his squad. Zia could not play the final weekend as he was sunning himself on a boat somewhere filming a rubber bridge series for the BBC — the rest of the team were not impressed, to say the least!

Although Zia is certainly one of the world's finest bridge players, his absolute specialty is rubber bridge. At the end of one of my recent sessions in the small game, I trotted over to see if I could learn the secret of how he supports his expensive tastes in wine, women, and gourmet cuisine.

Zia held:

♠ A K 9 5   ♡ 5   ◇ K J   ♣ K 10 8 7 4 3

He opened 1♣, it went pass on his left from the Trader, 1♡ from his partner, pass from the Australian professional, 1♠ from Zia. Now his partner bid 2♠, Zia bid 3♣ and heard his partner raise to 4♠ and his right hand opponent doubled. He received the lead of the ♡A and dummy tabled:

Lefty continued with a second heart to the king as Zia ruffed. He then laid down the ♠A, noting the fall of the ten on his right. How would you continue, and where is the club length?

Zia continued with the ♠9 which was won on his left

♠ J 8 3 2
♡ 10 7 4 3
◇ 6 5
♣ A J 2

```
      N
   W     E
      S
```

♠ A K 9 5
♡ 5
◇ K J
♣ K 10 8 7 4 3

as his right-hand opponent pitched a low diamond. Another trump was returned. Zia won, finessed the ♣J, drew the last trump with dummy's jack and claimed ten tricks. His reasoning was twofold. First, East has doubled with a trump singleton, no ♡A, and apparently no ◇A; he must surely have a surprise somewhere, which could only be a singleton club — he could not have the ♣Q. Second, West jumped up smartly (perhaps too smartly) with his trump queen to play a third trump, so he was likely looking at something in clubs.

Let's look at the whole hand. It is interesting that if West does not jump up with the ♠Q but plays low, Zia can ruff a heart in hand, guess clubs and play four rounds of the suit. On the fourth round, West can ruff high as Zia pitches his last heart but a trump exit to dummy now ensures that West will collect the last two tricks. Funny hand — on this defense, East would have been correct to double, as his partner would have taken four tricks!

♠ J 8 3 2
♡ 10 7 4 3
◇ 6 5
♣ A J 2

♠ Q 7 6 4
♡ A 8 2
◇ A Q 10
♣ Q 9 5

```
      N
   W     E
      S
```

♠ 10
♡ K Q J 9 6
◇ 9 8 7 4 3 2
♣ 6

♠ A K 9 5
♡ 5
◇ K J
♣ K 10 8 7 4 3

West	North	East	South Zia
			1♣
pass	1♡	pass	1♠
pass	2♠	pass	3♣
pass	4♠[1]	dbl[2]	all pass

1. Zia's playing it.   2. So? Let's confuse him.

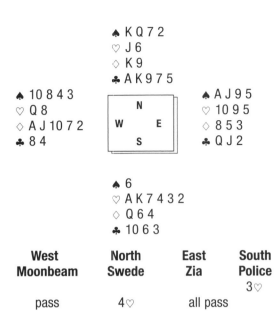

♠ K Q 7 2
♡ J 6
◇ K 9
♣ A K 9 7 5

♠ 10 8 4 3
♡ Q 8
◇ A J 10 7 2
♣ 8 4

♠ A J 9 5
♡ 10 9 5
◇ 8 5 3
♣ Q J 2

♠ 6
♡ A K 7 4 3 2
◇ Q 6 4
♣ 10 6 3

West Moonbeam	North Swede	East Zia	South Police
			3♡
pass	4♡	all pass	

Cutting into a new table Zia drew his compatriot Moonbeam and had to play against the Policeman and the Swede — a tough game.

Moonbeam led the ♣8, won in dummy, Zia contributing the deuce. Declarer played the ♠K and Zia shifted to the trump five. The Policeman gave this a look and let it run to Moonbeam. What would you do now?

Well, Moonbeam fell from grace by playing a second trump. Declarer won in dummy and cashed a high spade for a club pitch. He then took dummy's high club and ruffed a club before drawing East's last trump. A diamond up to dummy secured the contract. Zia was not amused as he pointed out the only defense was a heart from him and the ◇J from partner. 'But don't worry,' he said, 'it's only a game. We'll be more lucky on the next hand.' And so it proved.

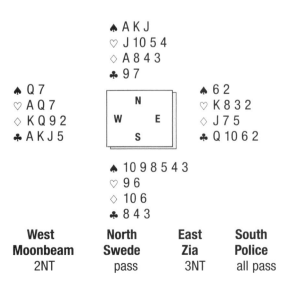

♠ A K J
♡ J 10 5 4
◇ A 8 4 3
♣ 9 7

♠ Q 7
♡ A Q 7
◇ K Q 9 2
♣ A K J 5

♠ 6 2
♡ K 8 3 2
◇ J 7 5
♣ Q 10 6 2

♠ 10 9 8 5 4 3
♡ 9 6
◇ 10 6
♣ 8 4 3

West Moonbeam	North Swede	East Zia	South Police
2NT	pass	3NT	all pass

North led the ♠A and his partner produced the ♠10. To Zia's consternation, he then tabled first the ♠K and then the ♠J. However, Moonbeam perked up when North could not find another spade. Just one more bit of luck was required, with the ◇A being with North. 'Paki luck!' shouted Zia, as his partner scored up his game to the accompaniment of a wry grin from the opponents.

On the next hand, Zia held:

♠ A J 5 ♡ 10 7 5 ◇ A 10 8 2 ♣ A 8 3

He opened 1◇, heard 2♣ from partner and rebid 2NT which was raised to three. The ♠6 was led and this was the dummy.

He put in the ♠9 which held, and led the ♣Q, which fetched the six, three, and four. How were those clubs — did East have a doubleton king or did West have doubleton ten? After only a few seconds of thought he continued with the ♣J which fetched the deuce from East and the ten from West. That gave him five clubs, three spades and a diamond — not a good contract but plus 600 anyway. He turned to East and

♠ K 9 4
♡ Q 6
◇ Q 4 3
♣ Q J 9 7 5

	N	
W		E
	S	

♠ A J 5
♡ 10 7 5
◇ A 10 8 2
♣ A 8 3

joked, 'You always play the six in this position; why don't you play the two and give me a chance to go wrong?' East was not amused, but Zia did not care: it was all part of a day's work in the life of the Wizard.

In 1999 I was invited by Zia to play with him in the Icelandair festival. The participants in this event, held annually in Reykjavik in

Zia Mahmood

February, consist of a large number of Icelandic players and a few invited international teams. The hospitality is excellent, the food good and the weather very fresh and, of course, very cold — just like Scotland. The general standard of play is higher than in most tournaments, perhaps because with very short days and long nights in the winter the Icelanders keep in practice with lots of bridge.

The pairs was won by Helness and Furunes from Norway, while Zia and I finished third. Magnusson and Vilhjalmsson

Both Vul.

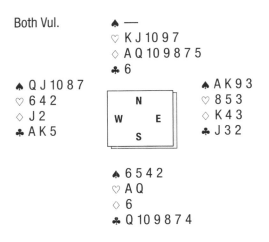

```
                 ♠ —
                 ♡ K J 10 9 7
                 ◇ A Q 10 9 8 7 5
                 ♣ 6
♠ Q J 10 8 7                        ♠ A K 9 3
♡ 6 4 2          N                  ♡ 8 5 3
◇ J 2        W       E              ◇ K 4 3
♣ A K 5          S                  ♣ J 3 2
                 ♠ 6 5 4 2
                 ♡ A Q
                 ◇ 6
                 ♣ Q 10 9 8 7 4
```

West	North	East	South
	Zia		Barnet
	2◇	pass	pass
2♠	3♡	4♠	pass
pass	4NT	pass	5♣
dbl	5◇	dbl	5♡
dbl	all pass		

from Iceland were second, and in fact, would have won had it not been for this board against us.

Zia opened 2◇ which purported to be a weak two-bid in diamonds, but with only four losers could pass for a strong two-bid! I was wrong to run from 5◇ — Zia was not seriously likely to be 6-7 and I knew in 5♡ he would need the hearts to be 3-3 so he could ruff a diamond, draw trumps and give up a diamond before claiming. However, he ruffed the spade lead, then cashed the ◇A and ran the ◇Q through East. He then ruffed a diamond with the trump ace, drew trumps and claimed twelve tricks for 1050 and all the matchpoints — more than a little lucky for us !

Playing with Zia was enjoyable, but I had to be on my toes. While the bidding was relatively straightforward, I found that I constantly had to be alert to keep up with the nuances in his defense. For example, he loves to play a zillion suit preference signals — I thought I played a lot of suit preference until I played with Zia. As well, he has the habit of watching your signals as well as making his! He also likes to use what he calls an 'alarm clock' signal. This tells partner to wake up, and comes in the form of the unexpected play of a nine or jack by a defender when a lower card would seem in order. It tells partner to be alert to an unusual play (like giving a ruff) that he might not otherwise consider. Strangely enough, it actually came up in Iceland. This deal is from the last round of the teams against Norway. My hand was:

♠ J 7 6 5 4   ♡ A 9   ◇ J 9 3 2   ♣ A 7

I led the ♠5 and saw the dummy in the diagram to the right. Declarer won Zia's king with his ace and played the king and queen of diamonds, Zia following with the eight and seven. We were playing upside-down count signals, so he had three. Declarer then led a low trump and I flew with the ace as Zia played the jack on the trick. The play of the diamonds had suggested I should play a spade and the jack of trumps seemed to be a wild signal for a ruff. I therefore played a second spade for Zia to ruff and he returned a club. When declarer played the king I won, gave Zia a second ruff, and we collected our ♣Q for down two and a useful swing, as eleven tricks were made by our teammates after the lead of the ♣A.

This deal came up towards the end of the tournament, and perhaps I was finally getting used to Zia's style. He had certainly given me a few problems in the earlier sessions. Let's try you out with some of them.

	♠ 10 3 2
	♡ Q 4 2
	◇ A 10 6 5
	♣ J 6 4

♠ J 7 6 5 4
♡ A 9
◇ J 9 3 2
♣ A 7

N
W   E
S

West	North	East	South
Barnet		**Zia**	
			1♡
pass	2♡	pass	4♡
all pass			

Barnet and Zia, with Steve Garner and Ralph Katz, win the teams event in Iceland

♠ A 9 7 6
♡ 8 5 4
◇ 8
♣ Q J 8 7 6

♠ 5
♡ A Q 9
◇ Q J 10 9 7 6
♣ 5 4 3

N
W   E
S

You lead the ◇Q and Zia wins the king to play the ♡3. Declarer hesitates slightly and plays the ♡J. What is your defense going to be?

West	North	East	South
You		**Zia**	
	pass	pass	1♠
2◇	3♠	pass	4♠
all pass			

♠ A 9
♡ K J 9 8 5 2
◇ 4 3 2
♣ 10 3

♠ 4 3 2
♡ Q 4
◇ K 9 6 5
♣ Q J 7 2

N
W   E
S

You lead the ♣Q to Zia's ace and he plays the ◇7 to the ◇8 and your ◇9. What is your next play?

West	North	East	South
You		**Zia**	
	2◇¹	pass	3♡

1. Multi.

P R O B L E M 3

♠ A Q 6
♡ K 10
♦ A 10 6
♣ A J 10 8 7

Zia leads the ♠K. Declarer wins in dummy, following with the ♠5 from hand. He then plays the ♠6 from dummy to his jack, as Zia plays the ♠7. Declarer now plays a heart to the ten. How do you defend?

♠ 8 3 2
♡ A Q J 5
♦ Q 9 7 5 2
♣ 5

West	North	East	South
Zia		You	
	1♣[1]	pass	1♦
1♠	pass	2♠	3♡
pass	4♡	all pass[2]	

1. Strong.
2. Chicken pass by you.

P R O B L E M 4

♠ Q J 9 4 2
♡ 9 7 6 2
♦ K 8
♣ K 4

Zia's double means 'I was bidding 5♦ but you can choose to defend if you like,' — so you do. You lead the ♠K, and Zia gives you the ♠6 playing upside-down count. You play the ♦Q to the king and ace and he returns the ♠7 to your ace. You have three tricks in and a sure fourth. A nice start, but what do you play now?

♠ A K 8 5
♡ J 10 5 4
♦ Q 10 4
♣ 8 7

West	North	East	South
You		Zia	
pass	pass	3♦	3♡
4♦	4♡	dbl	all pass

♠ K 5 4 2
♡ Q J 4 3
◇ 7 2
♣ Q 10 7

```
      N
  W       E
      S
```

♠ A Q 8
♡ A K 10 7 5
◇ A J 6 4 3
♣ —

West	North Barnet	East	South Zia
			1♡
pass	2♡	pass	3♣[1]
pass	4♡	pass	6♡

1. Zia game try.

Here we see an example of a Zia trial bid. When the charming Icelandic woman on lead asked about length of Zia's suit, I smiled and confidently replied he could hold anything between one and six. Well, I was close! She then led the ♣A and now you have to try to make your slam. The first time you play a trump West shows out. Also, if East gains the lead she returns a low club. Now you are in Zia's chair — how would you play your slam?

♠ A 9 7 6
♡ 8 5 4
◇ 8
♣ Q J 8 7 6

♠ 5
♡ A Q 9
◇ Q J 10 9 7 6
♣ 5 4 3

```
      N
  W       E
      S
```

♠ 10 8 3
♡ 10 3 2
◇ A K 5
♣ K 10 9 2

♠ K Q J 4 2
♡ K J 7 6
◇ 4 3 2
♣ A

West You	North	East Zia	South
	pass	pass	1♠
2◇	3♠	pass	4♠
all pass			

You led the ◇Q and Zia won the king to return the ♡3; declarer played the ♡J after a slight hesitation; what did you do? I played the ♡A and another heart and declarer made the contract. Zia could have made things easier by returning a diamond which would have conveyed the message that he had clubs under control. When he has shown up with the ◇AK I should not play him for the ♡K. If he held this card instead of the ♣K he would play the ◇A at Trick 1, concealing the king and in effect, forcing me to cash hearts out. If he actually held the ◇A without the king he should return his highest heart in all situations.

S O L U T I O N   2

You lead the ♣Q, Zia wins the ace and plays the ◇7; declarer plays the ◇8 and you win the ◇9. Now what? This was probably the most interesting defensive problem in the tournament. As the ◇7 was the lowest outstanding spot, I continued diamonds and declarer made his contract. Even if Zia held the ◇A we still needed an outside trick. The correct play is a trump, which will probably lead to down two. By leading low from ◇J107, Zia was guarding against declarer holding ◇KQ9.

♠ A 9
♡ K J 9 8 5 2
◇ 4 3 2
♣ 10 3

♠ 4 3 2
♡ Q 4
◇ K 9 6 5
♣ Q J 7 2

```
      N
  W       E
      S
```

♠ K J 6 5
♡ A 3
◇ J 10 7
♣ A 9 8 4

♠ Q 10 8 7
♡ 10 7 6
◇ A Q 8
♣ K 6 5

West	North	East	South
You		**Zia**	
	2◇¹	pass	3♡
all pass			

1. Multi.

♠ A Q 6
♡ K 10
♢ A 10 6
♣ A J 10 8 7

♠ K 10 9 7 4
♡ 7 2
♢ K 4 3
♣ Q 6 2

	N	
W		E
	S	

♠ 8 3 2
♡ A Q J 5
♢ Q 9 7 5 2
♣ 5

♠ J 5
♡ 9 8 6 4 3
♢ J 8
♣ K 9 4 3

West Zia	North	East You	South
	1♣¹	pass	1♢
1♠	pass	2♠	3♡
pass	4♡	all pass	

1. Strong.

Zia led the ♠K; declarer won in dummy and then played a spade from dummy to his jack, Zia playing the ♠7. Declarer now played a heart to the ten and your jack. What did you do now? At the table, I lazily returned a low diamond. Declarer won and took his diamond pitch and I realized I had blown it. He then played a trump to me and passed my low diamond return back to his ten. However, luckily for us, he misguessed clubs in the endgame to go down one. The ♢Q is the sure return to beat the contract. However, take full credit if you switched to your singleton club, which also works as the cards lie. A club shift removes declarer's entries prematurely, and he has trouble getting back to hand to play trumps.

Zia has made a specialized double which says 'I was going to bid 5◇ but pass if you like it'. You liked it and led the ♠K, Zia playing the ♠6 (upside-down count). You played the ◇Q to the king and ace and he returned the ♠7 to your ace. What did you do next?

I played the ◇10 and lost the second undertrick. Perhaps I should realize when Zia plays a second spade that he must hold a trump; if I play a third spade, he can ruff in and promote a second trump trick for me.

♠ Q J 9 4 2
♡ 9 7 6 2
◇ K 8
♣ K 4

♠ A K 8 5
♡ J 10 5 4
◇ Q 10 4
♣ 8 7

```
      N
  W       E
      S
```

♠ 7 6
♡ 8
◇ A J 9 6 5 3 2
♣ 10 5 2

♠ 10 3
♡ A K Q 3
◇ 7
♣ A Q J 9 6 3

| West | North | East | South |
You		Zia	
pass	pass	3◇	3♡
4◇	4♡	dbl	all pass

♠ K 5 4 2
♡ Q J 4 3
◇ 7 2
♣ Q 10 7

♠ 10 7 6
♡ —
◇ K 10 9 8
♣ A J 9 6 5 3

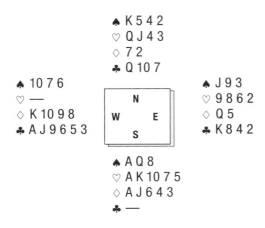

♠ J 9 3
♡ 9 8 6 2
◇ Q 5
♣ K 8 4 2

♠ A Q 8
♡ A K 10 7 5
◇ A J 6 4 3
♣ —

This was a great hand from the teams. Two Icelandic women, Anna and Gudrun were our opponents. Zia ruffed the opening lead and played the ace and jack of diamonds. West let that run to East who returned a second club, a low one. Zia ruffed and could no longer make the hand since trumps were 4-0. It was a pretty defense and Zia made a special presentation of $100 to this pair for this nice effort.

Had East returned a spade, Zia could win in hand, cash one high trump and then two more spades ending in hand. A diamond ruff with the queen and the last spade would leave East with no defense. If she ruffed Zia could overruff and ruff a second diamond and draw trumps; if she did not, he could crossruff. Had West won the second diamond and played a third diamond, then now East could pitch a spade and defeat the contract but this defense was not at all easy to find.

The only reasonable winning line for declarer is to duck a diamond at Trick 2 and if East wins this and plays a low club, to run this to dummy. If East plays anything else, declarer follows the previous line. Did you find the play or spot the clue that when West asked about clubs before leading she was unlikely to hold both the ace and the king? Although Zia knew this, it seemed wrong to put all his eggs in this one basket before he had found out about the bad trump distribution.

Can you beat Meckwell?

I f you play any kind of competitive bridge or have ever read a bridge magazine, you will have heard the names of Eric Rodwell and Jeff Meckstroth, who together comprise the partnership commonly known as 'Meckwell'. They have been playing as a pair since 1975, and they won the Bermuda Bowl for the first time in 1981. A victory in the World Open Pairs in 1986 and another in the World Teams Olympiad in 1988 gave them a set of the three major World Championships and membership in an exclusive club of eight players who can claim this achievement.

After the Nickell team was formed in the nineties, they achieved a whole bunch of victories in the Spingold and in the Reisinger which put them head and shoulders above any other USA team, and in the last three Bermuda Bowls (in 1995, 1997, and 2000) they have placed first, second and first. It would therefore be quite reasonable to regard them as the world's most successful bridge partnership in the modern era. Both players are in their mid-forties and so have plenty of time to add to their collection of World Championships.

As there is so little to choose among the skill levels of the world's top hundred or so bridge players, it is interesting to consider what actually makes this pair tick. First, they have played together for more than two decades, so they have had the opportunity to work on and develop a highly complex bidding system. Rodwell-Meckstroth Precision is a turbo-charged system which includes such features as a strong club opening, different opening ranges for 1NT according to vulnerability, and a Multi 2◇ opening. This system, developed in tandem but mainly by Rodwell, has the depth of an encyclopedia and includes hundreds of complex sequences that tax the memory. Usually they remember them, but occasionally they don't. On one deal in a Spingold semifinal against our team they played in 3-2 fit at the six-level when they could have made a grand slam in another denomination. Fortunately, the strength of the rest of their session meant they were more than able to stand one bad result. But that one result proves that they are fallible, and they have been known to have poor sets; unfortunately for the rest of the field, those sets do not happen often and when they do, their teammates are usually there to pull them out of trouble. It must give them confidence to have Bob Hamman in the other room (for many years with Bobby Wolff and now with Paul Soloway). Even the third pair on the team, Nickell-Freeman, have proved themselves no slouches.

Eric Rodwell finished third behind Michael Rosenberg and Bart Bramley in the World Individual Par Contest in 1998. The test involved some highly complex declarer play problems, and although the time allocated appeared generous (about two hours for three hands) the complexity of the hands was such that many players could not find the correct solutions. Rodwell has the right kind of problem-solving mind and was able to work his way through the possibilities to find the winning lines. At the table he acts in the same manner, and will not play until he is sure he is taking the line that he has calculated will have the best chance of success. Meckstroth enjoys having a partner who is not especially speedy, as he relishes the opportunity to take a smoking break while his partner handles the dummy!

Jeff Meckstroth appears to have the qualities of a streetfighter. A very tough competitor at the game, he reminds me in this respect of Bob Hamman — totally focused on the job in hand. Meckstroth likes to open the bidding very light. Once, in the Grand National teams in Florida, in a tight match he opened a strong notrump with eight points third in hand against my teammates, who were not playing penalty doubles. Confusion set in, and our partners missed a vulnerable game. Two years later in the same tournament, he opened 1♠

Eric Rodwell and Jeff Meckstroth

vulnerable in third chair with seven points and six spades, as he thought he was too likely to be doubled if he opened 2♠ — again he picked up a game swing. He likes to live dangerously, routinely opening a 14-16 notrump with thirteen points or even twelve. As a declarer, he differs considerably from his partner in that he generally likes to play quickly when he has made up his mind on a line of play, and seems to go along with his table feel rather than relying on percentages. He hates to be slowed down in his play. Like other very quick-thinking players I have encountered (Zia, Rose, Collings, Hoffman), the faster the game the more of an advantage Meckstroth generally has.

To give you a flavor of his style and that of the partnership, here's a hand from the USA Team Trials for the 2000 Olympiad.

This board was near the end of a close-fought match in the semifinal, so the pressure was on; the play was on VuGraph and could be followed on the Internet around the world. West opened 1◇ and Meckstroth overcalled 1♡. After East bid a 1♠, Rodwell called 2NT, an invitational

```
              ♠ 10
              ♡ Q 9 8 7 3
              ◇ K 10
              ♣ K J 10 7 6
♠ A J 7                        ♠ 8 6 5 4 3 2
♡ K 10 4         N             ♡ 5
◇ A J 7 6      W   E           ◇ Q 8 3 2
♣ A Q 2          S             ♣ 9 5
              ♠ K Q 9
              ♡ A J 6 2
              ◇ 9 5 4
              ♣ 8 4 3
```

West Weinstein	North Meckstroth	East Garner	South Rodwell
1◇	1♡	1♠	2NT
dbl	4♣	pass	4♡
4♠	pass	pass	dbl
all pass			

4-card heart raise. Weinstein doubled and Meckstroth jumped to 4♣. Even with a limited hand he wanted to show partner his distribution, so partner could later judge what to do knowing he had five clubs. As a result, Rodwell doubled 4♠ with two-plus defensive tricks.

Perhaps Rodwell should have led a club after his partner's jump to 4♣, after which they would have an easy set with one trick in each suit, but he led the ♡A. Meckstroth played the ♡9. They play upside-down suit preference signals so this was a clear signal for clubs, although Rodwell did not need it. He shifted to the club and declarer won in dummy and took a club pitch on the ♡K. It now looks as if declarer must make his contract, losing just a trick in spades and one in diamonds. After ruffing a heart to hand, he led a spade up and Rodwell carefully split his honors, playing the king. Then a club was ruffed in hand and a second spade resulted in Rodwell winning his queen and tapping declarer with his last club. This was the position:

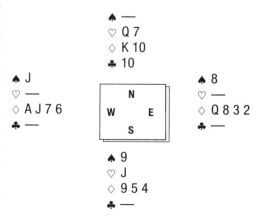

```
              ♠ —
              ♡ Q 7
              ◇ K 10
              ♣ 10
♠ J                            ♠ 8
♡ —              N             ♡ —
◇ A J 7 6      W   E           ◇ Q 8 3 2
♣ —              S             ♣ —
              ♠ 9
              ♡ J
              ◇ 9 5 4
              ♣ —
```

It appears certain that declarer will make the four tricks he needs for his contract. He leads a low diamond to the jack, North wins the king and if he plays his last club declarer can handle this by ruffing in hand. If South overruffs, dummy wins the ♠J and is now high; if he discards, declarer crosses to the ◇A and draws the last trump. However, declarer knew that North's pattern was 1-5-2-5 and saw that if North happened to hold the doubleton ◇109 he could lead the ◇Q and make an overtrick, so he led the ◇Q and when Rodwell played the ◇5, he played low. Although the VuGraph commentator was already mentally on to the next hand, crediting East-West with four spades doubled making, Meckstroth was not done — knowing the exact position, he played the ◇10 under the queen! This laid a dangerous trap for declarer, who could now in fact have made six by simply playing the ◇A. Could Meckstroth really have overcalled vulnerable and then jumped to the four-level holding only seven points? This had to be unlikely even for him, but declarer led a low diamond to dummy's jack, and Meckstroth pounced with his king and played his last club. Now when East ruffed, Rodwell was able to pitch his last diamond and in the three-card end position, declarer was unable to get to dummy to pull Rodwell's last trump and had to go down a trick!

Another of Meckwell's characteristics, and one of the Nickell team in general, is that of winning close matches rather than losing them. They are able to put bad results behind them and stay entirely focused on the game in hand. This was evident in their 2000 Vanderbilt quarterfinal match against Lev when they were some 30 IMPs down with four boards to go. Meckwell had had a couple of bad boards against the Polish pair including an early one; when, after intervening over the Polish 1♣ opening, Meckstroth had gone for 1100 against a game. However, they rallied and after collecting a penalty on the last board they compared scores with Hamman–Soloway to find that they had won by 1 IMP. Never count them out until the scores are done and dusted.

Before moving to the USA, I had only a few opportunities to play against Meckwell, mainly in invitational pairs events. We did play and win a match against them in Taiwan when I played with Rose but on that occasion it was Forrester-Sheehan who took them on while Rose and I played lesser mortals in the other room. After moving to the USA, I have had many more jousts against them at both National and Regional events. Of course, Regionals do not carry the same sense of importance or excitement but it is always enjoyable to play against the world's top pair and have the opportunity to play well. I have always found them to be pleasant opponents although Meckstroth can get a bit testy when I slow him down.

Jeff Meckstroth and Eric Rodwell, when they are going well, are undoubtedly the world's best bridge pair. That's not to say that they play perfectly, or that they are unbeatable. They are, however, extraordinarily difficult to beat. In the first place, they make life difficult when the hand belongs to the opponents. Look at this hand from the 1998 World Championship in Tunisia against Zia and Michael Rosenberg.

Here Rosenberg, having opened his shapely minimum, supports his partner's diamonds. Rodwell now comes in again with his good shape but few points and Zia bids a sensible 3NT. But Meckstroth, a tough street fighter, bids again with his one point and five spades, and now he has created a problem for his opponents. Rosenberg is not sure what to do as he is not certain Zia holds the ♣K. Zia knows his partner has a stiff spade but is worried about that there may not be ten running tricks in four

```
              ♠ J 9 7 6 5
              ♡ 10 6
              ♢ 10 6
              ♣ 9 5 3 2
♠ A 8 3                        ♠ 4
♡ Q J 9          N            ♡ 7 5 4
♢ A Q 9 8 4                    ♢ K J 7
♣ K J        W       E        ♣ A Q 10 8 7 6
                 S
              ♠ K Q 10 2
              ♡ A K 8 3 2
              ♢ 5 3 2
              ♣ 4
```

West	North	East	South
Zia	**Meckstroth**	**Rosenberg**	**Rodwell**
		1♣	1♡
2♢	pass	3♢	dbl
redbl	3♠	pass	pass
3NT	4♠	pass	pass
dbl	all pass		

notrump. Both players judge correctly that five of a minor is too risky because of the pending heart ruff. No one does anything terrible, but the result of plus 100 for Zia-Rosenberg is a poor exchange for a vulnerable game and costs 11 IMPs.

The Meckwell style is to make the opposition guess often — the more they have to guess, the more chances they have to guess wrong. They also have a reputation for bidding close and sometimes very unlikely games — and making them a lot of the time. When things are going their way, they are unstoppable. However, on a normal day tight defense may keep good and calm opponents in with a chance. Both Eric and Jeff are superb declarers, and will jump on any defensive mistake to let them get home — likewise, they don't give away a whole lot of tricks as defenders. See if you can get the better of them on these hands — I warn you, you'll have to play very well!

Your hand is:

♠ 9 5   ♡ Q 10 6   ◇ 8 7 4 2   ♣ A 7 6 2

You hear 1NT (14-16) from Rodwell on your left, 2♣ on your right, 2♡ on the left, and finally 3NT. Partner, who is informed that dummy has four

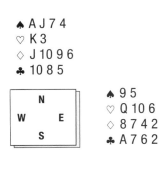

♠ A J 7 4
♡ K 3
◇ J 10 9 6
♣ 10 8 5

♠ 9 5
♡ Q 10 6
◇ 8 7 4 2
♣ A 7 6 2

spades, leads the ♣Q. You encourage in clubs, but declarer wins and plays a second club, partner winning the jack. Partner now plays the ♠10. Declarer thinks for a while and plays low; you play the ♠5 and partner holds the trick. Now the ♠K is ducked all round, declarer playing the ♠8.

Partner now exits with the ♡2, which goes to your ten and declarer's jack, and Rodwell plays a third club to your ace, partner throwing a spade. How do you stop Rodwell chalking up another game?

Your hand is:

♠ K J 9 7 5   ♡ 5   ◇ J 7   ♣ A Q 10 8 4

They are vulnerable, and RHO opens 1♠. You elect to pass, and the auction continues:

West	North	East	South
			1♠
pass	2♡	pass	3◇
pass	4◇	pass	4NT
pass	5♠¹	pass	6◇
all pass			

1. Two key cards and the ◇Q.

Perhaps you should lead the ♣A, but your spades are so good you decide to lead the ◇7 and see what transpires. This is the dummy (well, five trumps is as good as the queen for sure):

Meckstroth plays low from dummy, takes partner's ◇Q with his ace and ruffs a spade in dummy. Now he plays the ace and king of hearts pitching a club, as partner plays his hearts up the line. You curse yourself for not having led your ♣A, but can you recover to break Meckstroth's slam?

```
              ♠ —
              ♡ A K 9 7 4
              ◇ K 8 6 4 3
              ♣ 9 7 2
♠ K J 9 7 5   ┌─────────────┐
♡ 5           │      N      │
◇ J 7         │ W         E │
♣ A Q 10 8 4  │      S      │
              └─────────────┘
```

P R O B L E M   3

Your hand is:

♠ 8 4   ♡ A 7   ◇ 10 7 5 3 2   ♣ K Q 7 3

The vulnerability is favorable, and this is the auction. Given that North is a sound player, what do you lead?

West You	North	East	South Meckstroth
	1◇	2♣	2♠
4♣	4NT	pass	5◇
pass	5♠	all pass	

P R O B L E M   4

Here is a hand from the 2000 Memorial Day Regional at Safety Harbor. You have to play 4♡ after this bidding. You look at the following problem as the dummy goes down and West, an older pro, leads the ◇3.

West	North	East	South
	1♣	1◇	1♡
3♣[1]	3♡	pass	4♡
all pass			

1. 7-9 with four diamonds.

♠ A 10 6
♡ K 10 9 8
◇ —
♣ A Q 10 9 6 5

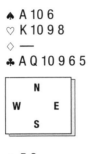

♠ 5 3
♡ Q 7 5 3 2
◇ K 10 7 4
♣ J 2

It looks as if you can't afford to lose a diamond as there is no quick way back to hand to take a spade discard, so you ruff and start by leading the ♡K trying to create an entry back to your hand. East contributes the jack with West pausing and then playing low. You know Meckstroth is in your chair at the other table. How would you continue?

S O L U T I O N   1

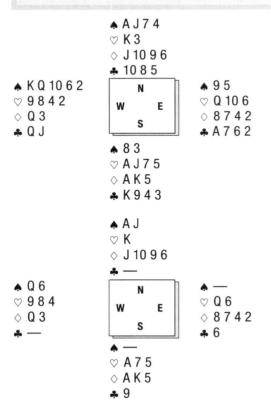

♠ A J 7 4
♡ K 3
◇ J 10 9 6
♣ 10 8 5

♠ K Q 10 6 2
♡ 9 8 4 2
◇ Q 3
♣ Q J

♠ 9 5
♡ Q 10 6
◇ 8 7 4 2
♣ A 7 6 2

♠ 8 3
♡ A J 7 5
◇ A K 5
♣ K 9 4 3

♠ A J
♡ K
◇ J 10 9 6
♣ —

♠ Q 6
♡ 9 8 4
◇ Q 3
♣ —

♠ —
♡ Q 6
◇ 8 7 4 2
♣ 6

♠ —
♡ A 7 5
◇ A K 5
♣ 9

This was the whole deal. Partner has made a great play by playing the ♠10, and the position now is shown in the lower diagram. If you return a diamond, declarer will go up ace and play his long club, squeezing partner in three suits. Partner will throw a heart but Rodwell will now make the hand with his long heart — he gets these situations right. If you return a heart, you force him to take a position without having played the club. You have four tricks in and, if he decides to cash the ♠A and finesse diamonds, he is going down. Did you give yourself a chance and follow up partner's nice defense?

You know that declarer has only one club, one heart and five diamonds, and his spades must be AQxxxx. Get over your unfortunate lead and realize that he needs three entries back to hand to set up spades and then one more to cash them. Another way of looking at it is that there are six losers in dummy. One can be

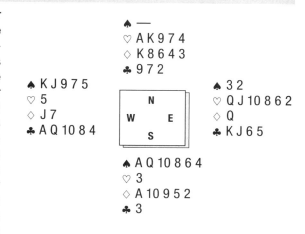

♠ —
♡ A K 9 7 4
♢ K 8 6 4 3
♣ 9 7 2

♠ K J 9 7 5
♡ 5
♢ J 7
♣ A Q 10 8 4

♠ 3 2
♡ Q J 10 8 6 2
♢ Q
♣ K J 6 5

♠ A Q 10 8 6 4
♡ 3
♢ A 10 9 5 2
♣ 3

discarded and four ruffed; however, declarer still has one loser left and you will score your ♢J as an overruff. If you ruff dummy's ♡K to play clubs, the last spade can now be established and cashed — try it and see. Did you discard and steal Meckstroth's slam? If you did, you did better than a young World Champion.

Don't lead the ♡A as there is no way you are cashing three tricks there. Your LHO has a spade fit, a good diamond suit, and controls in hearts and clubs. Your best chance is to try the ♡7 and play for the above layout. If you do lead the ♡7, you have a chance for a two-trick set. You could try the ♣K and a

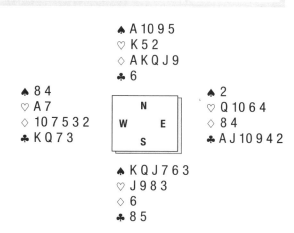

♠ A 10 9 5
♡ K 5 2
♢ A K Q J 9
♣ 6

♠ 8 4
♡ A 7
♢ 10 7 5 3 2
♣ K Q 7 3

♠ 2
♡ Q 10 6 4
♢ 8 4
♣ A J 10 9 4 2

♠ K Q J 7 6 3
♡ J 9 8 3
♢ 6
♣ 8 5

heart shift but Meckles always seems to get those guesses right! Although I believe a low heart lead is not so difficult to find, I must confess to having led a very stupid ♡A. Never having being scared to underlead aces, I was mad at myself for missing this easy one. The sequel to this is that the very next day playing in the Swiss, on the last board of the match and playing against random opposition, I led a low diamond against the auction 1♠-1NT, 4♠. The ◇K arrived in dummy and declarer played low. Partner won the queen, played one back to my ace and got a ruff along with a side trick for down one. As it happened, this was the only lead to defeat the contract. I was surprised not to hear some comment from the opposition at the time, but as the pair walked away from the table the woman turned to her male partner and said "Unlucky, dear, to have to play that hand against a beginner!"

S O L U T I O N   4

This is the position I left you in at Trick 3, you ruffed the opening diamond lead and played the ♡K off dummy (East producing the ♡J). If you lead ace and another club from the dummy now, West wins the king and East follows up the line to show three clubs. Now West pauses and unfortunately for you, plays another diamond. Had he played a spade instead, you could have won and played on clubs, conceding just two trump tricks.

♠ A 10 6
♡ 10 8
◇ —
♣ A Q 10 9 6 5

♠ 5 3
♡ Q 7 5 3 2
◇ K 10
♣ J 2

Now if you duck the diamond, East can shift to a spade and the defense will have established four tricks, so you must ruff the second diamond, coming down to this position:

The hand is pretty much double-dummy now — you need six more tricks and are in the dummy. You can't play winning clubs and discard as West can ruff in and draw dummy's last trump before cashing a diamond. You must first ruff one of your clubs in hand. It is always nice when you can afford to ruff one of your own winners, so you play any

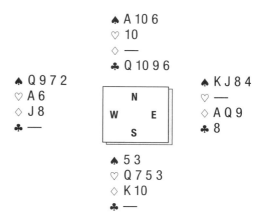

♠ A 10 6
♡ 10
◇ —
♣ Q 10 9 6

♠ Q 9 7 2
♡ A 6
◇ J 8
♣ —

N
W   E
S

♠ K J 8 4
♡ —
◇ A Q 9
♣ 8

♠ 5 3
♡ Q 7 5 3
◇ K 10
♣ —

club and ruff with the ♡7. It does not help West to overruff, so he discards. Now you ruff a third diamond in dummy, play a club and finally throw your ◇K. West can ruff this but when he plays a spade you can win in dummy and throw your last spade on another club. Good timing collects ten tricks.

The full hand is shown on the right. Did Meckstroth play it the same way? No, he received a spade lead and after flying ace and playing the ♡K, he was in a better position and was able to finesse clubs to make eleven tricks. However, if you played the hand well, you held your team's loss to 1 IMP — some-

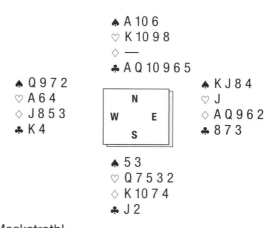

♠ A 10 6
♡ K 10 9 8
◇ —
♣ A Q 10 9 6 5

♠ Q 9 7 2
♡ A 6 4
◇ J 8 5 3
♣ K 4

N
W   E
S

♠ K J 8 4
♡ J
◇ A Q 9 6 2
♣ 8 7 3

♠ 5 3
♡ Q 7 5 3 2
◇ K 10 7 4
♣ J 2

times not so bad against Meckstroth!

Just to finish the chapter with a true story. Last year Mags and I were playing in the Sunday Swiss in Marco Island, and with two matches to play we got to Table 1 where we played Meckwell and Soloway. We lost — not a big surprise — and finished nowhere. When we got home, I turned on the television and looked at Mags, who was reading in bed.

"I see David Duval won the tournament," I said.

Looking round, she seemed surprised. "Oh, I didn't think anyone could catch Meckstroth!" was her quick reply.

C H A P T E R 12

Vive la france

Ask the proverbial man in the street what comes to mind when you mention the word France and he will probably say extraordinary cuisine, the world's finest wines and perhaps the world's most romantic city — Paris, with its unique atmosphere and elegant architecture. However, if you ask a bridge player you are likely to be told that France is one of the top bridge countries, and can boast a very strong group of international-caliber players. Out of the last five World Olympiads, France has won three in (1980, 1992 and 1996) and placed second once (in 1984) — a remarkable record. As well, on the way to their three victories, they twice defeated strong USA teams that included Hamman-Wolff.

Bridge in France has blossomed in the eighties and nineties and, like their best wines, their players have matured with age. Christian Mari and Michel Lebel were European Champions in 1974 and, along with Paul Chemla, Henri Svarc and Michel Perron, World Olympiad Champions in 1980. Alain Levy joined these stalwarts in the nineties and they emerged with three world team championships in a decade that saw the USA only capture one. Svarc, now seventy, is the oldest of the group, but still a top-class competitor. Perron is the youngest at forty-nine, while Chemla is fifty-five. Perhaps late middle age is the most productive time in a top bridge player's life, a time when he or she can draw on more than twenty years of experience.

In 1997 the French squad won the final of the Bermuda Bowl in Tunisia against Hamman-Wolff, Meckstroth-Rodwell, and Nickell-Freeman, the defending champions and most would say the strongest team of the era in world bridge. Not only had they dominated American bridge from their inception, having won three consecutive Reisingers and a like number of Spingolds, but they had added a World Championship in 1995 in Beijing. In doing so, they had defeated a good French team, including Chemla-Perron and Lebel, in the semifinal.

The French team are at their best when playing long knockout matches. Jean Paul Meyer, editor of *Le Bridgeur*, points out that the

French play a 'classical' style of bridge which tends to be more successful against the stronger teams. They do not play super aggressively but adopt sound tactics. As a result, they tend not to do as well in large Round Robin events, where you have to pound the weak teams, but if they make it through to the playoffs, watch out!

Alain Levy

Nevertheless, their success rate has improved quite remarkably, and the French were without doubt the bridge team and country of the nineties on the world stage. Much of this is due to a marked improvement in the players' temperament. In days gone by, the French team, although always one of the favorites, was not noted for team harmony and when (as inevitably happened) bad results were encountered or a couple of losses were sustained, they were not easily shrugged off. But the French teams in the nineties played tough bridge and winning bridge, without letting themselves be deflected from their goal by a setback or two.

In 1997, France qualified for the Bermuda Bowl in eighth and last position in the Europeans, and this only at the eleventh hour after some extraordinary results in other matches in the last round. They were third in the Bermuda Bowl Round Robin, then defeated a strong Polish team in the quarterfinals by 31 IMPs in a tight match, and in the semifinal they trounced a good Norwegian team by 63 IMPs. Curiously, the Nickell team were actually the official USA 2 as they had come through a repechage in the Trials to win their spot in the championship. Nickell slaughtered the other strong USA team in the semifinals, and certainly entered the final as the bookies' favorite. This did not worry the French underdogs, though; they took the lead at the half-way stage and never gave it up.

On this edition of the French team, Alain Levy partnered Christian Mari. Although Levy was a relative newcomer to the team, the new partnership blended well and in particular showed excellent bidding judgement. Let's look at some of the fine judgement they displayed in the final match.

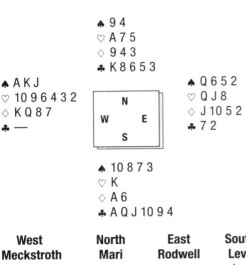

```
              ♠ 9 4
              ♡ A 7 5
              ◇ 9 4 3
              ♣ K 8 6 5 3
♠ A K J                      ♠ Q 6 5 2
♡ 10 9 6 4 3 2      N        ♡ Q J 8
◇ K Q 8 7      W       E     ◇ J 10 5 2
♣ —                S         ♣ 7 2
              ♠ 10 8 7 3
              ♡ K
              ◇ A 6
              ♣ A Q J 10 9 4
```

West Meckstroth	North Mari	East Rodwell	South Levy
			1♣
1♡	2♣	2♡	dbl
4♡	dbl	pass	5♣
dbl	all pass		

Levy doubled 2♡ to show some extra values and Mari doubled 4♡ to show some defense. Levy pulled the double to 5♣ and was delighted when Mari's value was the ♡A — plus 750. On this auction, Meckstroth thought the French pair were saving instead of bidding to make. In the other room the French found the good save in 5♡ which went down one for a gain of 12 IMPs.

A later board produced a similar theme.

```
              ♠ 10 9 6
              ♡ A Q 6 2
              ◇ 9 7 6
              ♣ 8 6 2
♠ 7 4                        ♠ K
♡ 10 5 4 3         N         ♡ K 9 8 7
◇ K Q 4 3     W       E      ◇ A J 8 5 2
♣ Q 7 4            S         ♣ A J 10
              ♠ A Q J 8 5 3 2
              ♡ J
              ◇ 10
              ♣ K 9 5 3
```

West Levy	North Nickell	East Mari	South Freeman
		1◇	1♠
dbl	2♠	4♡	4♠
pass	pass	dbl	pass
5◇	all pass		

Hamman	Perron	Wolff	Chemla
		1♡	1♠
2♡	pass	pass	3♠
pass	4♠	all pass	

Here again, Mari doubles 4♠ to show he has a good hand with offense and defense and Levy with his excellent diamonds pulls to his partner's suit. Another 11 IMPs to France as a result of good judgement. Even if Nickell had doubled 5◇, it would still have been a useful 8-IMP swing.

At the very top levels, bridge is a bidding game, with far more IMPs changing hands in the auction than as a result of play or defense. On this next deal, Mari-Levy outbid one of the world's best pairs.

Both East players could have cuebid 6♣ but thought they were too weak. Hamman could not bid more as he was likely missing the ♣A. When Rodwell took the save in 7♣, Levy (who thought that 7♣ reckoned to be a good save) hoped that he might receive a diamond lead should the ♣A be missing, but still felt that Mari (who had agreed hearts with 2NT) was certain to hold one of the minor aces. If it was the ♣A, the grand slam would be cold, so he took a calculated risk and bid the grand slam. Good judgement or just good luck? Perhaps a little of each, although Mari could certainly have improved the auction with a 6♣ cuebid. Since 7♡ has an easy thirteen tricks, this was a 13-IMP swing and built the French lead to 64 IMPs.

```
              ♠ Q 8
              ♡ 6
              ◇ 7 5 2
              ♣ K 10 9 8 6 4 2
♠ A K J 6 2                ♠ 3
♡ A K J 8 4 3 2       N    ♡ Q 10 7 5
◇ —               W       E  ◇ Q J 10 8 6 4 3
♣ J                   S    ♣ A
              ♠ 10 9 7 5 4
              ♡ 9
              ◇ A K 9
              ♣ Q 7 5 3
```

West Hamman	North Perron	East Wolff	South Chemla
1♣¹	3♣	3◇	5♣
pass	pass	5◇	pass
5♡	pass	6♡	all pass

1. Strong.

Levy	Meckstroth	Mari	Rodwell
1♡	1NT¹	2NT²	3♣
3♠	4♣	4♡	5♣
5◇	pass	6♡	7♣
7♡	all pass		

1. 15-18 or a weak one-suiter.
2. Four-card heart raise or strong two-suiter.

Christian Mari is well known as one of the world's finest players. A player of subtlety, he treats the game like a fine artist, an attitude which is also matched in his approach to life. He is often seen playing bridge wearing a classic silk suit — clearly a man of style. In 1997, Mari had already partnered the other top French players and in partnership with Chemla had won a World Championship in 1980. He showed me this key hand from the French Trials that qualified him for the team that was to win the Bermuda Bowl.

♠ Q 8 5 3 2
♡ J 10 6 5 3
◇ 3
♣ A 4

N
W E
S

♠ —
♡ A 9 2
◇ A K Q J 10 8 4
♣ K 5 2

Mari declared 6◇ after an uncontested auction. He received the lead of the ♠J which he ruffed; now he crossed to dummy with a club and led a low heart to the nine. West won the king and played a second spade. Now it looked as if Mari would take a club ruff before repeating the heart finesse for his contract. But the defenders were Chemla and Perron, and Mari wondered why they had not taken out dummy's trump when they were in with the ♡K. The only sensible answer was that the club ruff was not going to hold up. So instead, Mari drew trumps and when the ♡Q dropped under his ace, claimed his contract. Sure enough, the clubs were 6-2 and had he tried to get his ruff he would have gone down. It is interesting that had East risen with his doubleton ♡Q, or had West ducked the nine, then the contract could no longer have been made, but these would have been very tough plays.

Mari also showed his professionalism with this opening lead from the Tunisia final. He held:

♠ **Q 10 5**   ♡ **Q 10 8 7 6**   ◇ **J 9 4**   ♣ **A 3**

His partner opened 1◇ in first chair with neither vulnerable, and it went 1♡ on his right; Mari passed and so did his LHO. Partner now reopened with a double and this was passed to LHO, who redoubled. Now came 2♣ on his right; that went round to partner, who doubled. What would you lead?

Christian Mari found the only right answer when he led the ♣A and continued with another club.

Christian Mari

Levy had made an aggressive double with his minimum values. However, after Mari's opening lead, when declarer got in at Trick 2 to play a spade, Levy was able to win and play a third trump to stop the spade ruff. Accurate defense for down one and 5 IMPs when Perron brought home 1NT at the other table for plus 90.

Michel Lebel was one of the earlier French superstars. Now a family man, he spends most of his time making bridge

```
                  ♠ 7 6
                  ♡ A K J 5 2
                  ◇ 8 3 2
                  ♣ K Q 7
   ♠ K J 9 3                      ♠ Q 10 5
   ♡ 4 3              N           ♡ Q 10 8 7 6
   ◇ A K 7 5                      ◇ J 9 4
   ♣ 10 6 4     W        E        ♣ A 3
                      S
                  ♠ A 8 4 2
                  ♡ 9
                  ◇ Q 10 6
                  ♣ J 9 8 5 2
```

West	North	East	South
Levy	Nickell	Mari	Freeman
1◇	1♡	pass	pass
dbl	pass	pass	redbl
pass	2♣	pass	pass
dbl	all pass		

CD-ROMs, videos and other modern aids for the bridge student. His books have sold more than two million copies and have been published in twenty-six languages. As well, having been involved in developing the early theory around negative doubles, he also (along with some of the other French players) pioneered the use of a double in certain competitive auctions to show three-card trump support — a convention now commonly referred to as a 'support double'. Support doubles were used by the French in the World Championship as early as 1975.

In France, partnerships among the professional players do not seem to last as long as they do in USA, where up until very recently, there were five top pairs whose longevity averaged close to twenty years of play. However, it doesn't seem to matter, and Lebel attributes the French success to their bidding methods. These methods, which are based on five-card majors and a strong notrump, are sophisticated but at the same time, natural in style. Since they all play a similar system, any of their leading players can partner any of the others with half an hour's notice.

It helps to be a world-class card player too. I was sitting beside the USA captain Edgar Kaplan in Beijing when Lebel declared 3NT on this deal against Hamman-Wolff in the Bermuda Bowl final:

Perron
♠ A K Q 9
♡ A J 5 3
◇ A
♣ K 8 5 3

Wolff
♠ 7 6 4
♡ 7 6 4
◇ K 8 4 2
♣ Q 6 2

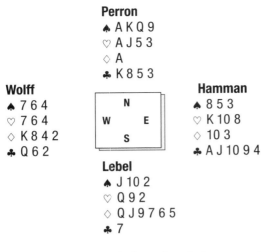

Hamman
♠ 8 5 3
♡ K 10 8
◇ 10 3
♣ A J 10 9 4

Lebel
♠ J 10 2
♡ Q 9 2
◇ Q J 9 7 6 5
♣ 7

Bobby Wolff led the ♡7 and Hamman's ♡10 lost to the queen. Lebel crossed to dummy's ◇A and then called for the ♡J. He reasoned that if West were to win this trick, he could still get back to his hand with a heart to knock out the ◇K (hoping that East had that card or if not, that West had the ♣A). However, everyone watching all four hands on VuGraph knew that this was not to be and that the defense could now cash five club tricks. Lebel, however, had given Hamman a problem by leading the ♡J. Perhaps declarer had diamond tricks to run and was trying to create an entry to hand with the ♡9. So Hamman, after a lot of thought, played low. Lebel now had nine tricks — four spades, four hearts now (with the king dropping under the ace) and the ◇A.

An elegant play by Lebel, but for Hamman's play to be right, his partner had to hold four spades or declarer would make his contract anyway, with the same nine tricks he actually took. If Wolff did actually hold a spade stopper, declarer would cash hearts and then play four rounds of spades putting him in. But now a switch to the ♣Q would still only enable the defense to take three club tricks along with the spade. The setting trick would have to come by way of the ◇K, and if Wolff had the ◇K, it was not necessary for Hamman to duck his ♡K!

Errors in bridge are very common but when Hamman makes an (extremely rare) error, people sit up and say to themselves 'If the world's leading player can make a mistake, maybe there is still hope for us all.' Kaplan, who was also providing his usual superb VuGraph commentary, said 'I know many players who think because they are confused. When Hamman thinks it is usually because we are about to win 10 IMPs.' In fact Edgar, who was so often right in these situations, nearly was this time too, because in the other

Michel Perron

room the French defenders, Chemla and Perron, also let the contract through. North was declarer, and after the ♣J was led there was *un petit accident*. When declarer lost a trick to the ♡K, East thought North had the ♣Q and switched to a diamond instead of cashing the club winners, so the board was a push.

Here is another hand featuring Lebel, this time a defensive gem from a 1995 match against Britain.

The contract was 6♠, and the opening lead was the ◇2 which Lebel won with the queen. After some thought, he made the only return to defeat the contract — another diamond! Now declarer was unable to enjoy his long hearts and had to go down one.

The youngest amongst this small group of especially successful French players is Michel Perron. He played on the French Junior team in the early seventies and won his first Olympiad title in 1980 at the age of twenty-nine. He then built up a very fine partnership with Paul Chemla which brought them two more world championships as well as silver and bronze medals. Perron is respected by his peers as a man who makes very few errors at the game. Look at a few deals which demonstrate why he is held in such high regard.

Perron declared 5♡ on the lead of a club to the king, which he ruffed. He drew two rounds of trumps, and when everyone followed he crossed to the

```
              ♠ 6 4
              ♡ A J 10 9 8 6
              ◇ A J 5
              ♣ 7 2
♠ 8 7 2                        ♠ 9 5 3
♡ 5 3           N              ♡ Q 7 2
◇ 10 7 2     W     E           ◇ K Q 8 6 4
♣ 10 9 6 4 3      S            ♣ K J
              ♠ A K Q J 10
              ♡ K 4
              ◇ 9 3
              ♣ A Q 8 5
```

```
              ♠ A K J 3
              ♡ J 6 4
              ◇ 7 5 3
              ♣ 9 6 2
♠ 10 9 5 4                      ♠ 8 6
♡ 10 7          N               ♡ Q 9
◇ A J 9 4    W     E            ◇ Q 8
♣ J 8 5           S             ♣ A K Q 10 7 4 3
              ♠ Q 7 2
              ♡ A K 8 5 3 2
              ◇ K 10 6 2
              ♣ —
```

West	North	East	South
		3NT	4♡
5♣	5♡	all pass	

♠J to ruff a second club. Next came the ♠Q and a spade to dummy where he cashed the last high spade, pitching a diamond, and then ruffed dummy's last club, reaching the position on the left.

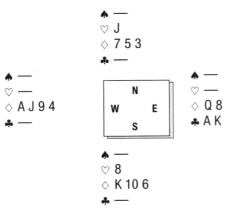

```
                ♠ —
                ♡ J
                ◇ 7 5 3
                ♣ —
♠ —                        ♠ —
♡ —          N             ♡ —
◇ A J 9 4  W     E         ◇ Q 8
♣ —            S           ♣ A K
                ♠ —
                ♡ 8
                ◇ K 10 6
                ♣ —
```

With his elimination accomplished Perron carefully exited with the ◇K(!) to endplay West, and the defense had to give him either the ◇10 or a ruff-sluff for the eleventh trick. This line would only lose if West held all three diamond honors, which was far less likely than a doubleton queen or jack with East.

The next two hands are from the 1992 Olympiad, the first being from the match against Sweden.

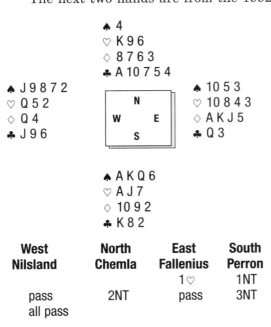

```
                ♠ 4
                ♡ K 9 6
                ◇ 8 7 6 3
                ♣ A 10 7 5 4
♠ J 9 8 7 2                   ♠ 10 5 3
♡ Q 5 2          N           ♡ 10 8 4 3
◇ Q 4        W     E         ◇ A K J 5
♣ J 9 6          S           ♣ Q 3
                ♠ A K Q 6
                ♡ A J 7
                ◇ 10 9 2
                ♣ K 8 2
```

West	North	East	South
Nilsland	Chemla	Fallenius	Perron
		1♡	1NT
pass	2NT	pass	3NT
all pass			

At both tables West led a spade against 3NT. The Swedish declarer won, cashed the ♣K and led a club to the ten and East's queen. Levy switched to a low diamond and the defense cashed four diamonds for down one. In the replay, Perron won the spade lead and at Trick 2 played the ◇10; when West played low, the hand could no longer be defeated. A very nice psychological play that Zia would have been proud of. Talking about Zia, the next hand from the French triumph in the 1992 Olympiad occurred when France faced Pakistan.

Zia led the ♠A which Michel ruffed in hand. He then laid down the ♡A, and Zia dropped the ♡Q! If this was a true card, it would be correct to play trumps and then use the ♣A as an entry to dummy in order to finesse the ♡8. But Perron knew Zia too well and continued with the ♡K, dropping the ♡10 from Zia. Zia had made a very good play. If he really did have a stiff ♡Q, declarer was going to have to cash the ♦A, cross to dummy and finesse in hearts — hoping that Zia had to ruff this with an honor and had no more trumps, so that a heart ruff in dummy would still be possible; not a likely position. So in fact, declarer's best chance would have been to continue with the ♡K and play Zia for ♡Q10 doubleton — which would work! So Zia, by playing the ♡Q instead of the ♡10, had offered Perron a losing option, which he had declined. "*Bien joué, Michel*," said Zia, with characteristic good sportsmanship, as they went on to the next hand.

France's best known bridge superstar is Paul Chemla. An extrovert with a quick wit and infectious laugh, Chemla is also a wonderful dinner companion — at least until the cigars come out! Last year we made arrangements to meet, and he picked up Mags and me at our Paris hotel. We clambered into his tiny car, which looked even smaller with Paul's bulk stuffed into it. Thrown across the back seat was his European Bridge Personality of the Year award for 1998. As we bobbed and weaved through the busy

♠ J 8 5 3		
♡ 9 5		
◇ 10 3		
♣ A 8 5 4 3		

♠ A 10 9 6 2	♠ K Q 7 4
♡ Q 10	♡ 7 6 2
◇ K 2	◇ Q J 4
♣ Q J 7 2	♣ K 10 6

♠ —
♡ A K J 8 4 3
◇ A 9 8 7 6 5
♣ 9

West Zia	North Chemla	East Nishat	South Perron
1♠	pass	4♠	4NT
pass	5♣	pass	5◇
all pass			

Paul Chemla

Paris traffic, he explained that he had not had time to move it to a position of slightly more prominence.

We abandoned his car almost in the middle of the road outside Henri's, a fine restaurant in Saint Germain. The owner greeted him warmly; clearly one of their best customers, Paul had a special table reserved for him. "I eat here only a few times a week," he laughed, "and always at the same table." As you would expect, Paul is a *gourmet spectaculaire* and you can rely on his choices of food and wine. A graduate in literature at a time when some of his friends went on to be prime ministers and philosophers, he chose to play bridge for a living. He seems to enjoy his lifestyle but his nocturnal habits mean he does not get the best from the mornings! "Call me after four p.m.," he would say.

I asked him about some of his most memorable hands. In each case, he said that the significance of the hand was heightened by the players it took place against. The first is the most exciting deal from the 1980 Olympiad (or indeed, from any Olympiad in which France opposed USA in the final), and it has been written up many times.

Soloway led a diamond and the slam went down one. Lebel selected to cuebid his singleton club rather than his diamond void in order to encourage the lead he wanted — a diamond.

Bob Hamman at the other table found himself on lead against a grand slam in a world championship final holding two aces — and knowing only one of them was the right lead! Unfortunately for Hamman, he select-

```
              ♠ 10
              ♡ K Q 9
              ◇ A 10 9 8 3 2
              ♣ K 9 8
♠ Q 9 5 3 2                   ♠ A K J 8 7 6
♡ J 8 5 4         N           ♡ A 10 7 6 3 2
◇ Q 6 4      W       E        ◇ —
♣ 7              S            ♣ 2
              ♠ 4
              ♡ —
              ◇ K J 7 5
              ♣ A Q J 10 6 5 4 3
```

West Perron	North Rubin	East Lebel	South Soloway
pass	1◇	1♠	2♣
4♠	pass	5♣	6♣
pass	pass	6♠	dbl
all pass			

Wolff	Mari	Hamman	Chemla
pass	1◇	2◇	2♡
4♠	4NT	5♠	6♣
pass	6◇	6♠	7◇
pass	pass	dbl	all pass

ed the ♡A for his opening lead and Mari scored up his doubled grand slam for plus 2330 and 19 IMPs. Had Hamman led the ♠A his team would have gained 9 IMPs — effectively a 28-IMP swing in a match which France won by only 20 IMPs. This was the first World Championship success for these talented players.

Seventeen years later in the Bermuda Bowl final, Chemla engineered another vital swing against the USA.

Chemla led the ♣K which went to the ace, and declarer passed the ♢8 to the jack. Chemla continued by cashing the ♣Q and playing a third club which Perron ruffed with the ♢K. When declarer overruffed this to play the ♢10, he had now lost control. Another club shortened him and he went down five for 500 to France. As soon as Nickell elected to bid over the double, the Americans were booked for a minus and the best they could have done was minus 200 in 4♠. Perhaps Nickell should have passed

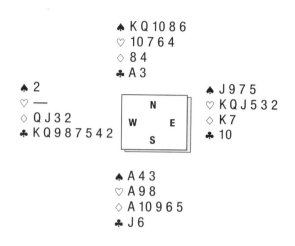

```
              ♠ K Q 10 8 6
              ♡ 10 7 6 4
              ◇ 8 4
              ♣ A 3
♠ 2                            ♠ J 9 7 5
♡ —              N             ♡ K Q J 5 3 2
◇ Q J 3 2    W       E         ◇ K 7
♣ K Q 9 8 7 5 4 2   S          ♣ 10
              ♠ A 4 3
              ♡ A 9 8
              ◇ A 10 9 6 5
              ♣ J 6
```

| West | North | East | South |
Chemla	Freeman	Perron	Nickell
			1◇
4♣	dbl	pass	4◇
all pass			

with his balanced hand and three aces — he would have collected 100 against 4♣ doubled. However it was not as easy for him as for his counterpart at the other table, where West overcalled 5♣. This was doubled and went two down for 300 to North-South.

So on this hand, Chemla earned his team a swing by giving the opposition a little extra rope. Time and time again in bridge you see that if you give your opponents the opportunity, they will make a high percentage of losing decisions. I like Chemla's bid here, particularly with his partner being an unpassed hand. There could even be occasions when his partner would be able to double the opponent's major-suit contract if they bid on, but this worked out just as well and earned his team 13 IMPs.

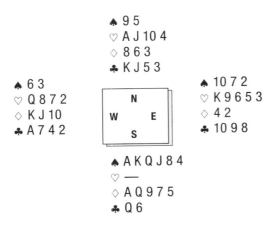

```
                ♠ 9 5
                ♡ A J 10 4
                ◇ 8 6 3
                ♣ K J 5 3
♠ 6 3                           ♠ 10 7 2
♡ Q 8 7 2        N              ♡ K 9 6 5 3
◇ K J 10      W     E           ◇ 4 2
♣ A 7 4 2        S              ♣ 10 9 8
                ♠ A K Q J 8 4
                ♡ —
                ◇ A Q 9 7 5
                ♣ Q 6
```

One of Paul's all-time favorite hands was played against Benito Garozzo during a match in the European Championship.

Benito led the ♠3 against Chemla's ambitious contract of 6♠, and Paul won that in hand to lead a low club which Benito won with the ace. Now Garozzo made a rare error by returning a low heart. Chemla played the ten from dummy and ruffed East's king, then ran trumps and reached the end position shown below.

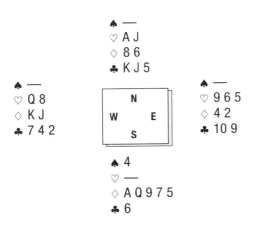

```
                ♠ —
                ♡ A J
                ◇ 8 6
                ♣ K J 5
♠ —                             ♠ —
♡ Q 8            N              ♡ 9 6 5
◇ K J         W     E           ◇ 4 2
♣ 7 4 2          S              ♣ 10 9
                ♠ 4
                ♡ —
                ◇ A Q 9 7 5
                ♣ 6
```

Chemla only had ten sure tricks at this point. However, when Chemla led his last trump, Benito was squeezed in three suits! A club or a heart would give declarer his eleventh trick, and when that winner was cashed, another squeeze would produce a twelfth. Instead, Garozzo parted with the ◇J, and Chemla ultimately dropped the ◇K to make his slam.

"A rare mistake from Benito, that heart return," said Paul, "perhaps the world's best-ever player and a good friend. I remember one year," he went on, "in the middle of an important European Championship match Benito and Lea's dog Snabu wandered into the playing area. 'Where is Mami?' called Benito to the dog. However Lea was also playing, so Benito got up from his seat to comfort the dog. When he returned to his chair, he proceeded to go down in a tricky slam. The next day his partner, Dano de Falco, brought to the playing area a large carrot. 'This is in case the dog shows again,' he laughed!"

Looking back on the last two decades, the French can be justly proud of their performance, and especially of their three wins and no losses in World Championship finals against USA. Eric Kokish commented in his summing up of the Tunisia final, 'If history is our guide the French players seem to have the Americans' number.' Taking no chances he then qualified this by saying that history is made afresh every year and any result between the two countries is of course uncertain. Nevertheless, you have to feel that the players from the world's leading professional bridge country are beginning to sense an unfortunate trend in their consistent losses to the French.

Polish Caviar

hen I first started to go to international tournaments in the early seventies, I learned two things about the bridge players from Poland. Firstly, as well as being fine players, they played very complicated systems and I did not enjoy playing against them. Secondly, they were always short of money and brought jars of caviar to sell at the tournaments. The caviar was of the best quality and the money it brought in helped with their expenses, so all in all everybody was happy. This went on for many years but recently, caviar aficionados have been hard put to find any at bridge tournaments; obviously times are better now in Poland. This increase in affluence has been matched by the growth in stature of Polish bridge players, several of whom now enjoy the reputation of being among the very best in the world. As World Olympiad Champion in 1984 and winner of the European title in Menton in 1993, Poland is always a contender for the Bermuda Bowl. As a European, I know the team that most people prefer not to play is Poland. They are excellent card players who like to defend, especially doubled contracts. All their pairs play complex systems, which often involve a number of unusual two-bids, including some where the suits are unspecified.

One of Poland's best-known players is Piotr Gawrys. Winner of the 1984 World Olympiad Teams in Seattle, Gawrys is one of the world's top players and travels the globe playing bridge. He showed me this little gem of a hand from a European Championship match against France. He held:

♠ K J 9 4   ♡ K J 8 7 5   ◇ 7   ♣ Q 8 2

After an opening bid of 1◇ on his right he overcalled 1♡ and the French bid to a contract of 6◇, declared by Jean Louis Stoppa. With no appealing lead, Piotr selected the ♣Q and this is what happened.

Declarer won the ♣A and ruffed two clubs in dummy while drawing three rounds of trumps to arrive at the position in the lower diagram.

What should happen now is that declarer leads a low spade to the queen and a low spade back to the ace. Gawrys now intended to drop the ♠K under the ace, pretending to be a man holding on to the ♣J and unblocking his spade from ♠Kxx. Declarer would not be able to afford to cash the last trump while the defense still had club winners, and so would attempt to exit to East's supposed ♠J. Gawrys could pounce on this with the ♠J to lead a fourth spade, endplaying dummy in

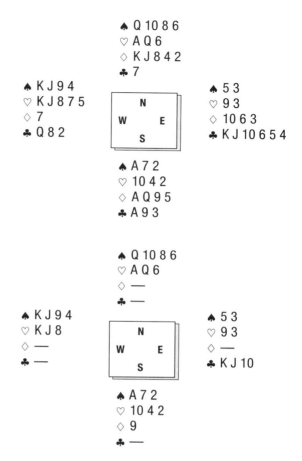

hearts for down one. This would be a flawless brilliancy. In real life, though, declarer played a spade to the ten which held, and a second spade to his ace, on which Gawrys dropped the ♠J. Now when declarer tried a third spade, Piotr was able to win his ♠K and play a fourth spade, endplaying the dummy to lead hearts away. Declarer erred though — after he had won the second spade trick, it was safe to play his last trump which would have squeezed West out of either his presumed ♣J (making it safe to exit in spades) or in actuality, his fourth spade. Then he could exit in spades or take the heart finesse to bring the contract home.

In 1994 in the World Championships in Alburquerque, Polish players won the gold medal in the Open Pairs, the silver in the Teams and the bronze in the Mixed Pairs. This was an amazing performance for a small country, only bettered by the USA which had one gold, two silvers and a bronze. One of Poland's best pairs, Cezary Balicki and Adam Zmudzinski, were on the team that lost the Rosenblum Teams final to Seymon Deutsch and the US 'team of destiny'. Deutsch had already gone home as he thought the semifinal match was lost beyond recovery, and Michael Rosenberg had to call him to return and play the final after an incredible comeback.

Balicki and Zmudzinski sometimes play the Suspensor system, which is the opposite of bridge as most of us know it — they open on worthless hands and make a 'forcing' pass with good ones. The idea is that their one heart or one spade openers, which are known as fertilizer bids or 'ferts', plant a seed which makes them difficult to play against. Many hours have been spent by the top teams in formulating defenses to these methods, but those less prepared have little chance. Remarkably, the Poles have proved that as well as being an effective obstructive tool, their system also works well constructively when combined with good judgement. Here is a hand from the semifinal of the World Championship against Brazil in Yokohama in 1991 (this was the year Poland lost in the final to Iceland).

North made a forcing pass with his twenty-one high card points and South was later able to show a negative hand. After North then showed a strong hand, South cuebid his spade control. With his hearts well-positioned over West, North bid the slam — a great one on this auction, with West highly likely to hold the ♡K. Not surprisingly, no pair in any other match bid this slam. This auction is a strange one indeed for many bridge players to see, with North passing a 2NT opener and South cuebidding with his four points after opening the bidding!

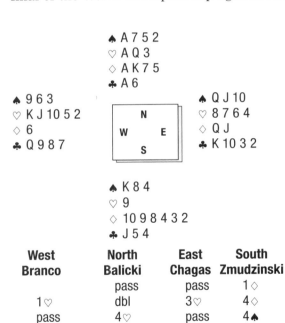

♠ A 7 5 2
♡ A Q 3
◇ A K 7 5
♣ A 6

♠ 9 6 3
♡ K J 10 5 2
◇ 6
♣ Q 9 8 7

♠ Q J 10
♡ 8 7 6 4
◇ Q J
♣ K 10 3 2

♠ K 8 4
♡ 9
◇ 10 9 8 4 3 2
♣ J 5 4

West Branco	North Balicki	East Chagas	South Zmudzinski
	pass	pass	1◇
1♡	dbl	3♡	4◇
pass	4♡	pass	4♠
pass	6◇	all pass	

The Z-men (so-called since their names contain so many Zs) can also play well without these complications and have won the Macallan Invitational playing a natural system — well, natural to them anyway! As you would expect, their card-playing ability is superb. Here is a hand Cezary Balicki showed me which could be called 'The Grand Sacrifice'.

Cezary declared 3NT after East had shown a major two-suiter, and West led the ♠Q. Declarer won in hand and played a heart to the king, ducked by East. Now a diamond from dummy went to East's king. The ♡A was cashed and East's ♡9 was won by South with the ♡10. The ◇Q went to the

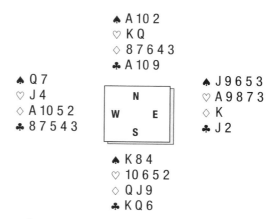

♠ A 10 2
♡ K Q
◇ 8 7 6 4 3
♣ A 10 9

♠ Q 7
♡ J 4
◇ A 10 5 2
♣ 8 7 5 4 3

♠ J 9 6 5 3
♡ A 9 8 7 3
◇ K
♣ J 2

♠ K 8 4
♡ 10 6 5 2
◇ Q J 9
♣ K Q 6

ace, West played a spade to dummy's ace, and Cezary played a diamond back to his hand. He could count eight winners: two spades, two hearts, one diamond and three clubs. The position was now the one in the diagram below.

Can you see what play Cezary made to make his contract, and also how the defense could have defeated him earlier?

The problem was to establish dummy's long diamond winner and then get there to cash it. Cezary played his ♣K and overtook it with dummy's ace before giving West his ◇10. Now West had to play a club and regardless of who had the ♣J, the ♣10 was secured as an entry to the long diamond. Well played — but did you spot how

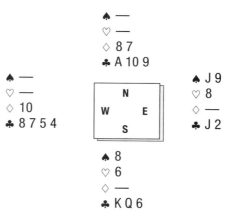

♠ —
♡ —
◇ 8 7
♣ A 10 9

♠ —
♡ —
◇ 10
♣ 8 7 5 4

♠ J 9
♡ 8
◇ —
♣ J 2

♠ 8
♡ 6
◇ —
♣ K Q 6

West could have beaten the contract? When declarer led the first diamond to his partner's king, he had to overtake with his ace and fire back a second spade. Now when East wins his ♡A he can cash his three spade winners. So both declarer and defender have to sacrifice their kings on the same hand — not a theme I have seen before!

This is a hand Balicki played in a Polish tournament. West led the ◇10 and East took the ace to play a trump. Cezary won in hand, cashed the ◇K and led a heart to the queen. He then ruffed a diamond and carefully watched East's card. Had East played the ◇Q, he would have led a club from hand and won the trump return to play a second club. When East played his third trump he would win in hand to run trumps and squeeze West who would be holding the ◇9 and the long hearts. However, when East followed with a low diamond on the third round, Balicki knew that he had started with a 3-2-4-4 distribution. He there-

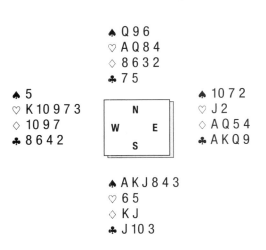

♠ Q 9 6
♡ A Q 8 4
◇ 8 6 3 2
♣ 7 5

♠ 5
♡ K 10 9 7 3
◇ 10 9 7
♣ 8 6 4 2

♠ 10 7 2
♡ J 2
◇ A Q 5 4
♣ A K Q 9

♠ A K J 8 4 3
♡ 6 5
◇ K J
♣ J 10 3

West	North	East	South
			Balicki
	pass	1NT	2♠
2NT[1]	dbl	pass	pass
3♡	3♠	pass	4♠
all pass			

1. Lebensohl.

fore now crossed to the ♡A and ruffed a heart as East pitched a club. The ♣10 went to the queen and a second trump was won with dummy's nine. The position was now as shown on the left.

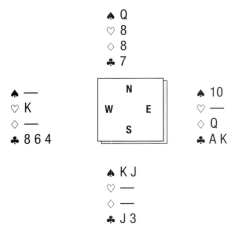

♠ Q
♡ 8
◇ 8
♣ 7

♠ —
♡ K
◇ —
♣ 8 6 4

♠ 10
♡ —
◇ Q
♣ A K

♠ K J
♡ —
◇ —
♣ J 3

South needs three tricks and leads a heart from dummy. If East pitches the ◇Q, declarer ruffs with the ♠K, goes to dummy with the ♠Q and cashes a diamond. If East pitches the ♣K instead, South ruffs low and leads a low club to East's ace. East must either let South make his two trumps separately or return a trump to South's king where the ♣J is the tenth winner. If East ruffs the heart, South makes his three trumps on a crossruff. A very good hand, worthy of a par contest!

In Albuquerque, the two Polish players who held off a strong challenge from Bob Hamman and Michael Rosenberg for the gold medal in the World Pairs were Marcin Lesniewski and Marek Szymanowski. Marek showed me this hand from the final of the Bermuda Bowl against Iceland.

He held:

♠ K 8 6 4 3   ♡ 4   ◇ A Q 8 6 2   ♣ 6 4

The bidding went 2◇ on his left, showing a weak two-bid in an unknown suit, 2NT on his right (enquiring), 3◇ showing hearts, then 6♡. What would you lead?

Marek found the only card in his hand to defeat the contract when he led the ♡4. Declarer had no choice about where to win this trick and found himself strangely stuck in hand with no way to reach dummy! The contract went two down and Poland gained 13 IMPs after this bizarre (but typical) auction by the Z-men at the other table. The 1◇ opener showed 0-7 and 1♡ was (maybe surprisingly) non-forcing. After East's takeout double, Adam tried a spade psyche and Cezary removed to 1NT. Adam then jumped to show his long hearts and they settled in 5♡ after this delicate auction! When East naturally led a spade, declarer had an easy twelve tricks after taking the club finesse. Bridge for the connoisseur.

```
              ♠ —
              ♡ A K Q J
              ◇ K 9 7 4
              ♣ A Q 5 3 2
♠ Q J 7 5 2              ♠ K 8 6 4 3
♡ 8 6          N         ♡ 4
◇ J 10     W     E       ◇ A Q 8 6 2
♣ K J 10 7     S         ♣ 6 4
              ♠ A 10 9
              ♡ 10 9 7 5 3 2
              ◇ 5 3
              ♣ 9 8
```

West	North	East	South
Marten	**Jonsson**	**Marek**	**Arnarson**
			2◇
pass	2NT	pass	3◇
pass	6♡	all pass	
Arnthorsson	**Balicki**	**Johannsson**	**Zmudzinski**
			1◇
pass	1♡	dbl	1♠
dbl	1NT	pass	3♡
pass	4♡	4♠	pass
pass	2NT	pass	3◇
pass	5♣	pass	5♡
all pass			

Marcin Lesniewski was a European Teams Champion in 1993 and World Pairs Champion in 1994. This is a hand he declared in the Polish Championships.

```
              ♠ 4 3
              ♡ A 9
              ◇ 10 9 6 3 2
              ♣ K J 10 8
♠ J 9 8 7 6                      ♠ Q 10 5
♡ K Q J 10 4 3      N           ♡ 7 2
◇ J             W       E        ◇ K Q 8 7
♣ Q                 S            ♣ 9 7 6 5
              ♠ A K 2
              ♡ 8 6 5
              ◇ A 5 4
              ♣ A 4 3 2
```

West had opened a Polish weak two-bid that showed six hearts and five spades. How did Marcin make his 3NT contract on the lead of the ♡K?

The opening lead was ducked and a second heart won in dummy with the ace. Marcin had to play for West to be either 1-1 or 2-0 in the minors. If East holds ◇KQx, he can make the hand by playing a diamond from dummy and either ducking East's queen or playing the ace if East plays low. However, he decided to go for the alternative line. This needed West to be 1-1 in minors with the singleton ♣Q and a diamond honor and also required that East hold the ♠Q. He led a spade from dummy to his ace and a club to the queen and king. When he led a second spade from dummy, East obliged by producing the queen. Marcin let this hold and

Cezary Balicki

won the third spade. Then he cashed his clubs and played the ◇A, West dropping the jack! A second diamond was won by East, who had to concede the last diamond trick to dummy for the ninth trick — bridge is an easy game!

Lesniewski-Szymanowski and the Z-men have recently teamed up with Grant Baze on a Spingold team. In 1997, sponsored by Tipton Golias, they

Marcin Lesniewski

won the final of the Spingold against Cayne. Having been behind at the half the four Poles made a great comeback to take the title — the first time that four non-Americans had won this premier teams event. The following year the Poles and Baze were back to defend their title, this time with Michael Whitman rather than Golias, who was unavailable. Again they reached the final, and it proved to be one of the most remarkable and certainly the closest in the history of the Spingold Trophy.

C H A P T E R 14

An IMP's an IMP for a' that*

hicago is a wonderful city in summer, with its downtown area full of beautiful and historic buildings overlooking Lake Michigan; the 1998 Summer Nationals in that city was well attended, with a large number of excellent teams playing in the Spingold. Many top foreign players added to the flavor of the event. In the first semifinal the defending champions, the Poles, Grant Baze and their new sponsor, Michael Whitman of San Francisco, had drawn the Richie Schwartz team: Mark Lair, Ron Smith, and Steve Weinstein-Bobby Levin, with the last two playing throughout. The second semifinal was won easily by the Nickell team, who had won three consecutive Spingolds prior to the Polish win in 1997. So Nick Nickell and Dick Freeman, along with Jeff Meckstroth, Eric Rodwell, Bob Hamman and Paul Soloway (who had replaced Bobby Wolff on the team) awaited the winner of the Schwartz-Baze match, which was featured on VuGraph.

Michael Whitman, who had never before played in the late stages of such an important event, played the first two quarters, but remarkably his team was up by 81-42 at the half with the super-strong Polish foursome to play the last half. However, in the third quarter the Schwartz team pulverized the Poles 86-8, making Schwartz the leader by 39 IMPs. Could the holders get it back in the last sixteen deals? A packed VuGraph audience watched the following story unfold.

Early in the set, a well-judged slam auction by a team 40 IMPs behind won back eleven; at the other table, Lair-Smith reached only 5♣ on a hand where twelve tricks were available. On Board 51, the Poles made an aggressive penalty double of a thin game, then beat it two to collect 6 IMPs against a partscore one down in the other room. Then a few flat boards brought us to Board 55.

---

* 'A man's a man for a' that.'— Robbie Burns, Scottish poet

After the lead of the ♡10, Smith drew trumps and played a heart up to the nine. Eventually, when South won his club trick, he was endplayed to allow declarer to escape for down one. The real excitement came in the Closed Room.

After the same opening preempt, Levin decided the time was opportune to psyche a 3♠ bid and an unsuspecting Weinstein raised with his stiff honor. For some reason, Levin decided this was where he wanted to play and Balicki saw no reason to disturb the contract.

```
                    ♠ 7
                    ♡ K J 8 4
                    ◇ A Q 10 7 5
                    ♣ 6 4 3
  ♠ 10 9 8 5 2                      ♠ A K Q 6 4 3
  ♡ A Q 9 7 5      ┌──────────┐     ♡ 6 3
  ◇ —              │    N     │     ◇ 4
  ♣ 9 8 2          │ W     E  │     ♣ A Q 10 5
                   │    S     │
                   └──────────┘
                    ♠ J
                    ♡ 10 2
                    ◇ K J 9 8 6 3 2
                    ♣ K J 7
```

West Lair	North Szymanowski	East Smith	South Lesniewski
			3◇
4♠	5◇	5♡	dbl
5♠	6◇	6♠	pass
pass	dbl	all pass	

West Balicki	North Levin	East Zmudzinski	South Weinstein
			3◇
pass	3♠	pass	4♠
all pass			

Although Weinstein played the hand carefully, he could score only two tricks for down eight and 800 for East-West. Perhaps Levin was unlucky; as if West had held the ♣K, North-South would have been cold for a slam. However, his team was considerably in front and he certainly created the opportunity for a substantial swing one way or the other. Some purists would say he got what he deserved. Anyway, the VuGraph audience loved it — they like to see great players have disasters just like they do. This was 14 IMPs to Baze, who had now scored an unanswered 31 IMPs, and on the next two hands small swings reduced the Schwartz lead to a mere six.

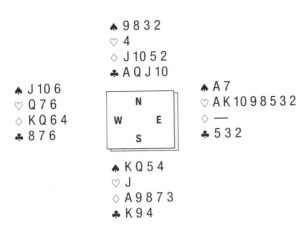

♠ 9 8 3 2
♡ 4
◇ J 10 5 2
♣ A Q J 10

♠ J 10 6   ♠ A 7
♡ Q 7 6   ♡ A K 10 9 8 5 3 2
◇ K Q 6 4   ◇ —
♣ 8 7 6   ♣ 5 3 2

♠ K Q 5 4
♡ J
◇ A 9 8 7 3
♣ K 9 4

On Board 60, however, Schwartz finally struck a blow.

In the Closed Room the Polish East opened 4♡, which was passed out, and when Weinstein led the ♠K, the contract had to go down one. However at the other table, Smith was able to open a Namyats 4♣ showing a good 4♡ opener and as a result, North ended up on lead. He selected the ◇J and Mark Lair pitched a club on this to lose only two clubs and a diamond — 10 IMPs to Schwartz, who led by sixteen.

Another 2-IMP swing and with Board 63 over, Schwartz was 13 IMPs ahead. Baze needed a 750-point swing to tie the match.

In the Open Room Lair-Smith played 3◇ for plus 130, but we noticed that it would take the defense of ♣A and ♣Q to break 5◇. South could then play another club when in to force the East hand to ruff and create a trump trick for North. Even making 5◇ wouldn't be enough to win, though.

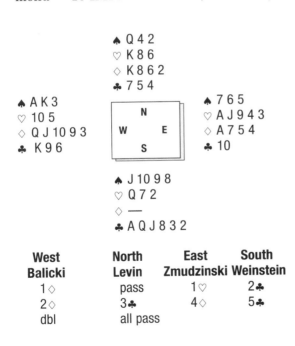

♠ Q 4 2
♡ K 8 6
◇ K 8 6 2
♣ 7 5 4

♠ A K 3   ♠ 7 6 5
♡ 10 5   ♡ A J 9 4 3
◇ Q J 10 9 3   ◇ A 7 5 4
♣ K 9 6   ♣ 10

♠ J 10 9 8
♡ Q 7 2
◇ —
♣ A Q J 8 3 2

West Balicki	North Levin	East Zmudzinski	South Weinstein
1◇	pass	1♡	2♣
2◇	3♣	4◇	5♣
dbl	all pass		

Again, however, Weinstein and Levin got too aggressive and got into trouble. Against 5♣ doubled, West led the ♡10. Declarer played low and won the queen in hand. After the ♣A by declarer, West pounced on the ♣Q to cash his spades and play another heart. Now a third and fourth heart set up a trick for the ♣9 — down four for 800. (Declarer could have saved a trick by rising with dummy's ♡K at Trick 1.) A great result for Baze, but not great enough; the net of plus 670 was worth 12 IMPs, so Schwartz had still won by 1 IMP. Or so everyone in the audience thought as they left the room. However, Adam Zmudzinski thought differently. His card showed two scoring errors from the third quarter which added up to two more IMPs for Baze. The defenders had not lost by one — in fact they had won by one! The poor Schwartz team went from elation to devastation as the Poles were buying triple vodkas at the bar. What a match!

The top two seeds were now booked to meet in the final — Nickell with six world champions against five very tough winners from last year along with the new boy, Michael Whitman. The smart money made Nickell around a 10-IMP favorite. Well, Michael Whitman played great for his two quarters and the score at the half was Nickell 45-Baze 39. The next quarter was a 26-IMP tie. The score was 71-65, one of the lowest scoring matches ever in the Spingold final, evidence of the high standard of play. At one stage there were nine well-played flat boards in a row. Could the Poles beat the Year 2000 USA team by seven in the last quarter or would we see a new champion?

On the first board of the last set, both teams played 5♣. When Zmudzinski declared he got the ◊A lead and made six. Against Hamman a trump was led, and with no clue from the bidding, he guessed to play North for four spades to the jack, finessed in spades and made a very important extra overtrick. Nickell had told his team

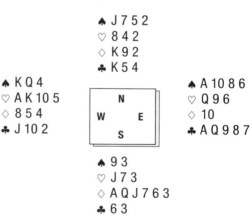

to pay attention to overtricks and also to the score! On the next two boards, first Meckwell then Hamman-Soloway bid to poor slams, going down three tricks and two tricks respectively. These two boards were worth 19 IMPs to Baze who now led by twelve. Nickell struck back immediately when Meckwell slipped through a 3NT when Marek could not find a club lead from:

♠ K 7 5 3   ♡ K Q 7 2   ◊ 5   ♣ 9 8 7 4

That was worth 10 IMPs. Then the Poles went for an extra under-trick in 3NT giving up 2 IMPs; the match was tied with nine deals left to play.

On Board 56, Hamman-Soloway played a quiet 2♡ making four, while the Poles overbid to a horrible 4♠ contract. Lady Luck was on declarer's side however, and Baze led by 6 IMPs now. Only two hands later, the luck changed.

Marcin's final pass was after a considerable pause. This looked like a chance for a pickup for Baze as Meckwell might find it difficult to put the brakes on, and 6◇ should lose a spade and a club. And indeed, the auction at the other table got very high.

South showed a 5-3-4-1 with no extras, 4♡ was Key Card, and North showed two with the queen as he had an extra trump. The slam has no play on a club lead, of course, but Zmudzinski took some time and then led the ♠Q. Rodwell, normally a deliberate and careful player, quickly played dummy's ace in case East was thinking of changing his lead! He now had a chance — the ♡Q with West, no more than three times. So it proved to be, and

```
                ♠ 6 2
                ♡ A K J 8
                ◇ A 8 6 5 4 2
                ♣ J
♠ J 5 4                        ♠ K Q 8
♡ Q 9 5          N            ♡ 6 3 2
◇ 10         W       E        ◇ 7 3
♣ A Q 8 7 5 2    S            ♣ K 10 6 4 3
                ♠ A 10 9 7 3
                ♡ 10 7 4
                ◇ K Q J 9
                ♣ 9
```

West Hamman	North Lesniewski	East Soloway	South Szymanowski
			1♠
pass	2◇	pass	2♠
pass	3♡	pass	5◇
all pass			

Balicki	Rodwell	Zmudzinski	Meckstroth
			1♠
pass	2◇	pass	3◇
pass	3♡	pass	3♠
pass	4♣	pass	4♡
pass	5◇	pass	6◇
all pass			

luck smiled on Nickell to the tune of 26 IMPs — winning thirteen instead of losing them. Six to go, and now Nickell led by seven.

Not for long, though. On Board 59, the Poles found an excellent save that was missed at the other table, while their teammates were allowed to score up their game for 8 IMPs — it was now Baze by one. Board 60 was a flat cold slam. On Board 61 Lesniewski tried for 3NT instead of four of a major, guessing he had four easy top losers. Had Soloway, who was on lead, held the ♠A declarer would have scored his game, but Hamman won it at Trick 1 and switched immediately to the open suit where the defense cashed five winners for down two. In the other room, a mundane 4♡ went down only one, which gave Nickell 3 IMPs and the lead by two. Board 62 was flat. Two to go, and nobody was leaving the packed VuGraph auditorium.

Paul Soloway

On Board 63, Paul Soloway reached 4♡ as East after North had opened 1♣. Marek hoped for good clubs with partner and started a club, but Paul was now in control and lost only two hearts and a club.

Rodwell had opened the North hand differently, with a 14-16 notrump, and just as the VuGraph commen-

```
                    ♠ K 4 3 2
                    ♡ A 10 9 8
                    ◇ Q 3
                    ♣ A J 10
  ♠ A J 9 7                        ♠ 5
  ♡ 6 5 2           N              ♡ K Q J 7 4
  ◇ 10 9 6      W       E          ◇ A K J 4 2
  ♣ Q 9 6           S              ♣ K 7
                    ♠ Q 10 8 6
                    ♡ 3
                    ◇ 8 7 5
                    ♣ 8 5 4 3 2
```

tators were discussing whether 4♡ could be made on a spade lead, Meckstroth duly led a spade. Zmudzinski won, passed the ◇10 and led a heart to his king. Rodwell was now in control and played spades both times he was in with his heart and club aces. It turned out the contract was doomed from the opening lead. Eric would certainly have gone in with the ♣A if declarer had tried a club at Trick 3, since he could see four tricks in his own hand. This was 10 IMPs to Nickell who now led by twelve going in to the last board. Was it over, or was there one more comeback left for the never-say-die Poles?

Here it was — Board 64. Marek reached 4♠ from the South hand, and received a heart lead. He finessed in hearts and pitched a diamond on the ♡A. He then played a club to the queen, ruffed a club and played the ace and king of spades. He was now okay as long as one of the black suits behaved, and duly scored up his game. To win the match Baze had to collect 300 at the other table.

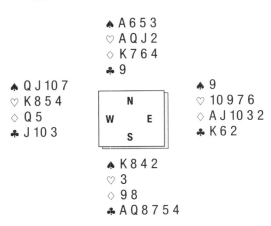

```
            ♠ A 6 5 3
            ♡ A Q J 2
            ◇ K 7 6 4
            ♣ 9
♠ Q J 10 7              ♠ 9
♡ K 8 5 4      N        ♡ 10 9 7 6
◇ Q 5      W     E      ◇ A J 10 3 2
♣ J 10 3       S        ♣ K 6 2
            ♠ K 8 4 2
            ♡ 3
            ◇ 9 8
            ♣ A Q 8 7 5 4
```

Well, Meckstroth received a heart lead against 4♠ and also finessed. However, he next played a club to the ace and found he had to go two down! Fortunately for Nickell, and unfortunately for Baze, nobody had doubled, so the swing was only 11 IMPs and, would you believe it, Nickell had won by one! And this time the score was accurate.

This surely was one of the finest and most exciting Spingold finals ever played. Neither team deserved to lose, and the game of bridge and the event as a whole was the real winner.

The 1998 Spingold winners. From the left: Jeff Meckstroth, Bob Hamman, Dick Freeman, Paul Soloway, Eric Rodwell and Nick Nickell

Things Nobody Tells You

The Sharp End of the Law

Director's rulings and Appeals Committees are two of the unfortunate crosses bridge players have to bear. Nobody likes them, but everybody has to put up with them. Apart from the usual humdrum stuff, I have been involved in two rather unusual situations in relation to rulings during the course of my bridge career. The first occurred in the European Championships in Lausanne in 1979. We were in contention towards the end and were having a good match.

I held as South

♠ K 9 6 ♡ A J 9 7 6 ◇ 8 ♣ A J 3 2

I bid 1♡, West bid a vulnerable 1♠, Goldberg bid 3♡ and I raised myself to game. The opening lead was a trump and I saw this dummy.

♠ 7 4 3 2
♡ K Q 4 2
◇ A 9 6
♣ 10 7

```
       N
   W       E
       S
```

♠ K 9 6
♡ A J 9 7 6
◇ 8
♣ A J 3 2

I had five heart tricks, a diamond, at least one club and two ruffs making nine in all. It looked as if I would need an endplay in spades to make the contract. I won the lead in dummy and led a low club to the jack and the king. Now a second trump came back which I won in my hand as East showed out. I was pleased — with eight cards in the majors, West was likely to be in trouble. I played the ♣A and then a small club ruffing in dummy, while West threw the ♠5, then I cashed the ◇A and led a small diamond off dummy. My plan was to ruff this, ruff my last club in dummy, and draw the last trump leaving myself with ♠743 in dummy and ♠K96 in hand. At that point I would be in my hand, and I would need to guess which spade to exit with to endplay my left-hand opponent. If he came down to ♠AQJ, a low spade would work, and he would have to give me a trick with the ♠K. If he had still the ♠8 in his hand, I would have to exit with the ♠K (or else he could play low and let East win the trick), and eventually I would score the ♠9.

Well, when I called for the diamond off dummy, West put his hand on the table and sank into a deep trance, after announcing that he was not thinking about *this* trick. A couple of minutes later he picked up his hand, I ruffed the diamond in hand and he followed. Now I ruffed my last club in dummy as he pitched the queen of spades. Another diamond ruff back to hand allowed me to to draw the last trump, and then I paused. What were West's last three cards and what had been his cards when he took his time out? The only problem he could have had was whether to unblock in spades from ♠AQJ8 — so now he must have ♠AJ8 left, and I knew what to do. I triumphantly played the ♠K from hand only to see West claim the last three tricks with the ♠AJ10. The full hand was as you see it here.

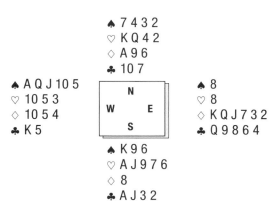

```
              ♠ 7 4 3 2
              ♡ K Q 4 2
              ◇ A 9 6
              ♣ 10 7

♠ A Q J 10 5      N        ♠ 8
♡ 10 5 3                   ♡ 8
◇ 10 5 4      W     E      ◇ K Q J 7 3 2
♣ K 5            S         ♣ Q 9 8 6 4

              ♠ K 9 6
              ♡ A J 9 7 6
              ◇ 8
              ♣ A J 3 2
```

Clearly, I would have made the hand if I had played a low spade from my hand instead of the king. For this to be right, when my opponent put his hand down on the table he had to have had the ♠AQJ10 remaining in his hand. He obviously could not have been thinking about pitching the ace, and surely with three equal cards in his hand he could not go into the tank and pretend he had a problem he did not have. Having taken some time to play this hand, and spent a fair amount of mental effort on getting the ending right, I was furious. I felt I had been deprived of the chance of making my contract by an unethical action, but the director ruled that the inference had been drawn at my own risk. In the other room, four hearts went two down, and as a result we only won the match 17-3, not by the blitz I felt we deserved.

We appealed the director's ruling in front of the Executive Appeals committee. I made my point as reasonably as possible, saying that I could not have found the winning play under the circumstances. My opponent was asked by the committee to explain his view and his play. He stated that he thought I was taking a double shot — I was trying for the brilliancy prize (a prize given at the tournament for the best-played hand) and if that line failed, I was trying to make the hand via a director's ruling. So why *did* he tank in this situation? He explained that he knew the hand depended on my view in spades and wanted to make sure he played the card which would most likely cause me to go wrong!

Well, the committee upheld the director's ruling but refunded our deposit, so they certainly didn't feel our appeal was frivolous. To this day this hand rankles me. Sour grapes by me or a bad ruling? Make up your own mind! Up to that point, we had been playing well and had received our share of the luck, but as so often happens, this ruling changed our momentum for the worse.

My second curious event came as a result of time pressure. First, I should explain that the rules for international bridge play provide for penalties for one or both sides if they are deemed to be guilty of excessively slow play. While this is not quite as draconian as the rules at chess events, where you lose the match if you exceed your allotted time, it can and has affected championship results (most recently in the 2000 Venice Cup where the USA lost the final by half an IMP after being assessed a time penalty earlier in the match).

Playing with Michael Rosenberg in Elsinore in my first European Championship, I held:

♠ 9 5 2   ♡ 8 7 5   ◇ K 6 2   ♣ 8 7 5 2

The auction was 1NT-3NT; what lead did I pick? Well, our team was up by 100 IMPs at the half, so we were guaranteed a maximum result; but we were in time trouble, and in order to avoid a time penalty we had to finish the hand in forty-five seconds. I picked the ◇K as likely to be the best lead for declarer, and he immediately claimed twelve tricks! Mission accomplished. Now, although I have the reputation of being a slow player, I am almost always able to make up for slow hands by playing quickly on others, thereby avoiding a time penalty. In fact, in thirty years of playing timed events I have received only three such penalties. The first was against Forrester-Robson in a Camrose trophy match, where penalties were assessed against both sides although in this case I felt my partner and I were not to blame. Tony quipped, "It's just like being charged with speeding when this is the one time you really were driving under the limit. You have to write it off against all the other occasions when you got away with it!"

The second time I was penalized was against the Poles in the European Championship. The Poles are intrinsically a very tough team to play, in part because of the unusual bidding systems they use. On this occasion their declarer took a very long time trying for an overtrick on the second-last board. By that stage he was already over the time limit and then found himself playing a grand slam on the last hand. A sound player, he missed two simple lines that would have given him his contract.

The third time penalty was a most unusual affair. We were playing on the last weekend of the 1993 Gold Cup; the previous year our team had lost the event in the final and here we were trying again. We won a tight quarterfinal but found ourselves 56 IMPs down at the half in the semifinal. However, a strong rally left our team only 13 IMPs behind going into the last eight boards. The tension was very high when I picked up the following collection as North — we were vulnerable against not vulnerable opponents.

♠ **Q J 7** ♡ **9 8 2** ◇ **J 10 8 3** ♣ **7 5 4**

The auction had taken a very strange turn of events — partner had bid diamonds for the first time at the six-level after showing a hand with a very long spade suit. I had decided to pass 6◇, but now had to make another decision. I thought for a long time. What would you have done?

West	North Barnet	East	South
		1♣	1♠
2♡	pass	4♡	4♠
6♣	pass	pass	6◇
pass	pass	6♡	dbl
pass	?		

The choices are to pass and lead a club (hoping partner is 7-1-5-0, and will ruff the club and cash a side winner) or to bid 6♠. I thought for a very long time and bid 6♠. Now I heard 7♣ on my right which partner doubled. He led the ♠A, and that lived because this was the whole hand:

So the perfect winning action on my part was to pass 6♡ and lead a club, but East went wrong too and we finished with plus 100. Since we collected 200 in the other room, that was worth 7 IMPs. The director was informed that I had taken all the time on the hand (more than fifteen minutes) and he ruled that as this was a timed event our side would be responsible if we went over the time limit, probably with an automatic penalty being assessed. However, as so often happens in these situations, everyone played quite quickly thereafter and

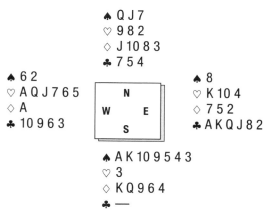

```
                    ♠ Q J 7
                    ♡ 9 8 2
                    ◇ J 10 8 3
                    ♣ 7 5 4
♠ 6 2                              ♠ 8
♡ A Q J 7 6 5        N             ♡ K 10 4
◇ A              W       E         ◇ 7 5 2
♣ 10 9 6 3           S             ♣ A K Q J 8 2
                    ♠ A K 10 9 5 4 3
                    ♡ 3
                    ◇ K Q 9 6 4
                    ♣ —
```

we finished about twenty seconds before the deadline. When we scored up, our team had gained 14 IMPs on the set to win by 1 IMP.

The match was not yet over, however. While we were celebrating, the opposition complained to the director that they had defended badly on the last hand to allow me to make an overtrick in two notrump when they might have held me or beaten me. They said that they had felt constrained to try to make up time to finish within the time limit. Moreover, had we not finished within the time limit, our side would have been penalized 3 IMPs and we would have lost the match. At about 1:30 a.m., the Scottish director discovered that under the rules he was allowed to assign a penalty for various nonspecific infractions. Even although we had finished within the prescribed time period, he therefore assessed us a 3-IMP penalty and our side was deemed to have lost by 2 IMPs. Needless to say, we appealed and when the meeting of the Appeals Committee was over, it was 3:00 a.m. The Appeals Committee, in an attempt to please everyone, produced a ruling worthy of Solomon — our team would be fined not 3 IMPs but 1 IMP, thereby making the match a dead tie! A further eight boards would be played to decide the result.

After getting very little sleep, we played the eight boards the following morning, won, and proceeded to play the final, where the same director became involved once again.

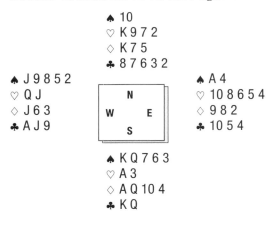

I played 3NT as North on a heart lead, winning the ♡A and playing the ♣K next. West won, and a second heart came back to my king. When a spade to the king held, I cashed all my winners ending in dummy before exiting with a low spade and setting up the ♠Q as my ninth trick. At the other table, Forrester was North in the same contract. He won the heart lead in hand and immediately passed the ♠10, losing to the jack. West switched to the ♣A, getting the ♣10 from partner, before playing a second heart. Declarer won and played the ♠K. East won this, but now played the ♡10 and another heart so now declarer only needed to play diamonds for four tricks to make his contract. However, at Trick 12 Forrester finessed in diamonds to go two down.

What happened here? Well, when East played the ♣10 under the ace, declarer had asked about it and had been told that it was a standard count signal (showing an even number of clubs) when actually it had been intended as a reverse attitude signal (discouraging a club continuation). Declarer, taking this information at face value, had counted East to be 2-5-4-2 with four diamonds, and now protested that he had been damaged. The director (the same director) upheld the table result but this time was overruled by the Appeals Committee, which allowed declarer to make his contract and score plus 400.

Although our team had a small lead at the half, we played without inspiration in the second half and in the end lost easily. Possibly the traumatic events of the day and the previous night, not to mention the lack of sleep, had taken their toll.

I felt we had been cheated by the strange time penalty ruling and wrote about it to the world's leading expert on the rules of bridge, my friend Edgar Kaplan. He replied that before the 'non-specific infraction' rule could be invoked there must be an 'offense'. Slow tempo in itself is not an offense, unless it is used as a weapon to disconcert the opponents or unless a pair exceeds a specific per-session time limit. Kaplan went on to say that if one pair chose to rush their play towards the end of the session in order to spare their opponents a penalty under the mistaken impression that they were being good sports, then that was their own affair. However, they could not then ask for redress if they suffered as a result. He went on to say that he had never before heard of a similar penalty being imposed when a table had finished within the limits set by the conditions of contest.

I then wrote to the British Bridge League asking for an explanation and making the following points. If the 7♣ board had come at the end and the same time had been taken, would there still have been a penalty? If a director can assess a penalty on any player who thinks for some lengthy but unspecified period of time, what happens to other players who think for longer periods at the same or other tournaments? Imagine Eric Rodwell or Michael Rosenberg trying to make a tricky slam towards the end of a Bermuda Bowl or a Spingold and not knowing how long they were allowed to think.

Of course they could not reply directly to the points I had made and instead I received a castigating reply from the Laws Committee. Their letter avoided responding to any of my points but set out their view that taking so much time was detrimental to the game, and that as such I was responsible for any misfortune that happened to befall me. In retrospect, I *should* have come to a much quicker decision and saved a lot of time — of that there can be no question. However, I still feel that had we actually strayed over the time limit, we would deservedly have incurred a penalty. The rules are the rules — everyone should know what they are, and transgress them at their own peril. However, since we had not in fact broken the rules, the subsequent proceedings were farcical.

Strange but True

H ang around the bridge table long enough, and you'll come across some very strange happenings, and some very wild hands. In this chapter, I've collected some of my favorites, most of which I was either involved in or was told about by one of the participants.

First, here's a taste of what it's like to sit in with the big boys. In the big money IMP game at the Regency in New York, Sam Lev held:

♠ **A J 9 4**   ♡ **Q 6**   ◇ **A Q 10 9 8 4 3**   ♣ **—**

Playing four-card majors, it went 1♡ on his right, he bid 2◇, and it went 2♠ from Ira Rubin on his left. His partner doubled, the meaning of which was undiscussed, righty passed and Sam chose to bid 3◇. Now he heard 7♡ (!) on his left which was passed back to him — both sides were vulnerable. He ruminated on this unusual situation and finally said double. It went redouble on his left, pass, pass! At this point Lev knew, as one might say, that all was not well in the state of Denmark. Clearly Rubin was up to some devilish scheme, but should he gamble and bid 7♠ or take his chances on defense? He opted for the latter and led the ◇A. This was the whole deal:

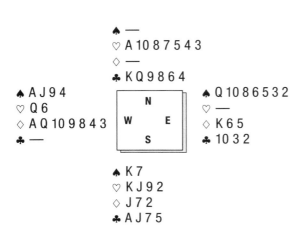

```
              ♠ —
              ♡ A 10 8 7 5 4 3
              ◇ —
              ♣ K Q 9 8 6 4
♠ A J 9 4                      ♠ Q 10 8 6 5 3 2
♡ Q 6            N             ♡ —
◇ A Q 10 9 8 4 3  W   E        ◇ K 6 5
♣ —                S           ♣ 10 3 2
              ♠ K 7
              ♡ K J 9 2
              ◇ J 7 2
              ♣ A J 7 5
```

Declarer had no trouble making seven hearts redoubled for a score of 2940. However, if Sam had taken the 'save' in seven spades he would have made that for a score of 2470, a difference of 5410 points. Fortunately for his side, his losses were limited as he was playing IMPs and not rubber bridge. His teammates, who came back after making 7♣, were not amused. Perhaps after Rubin's successful ploy had worked, Ira should not have raised the ante by redoubling and giving Lev one more chance.

On the track of more material for this chapter, I got wind of a recent unusual occurrence at the Regency club in New York; I went to TGR's club in London to meet Zia, who told me the following story.

"Playing in the big game at a dollar a point (about $1000 a rubber) I picked up:

♠ A Q 6　♡ A　◇ A K Q J 9 7 6 5　♣ 5

The bidding proceeded 3♣ from my LHO, pass from partner, 3♠ on my right. We were vulnerable against not. I bid 4NT, asking for aces, and my partner bid just what I wanted to hear — 6♡! I converted this to 7◇ and my LHO now bid 7♠ which partner doubled. Would you bid 7NT or take the money?" he asked.

Being a Scotsman and having a cautious outlook where money is concerned, I said I would make an opening lead — probably the ♠6. Zia went on, "I led the ◇A and when I saw the ♣A I sighed with relief that I had passed the double. I now switched to my ♡A and played a second diamond. Declarer ruffed, cashed the ♣A and led a club. Partner ruffed this and played the ♡K and another heart. Actually, we mis-defended the hand terri-

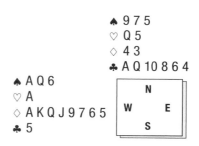

```
              ♠ 9 7 5
              ♡ Q 5
              ◇ 4 3
              ♣ A Q 10 8 6 4
♠ A Q 6            N
♡ A
◇ A K Q J 9 7 6 5   W   E
♣ 5                S
```

bly and let declarer make four tricks for down nine, or 2300. Of course declarer had psyched with:

♠ 10 8 4　♡ J 7 3 2　◇ 2　♣ K 9 7 3 2

"It was my best-ever result for such a horrible defensive screw-up. If I had led a trump we would have put them down thirteen for 3400 — but it was fun anyway. That's what rubber bridge is all about!" he laughed.

Having scribbled the hand down as good material, I sat down to play a few rubbers. The game was Zia, Gunnar Hallberg (a Swedish professional) and Tom Townsend from England. I won the first three rubbers and then cut Tom against Zia and Gunnar. Soon I was looking at:

♠ 10 5 2　♡ Q J 8 4　◇ 9 7 6 3　♣ K 5

With Tom and I passing throughout, I heard 1♣ on my right, 2◇

from Zia, 3◇ on my right, 4♣ from Zia, 4♠ on my right then 6♣ from Zia. At this point Hallberg gave the situation a little thought and bid 7♣, which ended the auction.

My worst scenario was that ♣A10xxx would hit the table as dummy while declarer had ♣QJxxx. Maybe I should lead the ♣5 and hope declarer played the ace. But what if declarer had the ♣A and Zia had five- or six-card support? In that scenario, I would look very foolish underleading my ♣K to say the least, so I led the ♡Q, anxiously awaiting the dummy as Zia spread it on the table.

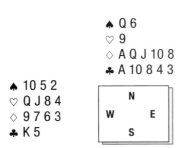

♠ Q 6
♡ 9
◇ A Q J 10 8
♣ A 10 8 4 3

♠ 10 5 2
♡ Q J 8 4
◇ 9 7 6 3
♣ K 5

An old fashioned jump shift with big support for partner. The opponents had exchanged hands and by the time declarer got his own hand back I was thinking furiously about what I was going to do when trumps got played. Suddenly, I saw the ♣Q on the table. Sure enough, declarer had won the ♡A in hand and tabled the ♣Q — quickly, now, what is your play?

Holding five clubs to the queen without the jack, declarer would have led low to the ace, hoping someone had a singleton king. The key declarer holdings for me were, therefore, ♣Qxxx or ♣QJxxxx. In the former case I had to cover, but in the latter, I had to play low very quickly and hope he didn't finesse. Which did you think was the more likely? Had Gunnar really pressed on to a grand slam with just the ♣Q and three teenies?

I thought not. I smoothly played my low club and when the next trick saw my king and partner's jack fall together, I suffered an acute pain. "A tough play," sympathized my partner, to his credit. As I saw the fruits of my afternoon's labor vanish in one hand I shook my head, but Zia was right there with a cheerful quip: "See how lucky you are, Barnet; you came here for a story about a grand slam and you got two for the same price!"

"Not quite the same price," I replied ruefully, but with half a smile.

Gabriel Chagas is one of the real characters in the bridge world. He is also top of my list of favorite dinner companions. As well as bringing his repertoire of funny stories, he always arrives with a special wine carrier, which contains two bottles carefully picked from one of his fine cellars; these he produces with a flourish in the restaurant and then talks his way into paying a minimal corkage fee. I remember bumping into him in a bridge club in Paris in the early seventies. I was there to play some rubber bridge but they were playing only Goulash, a game in which the cards are not shuffled between hands and are then dealt out four at a time. Wild distributions occur and although it is a very exciting game, it can also be very costly. I had never played it before but Gabriel said quickly, "Don't worry, Barnet, it is a very easy game to play. I will explain it as we go along!" I had heard that line before, but fell for it anyway.

In 1980 Gabriel was playing with his partner Pedro Paulo Assumpçao against Turkey in the World Teams Olympiad. The game was held in the 'pit' with many spectators watching, since Brazil had been one of the top qualifiers. Unfortunately for Brazil, the Turks had the upper hand and, as Chagas put it, 'were killing us' when this hand arose.

The contract was 4♠ played by the Turkish South, Ozdil, after West had opened 1♣. The opening lead was the ♡J and declarer won in hand to play a diamond to dummy. Pedro Paulo won the ace and Chagas dropped the ◇K at the same time as his partner was playing the ♡10 to the next trick. Declarer drew four rounds of trumps before leading a

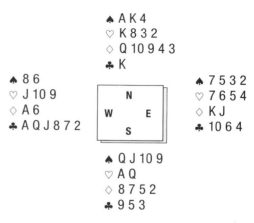

second diamond, and when West played a low diamond, South went into the tank. Clearly something was not right; why had West not given his partner two ruffs when he won the ◇A? Perhaps he had had too much wine with dinner! With the spectators holding their collective breath, the poor declarer put in the ◇10, losing to the jack, and the defense then cashed five more club tricks for down four!

Sometimes, when you think something is too good to be true, it really is. Playing in one of the later rounds of the Spingold, George Jacobs held the following hand:

♠ 8 2 ♡ J 6 2 ◇ 9 6 ♣ A K Q J 4 3

The opposition bid to 6NT. George was going to be on lead and thought for a while before passing. A carefully thought-out decision — perhaps they would run from 6NT doubled and find a better spot. Now, you may think that George was looking at a safe down five, but you would be wrong — six notrump made!

George led the ♣Q and his partner, Ron Smith, unfortunately dropped a spade on the table. "Play a spade, please," said declarer, trying not to laugh as he scored up his slam. George was philosophical. He turned to his kibitzer and said, "Lucky I didn't double."

Psychic bidding has been part of the game since it began — Oswald Jacoby was one of the earliest proponents of it, much to Sidney Lenz' disgust during the famous Lenz-Culbertson match. In December 1999 I had been playing golf at a friend's birthday celebration, and after the game, the conversation turned to bridge hands and in particular, to psychic bids. Michael Becker remembered one hand from a world championship when he was playing with Ronnie Rubin. The very next week I was reading an old book written by Jeremy Flint, with an entertaining foreword by my old friend Irving Rose, and I came across the same hand of Michael's that had given the boys some amusement. As Michael had no knowledge of this being in print anywhere, he was surprised. Flint had the wrong Rubin playing, though, Ira not Ronnie, and had guessed at his annotations. Here is the correct story, taken as it were 'straight from the horse's mouth'.

The match was the semifinal of the Bermuda Bowl held in Stockholm in 1983, and the two USA teams were playing one another as required by the rules.

```
              ♠ K J 9 7 5 4 3
              ♡ A K
              ◇ A 3
              ♣ 9 8
George Jacobs        ┌───────┐        Ron Smith
♠ 8 2                │   N   │        ♠ 10 6
♡ J 6 2              │ W   E │        ♡ 10 8 7 5 4
◇ 9 6                │   S   │        ◇ 10 8 7 4
♣ A K Q J 4 3        └───────┘        ♣ 6 2
              ♠ A Q
              ♡ Q 9 3
              ◇ K Q J 5 2
              ♣ 10 7 5
```

Mike Becker

"Ronnie and I used to psyche at favorable vulnerability," Michael told me, "and, although we were up in the match by quite a lot, I suspected right away that that was what had happened. So I thought that if he had psyched, he would pass 3NT although this did show a limited spade raise. When he bid, I assumed he had to have a real opener and he seemed to confirm this by showing what I thought were

```
                    ♠ 10 6 4 3
                    ♡ Q 9 8 4
                    ◇ 10 9 3
                    ♣ 10 6
 ♠ K Q J 5 2                      ♠ A 9 8 7
 ♡ J 6 5 3        ┌─────────┐     ♡ 10 7
 ◇ Q 5           │    N    │     ◇ 8 7 6 2
 ♣ 8 4           │ W     E │     ♣ A 7 3
                 │    S    │
                 └─────────┘
                    ♠ —
                    ♡ A K 2
                    ◇ A K J 4
                    ♣ K Q J 9 5 2
```

West Rosencranz	North Rubin	East Wold	South Becker
			1♠
	pass	3NT
	4♠	pass	4NT
pass	5♣	pass	7♣
pass	7♠	dbl	7NT
pass	pass	dbl	all pass

three key cards over 4NT. I was certain he would have passed 3NT or 4NT without an opening bid and so I bid a confident 7♣. This got past my left-hand opponent so my hopes were raised, but then the auction took an unsatisfactory turn.

"West led the ♠K and I called for the screen (or curtain as it actually was then) to be raised. Nothing happened from the other side and I called out louder, "Curtains!" As the dummy started to go down my partner Ronnie shook his head and remarked, "Curtains is right!", both a quick and an apt comment that at least elicited a smile from our opponents. I lost five spade tricks and the ace of clubs for minus 1100. After this hand we made it part of our system that the psycher had to pass at his first opportunity except to show a real suit. Fortunately we went on to win the match and the World Championship when we edged out the Italians by 5 IMPs after the famous hand where Belladonna and Garozzo bid to a slam off two cashing aces."

The Belladonna-Garozzo hand was another great true story that would fit admirably in this chapter. When I first thought about it, the 'strange but true' tag related to Michael's having mentioned this hand casually and then my finding it shortly afterwards in Flint's book. However, I later decided that it is much more strange to see the bidding on this hand and to realize that North-South had gone on to win the World Championship! Some would say that 'unbelievable' would be a more accurate description!

They say truth can be stranger than fiction, but there was a fascinating example recently of truth imitating fiction! Playing in a Fort Lauderdale, Florida Regional, Alan Sontag was partnering Jean Rahmey in a Swiss Teams event. They arrived slightly late at the table, just as the hands were being dealt. Soon Jean was looking at the following hand:

♠ **K J 9** ♡ **A K Q 10** ◇ **A K Q** ♣ **A K Q**

Holding thirty-one points and with both sides vulnerable she heard the auction go 2♠ (weak) on her left, pass from partner, 4♠ on her right, so she said double. It now went pass on her left, 5◇ from Sonty, and pass on her right, and she raised to 6◇. Now her LHO bid 6♠ which was doubled by partner, and that closed the auction. The ♣9 was led and dummy arrived.

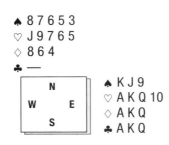

So far, despite Jean's monster hand, the auction had seemed reasonable. The play, however, was a different story. Declarer ruffed the opening lead in dummy, played a spade to the ten, ruffed a second club, then played a spade to the queen and a third club. Before Jean's ace hit the table, Sonty, even more agitated than his normal hyper self, started screaming at the opposition that he knew this hand, which was as shown below.

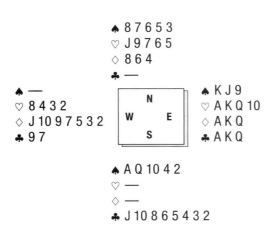

As you can see, no lead can defeat 7♠ by South. The hand is one that is well-known as the Duke of Cumberland's hand, or more recently as the James Bond hand — it appeared in the novel *Moonraker* and was used by 007 in a high-stakes rubber game to defeat the evil Hugo Drax. The South player at this stage turned to Sonty and said that if he didn't like his result they could redeal the hand. Sonty called the director. Not surprisingly, the hand was thrown out of the match but perhaps surprisingly, no disciplinary action was taken against the South player, who protested that it was just a coincidence. After all, surely if he'd known the hand he would have bid 7♠, not settled for six!

As you can see from this hand, distribution can overpower high cards any day. Here's a final example of exactly that. Playing one day in Benito Garozzo's rubber bridge game at his Florida home, I had spent all afternoon trying to get a little in front. My partner on this deal was the famous golfer Harold Henning, who although a sound card player tended to overbid frequently. For some reason, he liked to take chances. I picked up my last hand of the day and found myself looking at

♠ K   ♡ 7 6 4 3 2   ◇ 7 6 3 2   ♣ 8 5 3

With everybody vulnerable, Benito opened 2NT on my left. I was just hoping they would not bid a slam when Harold jumped in with 4♠. A sharp double was heard on my right and everyone passed. I had mentally written off another day's work when my RHO led a heart, Benito played the king and Harold ruffed. A spade went to the king and Benito's ace. Now the ◇K was played and Harold ruffed again! The ♠J went to the queen. I watched fascinated as Harold ruffed the return, drew the last trump and played out the ♣K, losing to the ace. He ruffed the return again, and when the clubs divided, claimed ten tricks! The full deal was as you see it here.

As a small slam can be made by East-West in either red suit or in notrump, my finances greatly improved when minus 1440 was turned into plus 790. Meanwhile poor Benito could hardly be blamed for cursing his ill-fortune, although he pointed out immediately that he could have defeated the contract by switching to a club when he won the first spade trick — his partner could then duck the first round, win the second and give him a ruff!

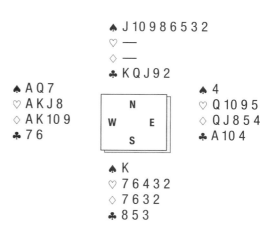

CHAPTER 17

Les Liaisons Dangereuses

I n contrast to many other games, it is not generally a good idea for husbands to play bridge with their wives. At golf or tennis a bad shot is easily excusable, but at bridge, a bad play gets criticized and the criticism often carries the implication that there is something wrong with someone's intelligence. From experience, I can say that it is usually the criticizer whose intelligence should be questioned, but it is from such small pebbles in the works that major breakdowns arise. Bridge is an unusual game in that a man can usually look forward to a much better sex life at home if he plays it with anyone else's wife but his own.

Having said that, you do get a good feeling when the tournament is over and the marriage has survived relatively unscathed. On a very good day, a win is even possible. For a long tournament like a National Championships, the trick is to have an early win and then not play together again. Then you can both say, "If only I had been playing with you, darling, you would never have made such a crazy bid."

In my younger years, I had some success in a mixed partnership, winning the British Mixed Pairs on two occasions with Barbara Kay, a friend and a Scottish international. My wife Mags has also won this event once; as an inexperienced player she pulled off a major surprise with Richard Benstead by just beating out Tony Forrester and Sally Horton. However, although Maggie and I tried, we could never win it as a pair — it was way too hard. Indeed, although occasionally Maggie and I have had some success at the table, more often the result has been despair.

One of our more memorable outings occurred when we decided to visit London for a three-day tournament on our wedding anniversary. This, I should point out, was in direct contravention to the advice of Roselyn Teukolsky, who wrote a very funny book about how to survive playing bridge with your spouse. She warned readers never to plan a romantic weekend playing bridge with a spouse or lover. Romance can be enjoyed, yes, she said, but play bridge with someone else — anyone else! The other good advice she offered to happy couples was not to discuss the hands at the table, or at least to say as little as possible. This, of course, is very sound advice for any aspiring bridge partnership, whether or not the pair are romantically involved. To the happy couples I would add that if they want to stay happy after a very bad result has been obtained through someone's idiocy (or perceived idiocy, which is not always the same thing), they should just skip it. If you must talk bridge, discuss your good results and forget your bad ones forever. The alternative is to have it out and be prepared for cold nights, a lot of them.

The irrepressible Mags

Anyway, we threw all caution to the winds on this the occasion of our anniversary, even though from previous experience I had good reason to be concerned. The first day, however, went splendidly when it was deemed that our entry for the main pairs event had been received too late and we were unable to play, and instead, spent a pleasant evening at a movie. We had actually traveled down the previous night but apparently most pairs had pre-entered and they had closed the list by the time we got there — not enough card tables! The second day went even better when I went to the Christmas sales and Maggie won the women's pairs with a pickup partner (of quality) after discovering that her intended had trundled off to Jamaica without informing her.

On the final day, however, we played together in the Swiss teams with Victor Silverstone and Gerald Haase, and we were leading the field when we sat down against a young Swedish player. Victor had warned Mags that although he was a good player, he tended to over-bid, and that she should therefore double him if he stepped out of line. This was the deal on which she took Stoney's advice to heart.

Against our team-mates, East-West bid to 4♡ and went quickly down after Gerald led a diamond and Victor played three rounds of the suit, promoting

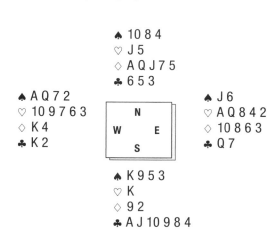

```
              ♠ 10 8 4
              ♡ J 5
              ◇ A Q J 7 5
              ♣ 6 5 3
♠ A Q 7 2                      ♠ J 6
♡ 10 9 7 6 3      N           ♡ A Q 8 4 2
◇ K 4          W     E        ◇ 10 8 6 3
♣ K 2              S           ♣ Q 7
              ♠ K 9 5 3
              ♡ K
              ◇ 9 2
              ♣ A J 10 9 8 4
```

South's ♡K. In our room, the Swede opened a vulnerable 2◊ as North and his partner tried 2NT; not finding anything extra in his hand, North bid 3◊, which whistled round to me. I liked my major-suit holdings, and balanced with a double. Mags remembered Victor's advice, so she decided to pass! She led the ♠J to the king and ace, and I switched to a trump. Declarer won the queen and played a heart. Mags won this and played another trump. Declarer won, cashed a high trump and crossed to the ♣A to play a spade to his ten, which won. He continued ace and another club, but we cashed out for down two and 500. A nice 11 IMPs courtesy of Victor! In spite of some late efforts to lose, we managed to hold on by a whisker when the team of young English stars lying second bid a grand missing the trump ace. So all ended well, and we didn't need to visit a marriage counselor.

For obvious reasons, not many husbands play in international competitions with their wives, but some do so in Mixed championships. One husband who has enjoyed some success is Poland's Marcin Lesniewski, who plays with his wife Eva Harasimowicz — they finished third in the World Mixed Pairs in Alburquerque. Here is a hand where Eva showed some nice technique.

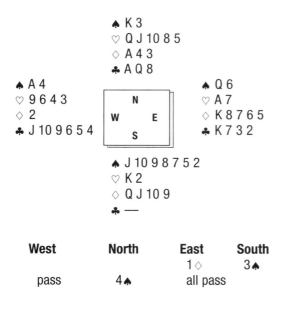

♠ K 3
♡ Q J 10 8 5
◊ A 4 3
♣ A Q 8

♠ A 4
♡ 9 6 4 3
◊ 2
♣ J 10 9 6 5 4

♠ Q 6
♡ A 7
◊ K 8 7 6 5
♣ K 7 3 2

♠ J 10 9 8 7 5 2
♡ K 2
◊ Q J 10 9
♣ —

West	North	East	South
		1◊	3♠
pass	4♠	all pass	

West led the ◊2 which was an obvious singleton, and declarer won the ace in dummy. How do you think Eva made her contract?

To have any chance, she needed the ♠A to be with West. East, who had opened the bidding, must then hold the ♣K so she could not break the defenders' communications by playing ♣A, ♣Q and pitching two hearts as East would cover the ♣Q with the king and could not be prevented from giving his partner a diamond ruff. She therefore played the ♣A, pitching a heart, and then the ♣8. When East did not play his king, she was home now when she pitched her ♡K. This neat Scissors Coup prevented the defense from getting their diamond ruff. Had East risen with his ♣K, declarer would have gone down; clearly he should have done so here, but the cover would have been easier to find if he had held a spot card in clubs higher than the eight. Often with these hands it takes fast thinking to see the position and take action without much delay.

Benito Garozzo

Another couple who play together are Benito Garozzo and Lea Dupont. While Benito was trampling the world beneath his feet he did not play so much with Lea, but in recent years she has become his regular partner and they have competed together very successfully. Benito, however, is not renowned for being reticent about his feelings; Lea, likewise, does not give in just because he is Benito and has been known not always to refer to him as her beloved Papi. All is therefore not always calm in the household. They have a very complex system and have played it for a number of years. They once found themselves playing in a tournament against the late Rixi Markus, partnered by Paul Chemla. Benito opened 1♡ and Lea bid 2♣ which was alerted as a relay. Now Rixi generally did not like being alerted and she asked them not to alert any more. The auction proceeded

West	North	East	South
Chemla	Benito	Rixi	Lea
	1♡	pass	2♣
2♠	pass	2NT	3♡
3♠	4♣		

At this point Rixi, with ♣KJx, doubled to show club values. Unfortunately for her, she did not realize that the relay system had just located a 5-4 club fit and when 4♣ was redoubled, declarer could not be prevented from making five!

Matthew and Pamela Granovetter have played with each other for many years, and you would think they would have the advantage of knowing each other's style, but Pamela relates this story about a hand against two elderly ladies in a pairs event. She held:

♠ J 8 3 2   ♡ 7 4 2   ◇ A 6   ♣ 9 8 7 5

With both sides vulnerable, it went 1◇ on her left from East and Matthew, usually a sound bidder, bid 1♡. Her RHO said double and Pamela judged it appropriate to bid what she called a 'strategic' 2♡ in order to prevent the opponents from playing 1NT. Happily for her, her LHO now bid 3◇, but unfortunately Matthew was there with 3♡ which her RHO now doubled; that ended the auction.

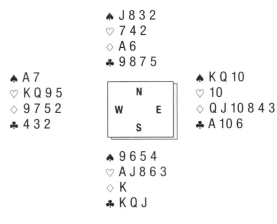

```
              ♠ J 8 3 2
              ♡ 7 4 2
              ◇ A 6
              ♣ 9 8 7 5
♠ A 7                        ♠ K Q 10
♡ K Q 9 5        N           ♡ 10
◇ 9 7 5 2    W       E       ◇ Q J 10 8 4 3
♣ 4 3 2          S           ♣ A 10 6
              ♠ 9 6 5 4
              ♡ A J 8 6 3
              ◇ K
              ♣ K Q J
```

Pamela had hoped that East's 3◇ rebid would have caused a problem for West, since it could have been made with quite a wide range of hands. Without the 3♡ bid, West was going to have to guess whether to bid on or not (in fact, accurate defense will defeat 3NT provided South switches to clubs after winning the ♡A). However, against 3♡ the defenders had no trouble winning their eight tricks, so that was minus 800 for the Granovetters. Matthew had calculated that with a suitable dummy he would only go down one. My own sympathies lie with Pamela rather than Matthew on this hand, although he did make his bid based on his partner's usual sound bidding practice. Perhaps, he said later, they should have checked on the first double to find out whether *it* was for penalties!

These days, the only husband and wife who name each other as their first choice partners and also represent their country internationally are Peter and Dorthe Schalz from Denmark. Peter, who won the European Junior Championship playing with his cousin in 1970, played with quite a few different partners before teaming up with his wife Dorthe in 1990. Having been successful in both Danish Teams Championships and Mixed Pairs, they have been on many Danish teams since 1992 and reached the quarterfinals of the Olympiad that year before losing to the eventual winners, France, by 2 IMPs. Second in the European Championships in Menton in 1993, they were again defeated at the world level in the quarterfinals, this time by a team from the USA. They have represented Denmark as partners 148 times, while Dorthe won a women's gold medal in the 1988 Olympiad before abandoning the women's game.

Here is a hand from Menton in 1993 where they were awarded a prize for the 'best-bid hand of the championship'.

Peter and Dorthe Schalz

Peter knew that Dorthe's shape was surely 1-4-3-5 and could count twelve tricks via two diamond ruffs in his own hand. Excellent judgement, as only an unlikely heart lead from West would beat the slam as the cards lay.

Although the bridge partnership is one of ten years, they have been married for twenty-two years. I had to smile when Peter told me that he thought it was an advantage to be mar-

```
                  ♠ 9
                  ♡ K Q 9 4
                  ♦ 10 6 2
                  ♣ K Q 7 4 2
♠ K J 10                          ♠ Q 7 5 4 3
♡ J 7 6 2            N            ♡ 5
♦ A J 9 8 3     W        E        ♦ K Q 7 5
♣ 3                 S            ♣ J 6 5
                  ♠ A 8 6 2
                  ♡ A 10 8 3
                  ♦ 4
                  ♣ A 10 9 8
```

West	North Dorthe	East	South Peter
pass	pass	pass	1♣
1♦	1♡	2♠	3♦
3♠	5♣	pass	6♣
all pass			

ried to your bridge partner! Their agreement is that they never discuss hands until they get home. Even then, they usually pick one night a week when they go over interesting hands or problems from the previous week's games — at one time they agreed to argue only on a Wednesday evening! That reminds me of David Berkowitz and Larry Cohen — when they started playing together, David was only allowed to yell at Larry once every six months. Larry tells me he has never exercised that particular option so far!

Possibly uniquely, Peter's parents also played for Denmark together in both the Olympiad in Palermo and the Europeans in Baden–Baden. Now in their mid-eighties, they still play together three times a week and have been married for almost fifty years. Perhaps, with the right temperament, a husband and wife can play at the top level together and still live to tell the tale after all. But perhaps, too, there is something more involved. Peter modestly states that Dorthe is regarded as the stronger player and it is that which gives the partnership its fine balance. It is very possibly this exception to the norm that is their catalyst for success.

It seems only fitting that having described the pitfalls of playing bridge in a married partnership, I should close with one of the real successes in mixed teams bridge. Earlier this year, when the Schalzes teamed up with the Aukens, Jens and Sabine, they reached the final of the strong European Mixed Teams event. Playing against Germany, the four spouses were down 13 IMPs with two boards to play.

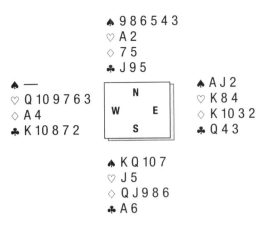

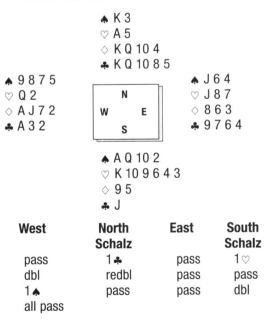

On the second last board, Sabine had to declare 4♡ as West after an opening 1◇ by South. Since the German pair had stopped in partscore, Sabine could keep the match alive by making her contract. After a spade lead, she won the ♠A to play a heart to the queen and ace, then ruffed the spade continuation and passed the ♡10, losing to the jack. Another spade was ruffed. She cashed the ◇A and ◇K and counting South to be 4-2-5-2, she confidently played a club to the king then ducked a club on the way back — 6 IMPs to the Danes, who now trailed by seven with one board to play.

This was the last deal:

With East-West vulnerable, the Germans bid the North-South cards to 3NT, making eleven tricks. It looked as if they were home and dry, but there was a final twist to come. Not knowing the title was in the bag, the West player in the Closed Room took a bid despite facing a passed partner at unfavorable colors. My own experience is that this is just asking the opposition to apply the axe and our heroes, the Schalzes, did just that. The only question was whether

West	North Schalz	East	South Schalz
pass	1♣	pass	1♡
dbl	redbl	pass	pass
1♠	pass	pass	dbl
all pass			

West could come to a third trick. The forfeit was 1100 and 11 IMPs, along with the title of European Mixed Teams Champions.

Maybe after all it is possible to live, love, play bridge and be happy all at the same time with the same person – but it's still quite an achievement!

Playing with the Bridge Legends

Life At The Top

Bridge at the Top

O nce I had attended my first World Championships as a spectator at the age of nineteen, I was hooked; as it turned out, it was not too long before my chance came to return to top-level bridge. My friend Patrick Jourdain, who was by then editor of the IBPA Bulletin, had moved to Glasgow and we had become a successful partnership, especially in pairs events. In 1974 we traveled to London to play in a large sponsored pairs tournament, the prize being an all-expenses-paid trip to Las Palmas to play in the World Open Pairs. We won the three-session event, just finishing ahead of Jeremy Flint-Jonathan Cansino and Rixi Markus-Fritzi Gordon. Flint and Cansino were Britain's top pair at that time, so we were delighted with our victory. Patrick and I had a great time in Las Palmas. We led the field after Day 1, qualified for the final and finished in eighteenth spot, which was very respectable. I remember playing against Rose and Sheehan while they were leading in the final, just before they moved across into the wrong line of pairs (an incident you may remember from Chapter 8).

Patrick Jourdain and Barnet

In 1976 there was an unusual occurrence on the world bridge scene. Following the Bermuda Bowl for the World Teams Championship, there was also to be a World Bridge Teams Olympiad. These tournaments were scheduled one after the other and were to determine two separate World Champions. Strong teams from both the USA and Italy were playing in both events so spectators and journalists were getting excellent value for the trip to Monte Carlo. Two championships for the price of one! I had just failed to qualify for the British Olympiad team in partnership with Michael Rosenberg, but being Scottish, I could not resist the lure of a bargain.

The final of the 1976 Bermuda Bowl turned out to be the match-up all the non-partisans wanted to see — USA versus Italy. Italy were the holders of both the Olympiad title and the Bermuda Bowl. Amazingly, still showing their dominance in world bridge, they had won the 1972 Olympiad and the 1973, 1974 and 1975 Bermuda Bowls, each time defeating a strong US team. For the Italians, Belladonna and Garozzo had been a constant in their four victories and Forquet had played in

Billy Eisenberg

three. Hamman-Wolff had played in all four losing finals for the USA with Goldman playing in three of them. Up until this point, then, the USA had never beaten an Italian team that included the great Blue Team players. This year Belladonna, Garozzo and Forquet, the three greatest Italian players, were to be joined in both 1976 championships by Arturo Franco, a younger, very talented but volatile player. Meanwhile, the USA was fielding new partnerships: Eisenberg-Hamilton, Rubin-Soloway and Ross-Paulsen. Could they break the dominance of the Italians?

I remember watching the most sensational deal from the final on VuGraph. It was standing room only in the theater as many of the Olympiad contestants had arrived, and they crammed into the room along with the rest of us. For the USA, Billy Eisenberg was East and Fred Hamilton, West.

The players, who were using screens for the first time, could only see the one opponent on their side of the screen. West's 6♡ bid was made after a considerable pause and East then raised to 7♡. As you can see, fifteen tricks are readily available.

	♠ A 2			♠ K 8 6
	♡ K Q J	N		♡ A 9 8 6 5 4 2
	◇ A K J 7	W E		◇ Q 4
	♣ A 8 7 5	S		♣ 10

West	North	East	South
Hamilton		**Eisenberg**	
	pass	3♡	pass
4NT	pass	5◇	pass
5NT	pass	6◇	pass
6♡	pass	7♡	all pass

The Italians protested that East should not have bid 7♡ after his partner's lengthy pause, and the director rolled the contract back to 6♡, which created a swing for the Italians. The USA appealed the ruling.

Eisenberg made an excellent case to the committee. He said that he had to wait until he knew where his partner was planning to play the hand before he could bid the grand slam. When he found out it was hearts, he had the maximum possible for his bidding including the extras of a side queen and a singleton. The Appeals Committee agreed with Eisenberg and reversed the director's ruling, so there was no swing on the board after all. As the match was still in progress at this point, the decision generated a lot of controversy and was the source of many arguments among both the participants and the spectators.

The committee, applying the criteria in force at the time for such rulings, felt that more than 75% of Eisenberg's peers would make the same bid. Today the rules for such cases are more stringent and it is perhaps less likely that the 7♡ bid would be allowed to stand. However, I also know that Billy would still be able to argue his case very eloquently and you can never be sure of the outcome with appeals. Curiously, I now live across the street from Billy, and I often see him walking his dog. I have this picture of Billy saying to the committee, "Really, guys, even my dog would have bid seven hearts!"

USA went on to win the match by 34 IMPs, which fortunately for all concerned, was more than this one hand was worth. They had finally broken their jinx against the Italians in the Bermuda Bowl, and the Olympiad was next up. In those days, with fewer teams involved, the Olympiad consisted only of a Round Robin and there were no playoffs. As the last round began, Italy (still the favorites) were leading, closely followed by Brazil. In their final match against Greece, Italy required only a tie to win the event. Around a thousand spectators saw Greece take an early lead and eventually the title was decided by this one hand.

Greece had stopped in game with these cards but Garozzo-Franco had bid to 6◊ played by Franco in the South chair. Work out how you would play the hand on the lead of the ♣J.

♠ K Q 7 2
♡ 8 7
◊ A Q 6 4 2
♣ 6 4

♠ A 5 3
♡ A K 6 5
◊ K J 5
♣ A 8 5

Franco played very quickly. He ducked the club, won the next club and then drew three rounds of trumps. He next played three rounds of hearts, ruffing in dummy. He now needed either a 3-3 spade split or for the defender with the long spade to hold the long heart, in which case, he would be squeezed on the the play of the last trump. A perfectly reasonable line but alas for Italy, on this occasion not the winning one.

The winning line as the cards lay, would be to embark on a dummy reversal: duck the first club and win the second one. Ruff a club and then cash the ◇A. Next, after playing the ace and king of hearts, ruff a heart in dummy. Now a spade to the ace to play another heart, ruffed with the queen, before returning to hand with a diamond to

	♠ K Q 7 2	
	♡ 8 7	
	◇ A Q 6 4 2	
	♣ 6 4	
♠ J 9 6 4		♠ 10 8
♡ Q 10 3	N	♡ J 9 4 2
◇ 7 3	W E	◇ 10 9 8
♣ K 10 9 7	S	♣ Q J 3 2
	♠ A 5 3	
	♡ A K 6 5	
	◇ K J 5	
	♣ A 8 5	

draw the rest of the trumps and claim. Declarer would make three spades, two hearts, a club and six trumps. Like Franco's, this is a reasonable line, but it has the added virtue of working on the actual hand. A third line, which would also fail as the cards lay, would be to take two rounds of trumps and then play four rounds of spades, relying on either a 3-3 spade break or the hand with two spades having only two trumps. Benito told me that this was the best line with Franco's line the middle one, while the play that worked at the table actually had the lowest likelihood of the three to succeed!

So Franco's slam went down and Italy went with it. A very popular Brazilian team, led by their superstar, Gabriel Chagas, became the World Olympiad Champions. Garozzo and Belladonna, who had never previously been defeated, now had lost twice in the space of two weeks and poor Italy had lost both its titles. In fact, the championships of 1976 marked the end of an era in bridge; although Italy was able to reach the finals of the Bermuda Bowl on two later occasions, the Italians would suffer

Gabriel Chagas

narrow defeats both times, and were not to win another World Championship until they had suffered more than twenty years in the wilderness.

In 1984 the Olympiad was held in Seattle. The British team played their first match against the holders, France, and I played with my partner Willie Coyle against Perron and Chemla. Screens were in use and Michel Perron was my screenmate. On Board 1, after making his bid, Perron pushed the bidding tray through the screen and we heard a groan from the other side. He had hit his poor partner in the stomach! (In those days Paul was a lot heavier than he is today.) There were some heated exchanges in French and the outcome was that Michel was told he had to tap the table in warning before pushing the tray through. I remember that Willie and I had a good set, and that Rixi Markus was kibitzing us. Rixi hated the weak notrump and was chagrined to watch us pick up three or four swings as a result of her *bête noire*. In the morning she wrote in the Bulletin, 'Coyle is an excellent player and Shenkin is very lucky!' I have always looked back on that as being a great backhanded compliment. In bridge you *need* to be lucky to win, and I have won more than my share.

Our captain, John Armstrong, watched us play a match in a later stage of the event. On one hand, after I had opened 1◊, my LHO overcalled 1♠. It went 2♣ from partner and I bid 2♠, looking for a stopper. Partner bid 3♣ and I bid 3♠, hoping to find half a stopper. The next bid I saw from partner was 4♠! Now I was endplayed — I had to bid 5♣, and this went down three vulnerable for minus 300.

Armstrong, who had seen that Coyle held ♠QJx and that 3NT was cold, came up to me after the match.

"Can you explain the bidding on this hand?" he asked.

"Sorry," I said, "but our agreement is never to discuss any hands; we found from experience it only led to arguments. However, please let me know if you find out the answer."

The next day I sought out the captain to find out what had happened. It was explained that the whole fiasco had been my fault — when the tray had been pushed through by me, the opponent's 1♠ bid had not been clearly visible and my partner subsequently thought that I had bid and rebid spades naturally! Such is life.

My other main memory from this Olympiad was a bidding accident we had against Poland on VuGraph that led to a slam off two quick cashing tricks. In the end, we did not qualify for the playoffs but were not too far away; Poland won the event, beating France in the final.

Going to the Wall

After making a brief and unsuccessful visit to Geneva to play in the World Mixed Pairs, my next extended visit to the World Championships, after the Seattle Olympiad, was to Beijing, China in 1995. China was a familiar country to me since I had visited it about four times a year over the previous ten years in the course of my rug business. I even knew some of the Chinese bridge players. Any of their players who worked in government-sponsored jobs and were competing in the 1995 championships were given a year's sabbatical to practice for the upcoming Bermuda Bowl. They all lived in a hotel in Beijing and played two sessions a day before spending time discussing the hands. It must have helped, as their Open team narrowly lost to France in a semifinal match that was up for grabs right to the end. The Chinese women lost to the strong USA team in the semifinals, their best performance up to that time in world competition.

I managed to time a business trip to coincide with the Bowl and was able to make time to take in a lot of the matches. The first big surprise was the failure of the Jimmy Cayne USA 1 team to make the playoffs. They had to finish in the top four of eight teams, playing in the softer of the two groups. However, the squad (which included Paul Soloway and Bobby Goldman) never seemed to get going and finished a poor fifth. Paul could be seen on the sidelines wryly shaking his head at the way things were going. It seemed strange to me that a pair with their experience were not being put in for virtually every match. The Brazilian team, including Chagas and Branco, also just missed out on the playoffs in a photo finish, two Victory Points behind USA 2 — the Nickell team, with Hamman-Wolff, Meckwell and Nickell-Freeman. The top two Italian pairs, Lauria-Versace and Lanzarotti-Buratti, also could not win their final match by a big enough margin to get through, but their time was to come in the Rosenblum World Teams three years later.

USA 2 (Nickell) played France in the semifinal. I remember getting my press pass and as it turned out, I was the only journalist present in the Closed Room to watch two of the world's best pairs do battle as Hamman-Wolff took on Chemla-Perron. As a result, I was fortunate enough to witness first-hand one of the most intricate hands of the entire Championship.

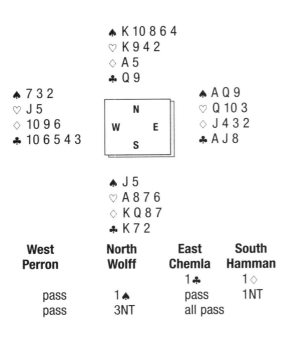

```
                  ♠ K 10 8 6 4
                  ♡ K 9 4 2
                  ◇ A 5
                  ♣ Q 9
  ♠ 7 3 2                        ♠ A Q 9
  ♡ J 5                          ♡ Q 10 3
  ◇ 10 9 6                       ◇ J 4 3 2
  ♣ 10 6 5 4 3                   ♣ A J 8
                  ♠ J 5
                  ♡ A 8 7 6
                  ◇ K Q 8 7
                  ♣ K 7 2
```

West Perron	North Wolff	East Chemla	South Hamman
		1♣	1◇
pass	1♠	pass	1NT
pass	3NT	all pass	

Having avoided the tricky 4♡ contract in favor of notrump, Hamman received a club lead which went to dummy's nine and East's jack. Hamman ducked and Chemla continued with the ♣A and a third club. Hamman now had time to develop three spades along with his three diamonds, two hearts and a club. It looks as if Chemla might defeat the contract if, instead of continuing clubs, he shifts to a diamond in order to set up his long diamond as the setting trick. However, if he does so, then it turns out that when Hamman cashes his long spades, throwing two hearts from hand, the last spade embarrasses Chemla in three suits. He can pitch one club, but then must throw a diamond, establishing South's ninth trick in diamonds — and when that is cashed, Chemla gets squeezed again for an overtrick! Difficult as it is to see and perhaps even more difficult to do at the table, to defeat the contract East has to switch to a heart at Trick 2 while he maintains control in the black suits. Playing partner for the ♡J, he establishes his own heart honor as the setting trick.

At the other table, Replinger got to 4♡ from the North hand, and

West Nickell	North Replinger	East Freeman	South Soulet
		1◇	pass
pass	dbl	pass	2◇
pass	2♠	pass	2NT
pass	3♡	pass	4♡
all pass			

won the diamond lead in hand in order to play the ♣9 next. Freeman hopped ace and played a second diamond. Declarer won this and cashed his ♣Q before taking the ♡K and ♡A. He then cashed the ♣K followed by dummy's ◇Q, ruffed the last diamond and exited with a trump to East who found himself endplayed. Well played, but if East had not risen with the ♣A declarer would have had to play another club. At this point in the hand, a second diamond play by the defense would break declarer's communications. After taking the club ruff in hand declarer would have to cross to dummy with a trump in order to ruff the last diamond. He would thus no longer be able to throw East in. It might seem that Replinger could succeed after the ♣A is ducked by throwing his club loser on the ◇Q, but the defense has a counter. If declarer draws two trumps before setting up spades, East can win the first spade, cash a high trump, and force declarer to ruff, taking out his only entry prematurely. If declarer does not draw trumps, East wins the first spade and plays the ◇J, forcing declarer as West pitches a spade. Now when declarer plays a second spade, East can win and give his partner a ruff.

All in all, a very interesting hand but, as P. O. Sundelin of Sweden pointed out, the Morton's Fork strategy of leading the ♣9 was actually an illusion — if North leads the ♣Q instead at Trick 2, the contract is secure. Declarer has time to ruff a club and then play three rounds of diamonds, ruffing the third in hand. Now the ♡K and ♡A followed by cashing the last high diamond in dummy, strips East of his exit cards and he can then be thrown in with a heart to give up the tenth trick.

USA 2 won their semifinal and now faced a surprise team, Canada, in a David against Goliath final. The Canadian team of Kokish-Silver, Mittelman-Gitelman and Molson-Baran had been in fine form but were nevertheless heavy underdogs against USA 2, and they knew it. Most of the non-Americans were rooting for them, of course, but they had already surpassed everyone's expectations, including their own, just by getting to the final. Would there be a fairy tale ending?

The match proved to be an exciting affair. After sixty-four boards, USA led by a mere 1 IMP. However, in the next set they added 49 IMPs to the lead, and began to pull away. Later, after the lead had grown to nearly 100 IMPs the Canadians staged a comeback, and in fact brought the deficit down to 13 IMPs during the final set before losing out to a power session by Meckwell. The final score was 339 – 296 to USA. Edgar Kaplan took on a dual role — American captain in the first instance, but also a magnificent VuGraph commentator — and it was he who calmed his troops to withstand the Canadian charge.

Although the match was a thrilling affair, the bridge was very up and down and both teams made a lot of errors — perhaps inevitably after such a long event. Here are a couple of the hands that got the Canadian counterattack started:

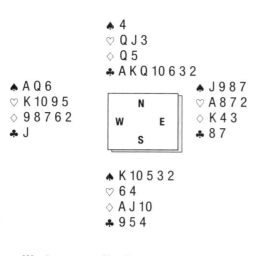

```
                    ♠ 4
                    ♡ Q J 3
                    ◇ Q 5
                    ♣ A K Q 10 6 3 2
♠ A Q 6                              ♠ J 9 8 7
♡ K 10 9 5          N                ♡ A 8 7 2
◇ 9 8 7 6 2     W       E            ◇ K 4 3
♣ J                    S             ♣ 8 7
                    ♠ K 10 5 3 2
                    ♡ 6 4
                    ◇ A J 10
                    ♣ 9 5 4
```

West Meckstroth	North Silver	East Rodwell	South Kokish
		pass	pass
1♡	3NT	all pass	

With Canada 66 IMPs down, Joey Silver had not traveled round the whole world to get walked all over in the final and he was right there with his bold 3NT call. Rodwell showed what he thought of Meckstroth's third-hand openers by passing rather than doubling, and when he chose a diamond lead Silver wrapped up his contract. Only with second sight could Rodwell have found the killing opening lead — a spade. When Hamman removed Wolff's Gambling 3NT opening to 4♣, that was 7 IMPs to Canada. Maybe Meckles should have opened with 1♠ rather than 1♡! This was the very next board:

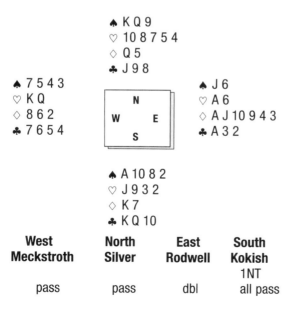

```
                    ♠ K Q 9
                    ♡ 10 8 7 5 4
                    ◇ Q 5
                    ♣ J 9 8
♠ 7 5 4 3                            ♠ J 6
♡ K Q              N                 ♡ A 6
◇ 8 6 2        W       E             ◇ A J 10 9 4 3
♣ 7 6 5 4             S              ♣ A 3 2
                    ♠ A 10 8 2
                    ♡ J 9 3 2
                    ◇ K 7
                    ♣ K Q 10
```

West Meckstroth	North Silver	East Rodwell	South Kokish
			1NT
pass	pass	dbl	all pass

I like the weak notrump, having played it most of my life. It leads to more excitement and creates plenty of opportunities for swings one way or the other. The best time to open it is in first seat, when all the hands are unknown quantities. With Gitelman quietly down one in 3◇ on the East-West cards at the other table, there was sure to be a swing here when Rodwell doubled

Kokish in 1NT and Joey Silver, looking for IMPs, stood his ground rather than run to 2♡. Meckers led the ♣7 to the ace and Kokish dropped the queen. Rodwell, not knowing the diamond position, switched to the ♠J, and that ran to dummy. When West won the ♡Q he played a second spade, and now another heart established nine tricks and plus 580 — a vital 10 IMPs to Canada.

Put yourself in the Canadian shoes on these next eight deals from the late stages of the final, and see if you can make the fairy tale ending happen. Can you bring a World Championship home to Canada?

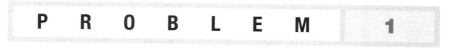

P R O B L E M   1

Both are vulnerable, and you hold:

♠ Q   ♡ A K 10 8 5 2   ◇ Q 6 4   ♣ J 6 3

You open 1♡ and Rodwell on your left overcalls 1♠. Partner bids 2♣ and it goes 4♠ on your right. Perhaps you should pass now, but you bid 5♣ under pressure and are pleased not to hear 6♣ from partner. When this goes round to Meckstroth, he bids 5♠ which you double. Partner leads the ♡Q and you see the dummy:

You overtake the ♡Q with the king. What is your next play?

You
♠ Q
♡ A K 10 8 5 2
◇ Q 6 4
♣ J 6 3

Dummy
♠ A 10 7 6 4 2
♡ 9 7 6 4 3
◇ 2
♣ 9

P R O B L E M   2

What would you open with this hand (neither vulnerable):

♠ A K J 9 4   ♡ A K 10 4   ◇ —   ♣ A K 7 5

♠ K 9 ♡ A K Q J 10 4 ◇ A ♣ A 9 8 7

This time you are vulnerable, and they are not. You open 1♡, and it goes 1♠ on your left. Partner bids 2◇, righty raises to 3♠, you double to show extra values and partner bids 4♡. You try 4NT next and partner jumps to 6◇, which according to your methods (if he is responding to Key Card) shows one key card and a diamond void, and you know he can't have that. What would you bid now?

West Meckstroth	North partner	East Rodwell	South You
		1♣ [1]	pass
2♣ [2]	pass	3◇ [3]	pass
3NT	all pass		

1. Strong.
2. Positive response with a diamond suit.
3. 4-4-4-1.

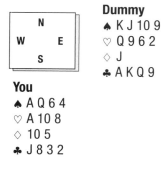

Dummy
♠ K J 10 9
♡ Q 9 6 2
◇ J
♣ A K Q 9

You
♠ A Q 6 4
♡ A 10 8
◇ 10 5
♣ J 8 3 2

Your partner leads the ♡7 and you see this dummy. Meckstroth plays the ♡9 from dummy, you play the ♡10 and he wins in hand with the ♡K. He now leads a spade to the jack, partner playing the ♠2 (standard carding). How do you defend?

PROBLEM 5

♠ — ♡ AK10 ◇ AQ63 ♣ AQJ965

You are in fourth chair and open 1♣ with this hand. It goes 2◇ overcall, negative double from partner. You cuebid 3◇ and partner bids 4♣. You encourage with 4◇ and he bids 4♠. Not what you wanted to hear, but you try 5♡ anyway. When partner bids 5♠ over this, do you sign off in 6♣, bid 5NT (one more try) or just bid 7♣ anyway?

PROBLEM 6

You reach 7♣ from the South hand and Meckstroth leads the ♣J. You win and play four more rounds of clubs. Meckstroth throws three diamonds and then a spade. Rodwell throws two diamonds and then a heart. How would you proceed in your grand slam?

♠ A K J 3
♡ A K 9 4
◇ J 9
♣ K 7 4

N
W E
S

♠ 10 2
♡ J 10
◇ A 10
♣ A Q 10 9 8 5 2

PROBLEM 7

♠ K975 ♡ Q10974 ◇ A83 ♣ 6

With both vulnerable, partner passes and you hear 1◇ on your right. You overcall 1♡, it goes 2♣ on your left and partner doubles to show spades. Opener now rebids 3♣ on your right; do you bid now? If you pass, it goes back to partner who calls 3♡. Now what do you do?

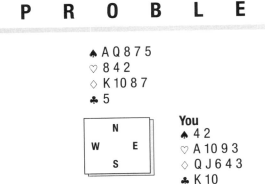

♠ A Q 8 7 5
♡ 8 4 2
◇ K 10 8 7
♣ 5

You
♠ 4 2
♡ A 10 9 3
◇ Q J 6 4 3
♣ K 10

Partner leads the ♣Q against 4♠ played after a transfer auction by South, who opened a 14-16 1NT. Declarer wins the ♣A in hand, and plays the ♡K, which you take with the ace in order to play a second club. South ruffs and crosses to the high heart queen, then plays a spade to the queen and cashes the ♠A. Next he ruffs a heart in hand and another club in dummy. He now leads the ◇K from dummy, which holds the trick, and then the ◇7. Which diamond do you play to this trick?

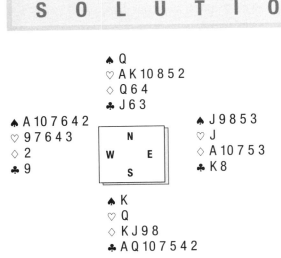

♠ Q
♡ A K 10 8 5 2
◇ Q 6 4
♣ J 6 3

♠ A 10 7 6 4 2
♡ 9 7 6 4 3
◇ 2
♣ 9

♠ J 9 8 5 3
♡ J
◇ A 10 7 5 3
♣ K 8

♠ K
♡ Q
◇ K J 9 8
♣ A Q 10 7 5 4 2

Did you play a second heart at Trick 2 and allow partner to score his trump king? To beat the hand, partner needs both minor aces or one ace and the trump king. As the aces are not going anywhere if he has them, it is correct to lead a heart now. You should lead a high heart, of course, just on the off chance that partner has eight clubs and declarer can pitch his losing club if you lead low. Fred Gitelman did not find this tough defense and when Hamman–Wolff bid the North-South hands to 6♣ down two in the replay, it was a 12-IMP loss for Canada instead of a 9-IMP pickup. Of course, had Mittelman led his ♣A the defense would have been more clear, but he was not sure it was going to stand up.

If you open 1♠, you get to play there. If you open 2♣ you will get to 4♠, which makes. In fact, Meckstroth got to game and made five after a strong club opening and a club lead. Opening 2♣ would therefore save your side 7 IMPs. Notice that if North's minor suits are interchanged, 7♣ is laydown — try to explain that away if you end up playing in 1♠!

```
            ♠ 8 6
            ♡ 9 7
            ◇ J 8 7 5 3 2
            ♣ 10 6 4
♠ Q 10 3              ♠ 7 5 2
♡ Q 6 5      N       ♡ J 8 3 2
◇ A Q 6 4  W   E     ◇ K 10 9
♣ J 9 3      S       ♣ Q 8 2
            ♠ A K J 9 4
            ♡ A K 10 4
            ◇ —
            ♣ A K 7 5
```

This is a very tough problem; something has gone wrong, but what is it? Silver did not take Kokish's 4NT bid as Key Card and jumped to show a possible alternative strain. Kokish knew the wheels had come off but gambled by bidding 7♣, which he intended to mean 'pick a grand slam' in case his partner had solid diamonds and a spade void. This was doubly unfortunate as the opposition had stopped at the five-level. If you bid 6♡ you win 11 IMPs instead of losing them.

```
            ♠ 6
            ♡ 5 3 2
            ◇ K Q 10 8 7 5
            ♣ K 3 2
♠ A Q 10 8 7 5         ♠ J 4 3 2
♡ 9 7 6       N      ♡ 8
◇ 2        W    E    ◇ J 9 6 4 3
♣ Q 5 4       S      ♣ J 10 6
            ♠ K 9
            ♡ A K Q J 10 4
            ◇ A
            ♣ A 9 8 7
```

West	North Silver	East	South Kokish
			1♡
1♠	2◇	3♠	dbl
pass	4♡	pass	4NT
pass	6◇	pass	?

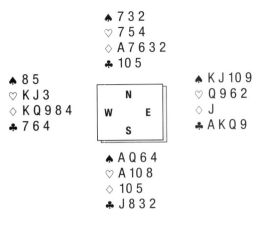

♠ 7 3 2
♡ 7 5 4
◇ A 7 6 3 2
♣ 10 5

♠ 8 5
♡ K J 3
◇ K Q 9 8 4
♣ 7 6 4

♠ K J 10 9
♡ Q 9 6 2
◇ J
♣ A K Q 9

♠ A Q 6 4
♡ A 10 8
◇ 10 5
♣ J 8 3 2

Against West's 3NT, partner led the ♡7 to dummy's ♡9, your ♡10 and declarer's ♡K. He now led a spade to the jack. You must win this and attack declarer's entries by playing ace and another heart. You can then win the second spade and cross to partner's ◇A, and he can then put declarer in the dummy with a third spade, leaving you to collect the setting trick in clubs in the endgame. Perhaps Meckstroth should have played a diamond at Trick 2 to set up a later club pitch from dummy. Did you find the winning defense and win 10 IMPs for your team?

♠ A K 9 6
♡ J 9 6 4
◇ 5
♣ K 8 4 2

♠ J 8 5 4
♡ 7 5
◇ K J 10 8 7 4
♣ 7

♠ Q 10 7 3 2
♡ Q 8 3 2
◇ 9 2
♣ 10 3

♠ —
♡ A K 10
◇ A Q 6 3
♣ A Q J 9 6 5

At this point, Canada's Boris Baran, who had heard his partner cue-bid his void twice, signed off in 6♣, when a final try of 5NT would have got them to 7♣. However, Mark Molson who had a great hand might have bid 7♣ over 5♡. How did Meckwell do on these cards?

West	North	East	South
pass	pass	pass	1♣
2◇	dbl	pass	3◇
pass	4♣	pass	4◇
pass	4♠	pass	5♡
pass	5♠	pass	?

What price technology? Meckwell were able to bid the grand slam in two bids! They actually won three swings in this match by

West	North	East	South
Kokish	**Meckstroth**	**Silver**	**Rodwell**
pass	2♡¹	pass	7♣
7◇	dbl	all pass	

1. 4-4-4-1, 11-15, short diamonds.

bidding grand slams but this was the best. Kokish the brave scored four tricks in his sacrifice — a good try, but minus 2300 lost 14 IMPs. Had his teammates bid the grand, they would have lost only 4 IMPs, so 10 IMPs would have been saved.

S O L U T I O N   6

Playing 7♣, you received a club lead and played off five rounds of trumps. West threw three diamonds and a spade and East threw two diamonds and a heart. All the discards had been forced. Should you decide that West is unlikely to have five spades, it looks reasonable to play the ace and king of spades and ruff a third round, and if

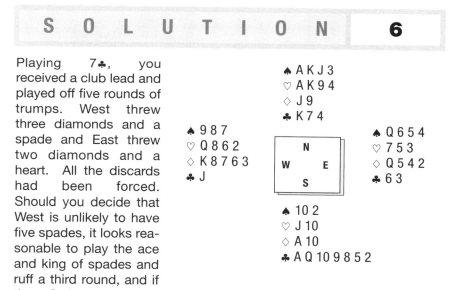

the ♠Q does not appear, take a heart finesse. However, Kokish tried three rounds of hearts instead, and when the ♡Q did not drop, took a spade finesse. Although this was wrong on the hand, he had the consolation that Bob Hamman took the same line of play. However, Hamman had played off only four trumps so he did not obtain quite as much information. If you played three rounds of spades and then took a heart finesse you win sixteen invaluable IMPs going down the stretch.

```
                ♠ A 3
                ♡ J 8 5
                ◇ 7 4 2
                ♣ K Q J 8 7
♠ Q 10 6 4 2              ♠ K 9 7 5
♡ A K          N         ♡ Q 10 9 7 4
◇ J 9 6 5    W   E       ◇ A 8 3
♣ 9 4          S         ♣ 6
                ♠ J 8
                ♡ 6 3 2
                ◇ K Q 10
                ♣ A 10 5 3 2
```

West Baran	North	East Molson	South
pass	1◇	1♡	2♣
dbl¹	3♣	pass	pass
3♡	pass	?	

1. Shows spades.

If you bid 3♠ over 3♣, partner will raise himself to four. Having passed over 3♣, you also might try 4♠ directly over 3♡, but Molson settled for 3♠ only and Baran passed. Hamman-Wolff had no problem — after North failed to open, they bid 1♡-1♠, 2♠-4♠. Four spades may not be a wonderful contract but if you're in it, you're going to make it. Did you save 10 IMPs?

```
                ♠ A Q 8 7 5
                ♡ 8 4 2
                ◇ K 10 8 7
                ♣ 5
♠ K 10 9                 ♠ 4 2
♡ J 7 6 5      N         ♡ A 10 9 3
◇ 2          W   E       ◇ Q J 6 4 3
♣ Q J 9 4 2    S         ♣ K 10
                ♠ J 6 3
                ♡ K Q
                ◇ A 9 5
                ♣ A 8 7 6 3
```

Partner led the ♣Q against 4♠, and declarer won in hand to play the ♡K. You took your ace and played a second club, ruffed in dummy. Now a heart to the queen and a spade finesse was followed by the ♠A, a heart ruff and a club ruff, arriving at this position:

When declarer cashes his ◇K and leads the ◇7 from dummy, you had better split your honors. Then partner can ruff declarer's ace and tap dummy with a high club; later, when you win your diamond trick you can cash a heart winner. Rodwell was trying to catch a stiff diamond honor with West, who had not led a diamond and by now was known

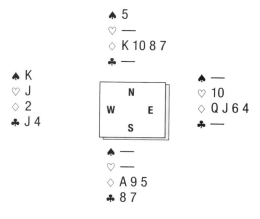

to have had a singleton. When Molson played low on the ◇7, Rodwell let it ride and scored a cheap trick as West had no winning play now! If you split your diamonds you win 10 IMPs.

These eight deals were chosen for their intrinsic interest. In some cases, the winning answers were clearly also the correct ones; in others, it was not so clearly the right action that turned out to be the winning one. As you would expect in a long contest, there were many other mistakes made by both teams, but there was also a lot of good bridge played. It is tough to play against a team of the caliber of the winners and probably the bookies would have spotted Canada more than the 43 IMPs that proved to be the winning margin. However, in reality, the Canadians surely had their chances to win the title. On these eight hands Canada lost 56 IMPs, while the margin of victory was only 43 IMPs.

Check your play against the actual Canadian results and see if you would have won the World Championship!

	Closed Room		Open Room		IMPs
Board 1	6♣–2	+200	5♠$^{\times}$=	–850	–13
Board 2	4♠+1	–450	1♠+3	+170	–8
Board 3	5♡+1	–480	7♡–1	–50	–11
Board 4	3NT=	+400	3NT=	–400	0
Board 5	7◇$^{\times}$–9	–2300	6♣+1	+1390	–14
Board 6	7♣–1	+100	7♣–1	–100	0
Board 7	4♠=	–620	3♠+1	+170	–10
Board 8	4♠=	+620	4♠=	–620	0

C H A P T E R 20

Bermuda 2000

It was designed to be a showcase for bridge, part of a carefully planned and orchestrated campaign to make bridge an Olympic sport. It was the fiftieth contest for the Bermuda Bowl, the half-century celebration of the one event most associated with world supremacy in bridge. Since the first Bowl competition actually took place in 1949 (in Bermuda, hence the name), the real anniversary year was 1999, but the Bermudans wanted to host the first world championship of the new millennium, so the event was postponed a few months until January 2000. The format has changed over the last half-century, and whereas in 1949 only three teams took part, twenty teams arrived for the 2000 tournament.

The surroundings had changed too. This year the WBF was working with a sponsor (the investment company Orbis), and largely as a result of this, Bermuda 2000 will be remembered as one of the best-run competitions in the history of the Bowl to date. Playing conditions were excellent. Spectators were treated to a lavish VuGraph show and the press enjoyed full access to all the hand records and to the Internet. Bridge players from all over the world could therefore get the results pretty much as soon as they came in. Indeed, it was even possible to watch play-by-play from the VuGraph matches, since these records were posted to the Web site thirty minutes or so after the end of each session. The only bleak spot was the weather — Bermuda is on the same latitude as the Carolinas, and it was January, after all. After some early feeble sunshine, the second week consisted totally of scattered rain and very strong winds. In fact, the plane Mags and I traveled on almost had to return to New York because the high winds made landing very dangerous; after a couple of missed approaches, the pilot decided to make one last attempt and fortunately was successful. I brought my golf clubs, but when I finally got out to play with Zia he complained that the standard Scottish weather gave me too much of an advantage!

Back at the bridge table, both USA teams were strong contenders. USA 1 was Nickell-Freeman, Hamman-Soloway and Meckstroth-Rodwell — the same team that, with Bobby Wolff playing instead of Paul Soloway, had finished as winners in 1995 and runners up in 1997. They would have been clear favorites except that Soloway was recovering from having undergone heart surgery the previous month and was also suffering from a bad flu-bug — an unfortunate cross to bear in a championship of this length and stature. USA 2 featured Zia playing with Rosenberg, Martel-Stansby and Wolfson-Silverman — the first two pairs having been losing finalists to the Nickell squad in Tunisia two years earlier. Zia was trying to win his first World Championship and Rosenberg his first Bermuda Bowl.

The European contenders were Italy, Poland, France, Norway, Sweden, and Bulgaria. The first three countries were all capable of fielding teams who would be amongst the favorites, while Norway and Sweden could never be ignored. In practice, France did not field anything like its best team, with only Mari returning from the 1997 winners in Tunisia. Italy, who perhaps surprisingly had won the European Championship without Versace-Lauria and Lanzarotti-Buratti, kept their European team intact with Bocchi-Duboin and Ferraro-de Falco as their leading pairs. Poland's team was a good one but not their best, as some internal political wrangling had deprived them of the services of their best pair, Balicki-Zmudzinski. Both Norway and Sweden had good teams, although Helgemo and Helness were separated and playing with new partners on the Norwegian team. The young Bulgarians, surprise qualifiers from Europe, were not considered to have a realistic chance. Outside of this group, nobody was rated to have any serious hope except perhaps Brazil, who fielded a strong team led by Chagas-Branco and who had a reputation for performing beyond expectations, and possibly Indonesia, who had made the final of the last Olympiad in Rhodes.

The initial stage of the event was a full Round Robin, from which eight teams would make the cut for the knockout stage. There are always surprises in large Round Robins, and this was no exception. An inexperienced Canadian team lost heart early and barely stayed out of last place — fortunately for them, the host country had entered a team. In contrast, the Bulgarians, playing very well, jumped out to a surprise early lead, began to fade towards the end and finally just failed to make the cut. Their young team was in tears, but they did go on to win a bronze medal in the Transnational Teams event that followed. There would also be no French team to defend its title — they, too, had been eliminated. USA 2 had started slowly, but in the end had done enough to stay in. The young Norwegian team, however, had been impressive, and were worthy winners of the qualifying rounds.

The top eight finishers were

1	Norway	345
2	USA 1	340
3	Poland	334
4	Brazil	330
5	Indonesia	329
6	Italy	327.5
7	USA 2	322
8	Sweden	320

Before leaving the qualifying stages, let's look at a couple of significant hands from the match between USA 1 and Italy — you'll see why they were so significant later on.

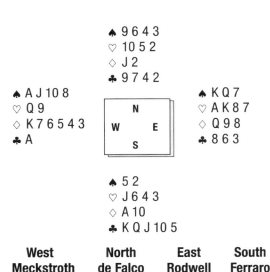

```
                    ♠ 9 6 4 3
                    ♡ 10 5 2
                    ◇ J 2
                    ♣ 9 7 4 2
♠ A J 10 8                          ♠ K Q 7
♡ Q 9                               ♡ A K 8 7
◇ K 7 6 5 4 3                       ◇ Q 9 8
♣ A                                 ♣ 8 6 3
                    ♠ 5 2
                    ♡ J 6 4 3
                    ◇ A 10
                    ♣ K Q J 10 5
```

West Meckstroth	North de Falco	East Rodwell	South Ferraro
		1NT	pass
2♣	pass	2♠	pass
3◇	pass	3NT	all pass

Duboin	Hamman	Bocchi	Soloway
		1♣	pass
2♠	pass	2NT	pass
3NT	pass	4♡	pass
5◇	pass	6♠	all pass

Meckwell located their diamond fit but chose to play 3NT. When South led the ♣K, Rodwell had only one small chance — he needed one defender to hold five clubs, the ◇A and four hearts. He therefore played off his four spade winners hoping something good would happen, and as it so often seems to for this pair, it duly did. After South pitched a club on the third spade he had no further idle card for the fourth, and had to concede declarer his nine tricks. In the Open Room, a bidding misunderstanding meant Italy reached 6♠, which is not without its chances, although clearly 6◇ and 5◇ are both better contracts. Hamman found the only lead to sink 6♠ — a club. Now when Soloway won the ◇A, he could play a second club and reduce declarer's trumps to three, promoting a trump trick for his partner. In fact declarer lost control after that and went down four, so USA 1 scored up a 12-IMP gain when the swing might easily have gone the other way.

And then another slam came up only three boards later:

```
                    ♠ A Q J 10 7
                    ♡ 7 6 4
                    ◊ 5
                    ♣ K 7 6 2
♠ K 8 5 4 3                          ♠ 9 6
♡ J 10 9 5          N                ♡ K 8 2
◊ J 10 7        W       E            ◊ K 9 8 3 2
♣ 8                 S                ♣ Q J 3
                    ♠ 2
                    ♡ A Q 3
                    ◊ A Q 6 4
                    ♣ A 10 9 5 4
```

Hamman-Soloway investigated slam but eventually decided to play in game. The slam was in fact quite a good contract, but with the bad trump break, Guido Ferraro was going to have to guess well. Meckstroth led the ◊J. Declarer should win this with the queen and play ♠A, ruff a spade, ♣A, ♣K, and ruff another spade. If the clubs break or the ♠K comes down in three rounds, he is home; if not, he plays ◊A, diamond ruff, heart finesse, ♡A and another diamond ruff to bring about this position (see next page):

West Duboin	North Hamman	East Bocchi	South Soloway
	1♠	pass	2♣
pass	2◊	pass	3◊
pass	4♣	pass	4♡
pass	4NT	pass	5♣
all pass			

Meckstroth	de Falco	Rodwell	Ferraro
	1♠	pass	2♣
pass	2♡	pass	2♠
pass	3◊	pass	3♡
pass	6♣	all pass	

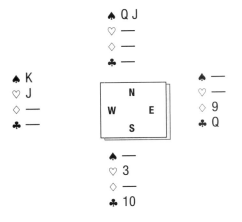

```
              ♠ Q J
              ♡ —
              ◇ —
              ♣ —
 ♠ K                        ♠ —
 ♡ J        ┌────────┐      ♡ —
 ◇ —        │   N    │      ◇ 9
 ♣ —        │ W    E │      ♣ Q
            │   S    │
            └────────┘
              ♠ —
              ♡ 3
              ◇ —
              ♣ 10
```

East's best chance was to hold on to the ◇9, hoping South would try to ruff his heart rather than his last diamond; but if declarer does reach this position he can score his ♣10 *en passant* to make his slam. However, a key part to the story is that Ferraro had explained his partner's bidding as showing 5-2-2-4 distribution. When Meckstroth gave him a favorable diamond lead, he felt under some pressure not to take advantage of the lead lest his opponents call the director and ask for an adjusted score. So he won his ◇Q and cashed the ♣K and ♣A before playing the ♠A and running the ♠Q and going down a trick.

In fact, if West leads the ♡J (as he might well have, had he known that the dummy had a singleton diamond) the play is not so easy. It seems reasonable for declarer to play the ♠A and ruff a spade before cashing the top trumps and taking another spade ruff. Now when the ♠K fails to appear, declarer is in the wrong hand for the diamond finesse and he will go down one. So maybe Ferraro was right. How many times have you heard that — "He played it right, but he was wrong on the hand!" ? Anyway, that was another 11 IMPs for USA 1, who ran out winners by 27 IMPs.

Norway, as the winners of the Round Robin, had the right to pick their quarterfinal opponents, and they selected Indonesia. They started the match with a 5.5-IMP carryover and had built up a lead of 35.5 going into the last session. There were a couple of mishaps in the last few boards, however, and in the end Norway just held on to win by 8.5 IMPs. Brazil took 6 IMPs of carryover into their match against Sweden but quickly built up an 80-IMP lead. Although Sweden came back somewhat to make it a match at least, Brazil were comfortable winners by 30 IMPs.

The other two matches were not short of excitement however, and indeed were to provide two of the most dramatic finishes in the long history of the Bermuda Bowl. USA 1 faced Italy with a carryover of 13.5 IMPs and Poland had, perhaps surprisingly, selected an even match against USA 2 rather than taking on Sweden, against whom they would have started with a slight edge. No doubt they were mindful of Poland's poor record over the years against Swedish teams.

Here are a couple of interesting defensive hands from early in the

USA 2-Poland match. First, a typical Zia opening lead special.

Against 4♣, Zia led a prompt ◇J. Declarer won the ace and played the ♣K, which North won to lead a second diamond, and declarer ran this to Zia's blank queen. Now a spade to North and a diamond ruff resulted in down two, 200 to North-South, and a wry smile from East. Without this lead, declarer can make his contract if he finds out South's distribution is 5-4-2-2 before playing diamonds. This was a gain of 3 IMPs to USA 2 when the Poles made 2♠ for 110 in the other room.

On this next deal, Zia led the ♣5 and Kowalski ducked Rosenberg's jack. Now Michael switched to his singleton diamond, won by the ace. A trump was led next. Zia rose with the ace to give Rosenberg a ruff, and when he exited with a club to the ace, Zia carefully played the ♣3, not a MUD ♣9. See how important this was as the hand developed further. Declarer ran all his winners, hoping to squeeze

```
                 ♠ A 10 8 4 2
                 ♡ A 5
                 ◇ 7 4 3
                 ♣ A 8 5
♠ Q                               ♠ K 7
♡ Q 10 4 3        N               ♡ K 8 7
◇ A 10 8 2    W       E           ◇ K 9 6 5
♣ K 10 7 6        S               ♣ Q J 4 3
                 ♠ J 9 6 5 3
                 ♡ J 9 6 2
                 ◇ Q J
                 ♣ 9 2
```

West Romanski	North Rosenberg	East Kowalski	South Zia
			pass
pass	1♠	pass	2♠
pass	pass	2NT	3♠
3NT	pass	4♣	all pass

```
                 ♠ K J 5 3 2
                 ♡ 4 2
                 ◇ 4
                 ♣ K Q J 8 4
♠ A Q 10 7 4                      ♠ 9
♡ K Q 5           N               ♡ 10 9 7 6 3
◇ Q 9 8       W       E           ◇ A K J 6
♣ 10 6            S               ♣ A 7 2
                 ♠ 8 6
                 ♡ A J 8
                 ◇ 10 7 5 3 2
                 ♣ 9 5 3
```

West Romanski	North Rosenberg	East Kowalski	South Zia
	pass	1♡	pass
1♠	2♣	2◇	3♣
4♡	all pass		

Rosenberg, but Zia pitched two spades, forcing Rosenberg to keep his guarded spade king. Michael knew to pitch his clubs, leaving Zia with the vital ♣9.

"Lucky I didn't lead it!" Zia joked, but the funny thing is that the ♣9 was his correct systemic lead. I guess it just didn't feel right, and when it doesn't feel right, Zia really doesn't care what he's *supposed* to do. When Martel-Stansby picked up 500 defending 3♣ doubled, this was a gain of 12 IMPs to USA 2.

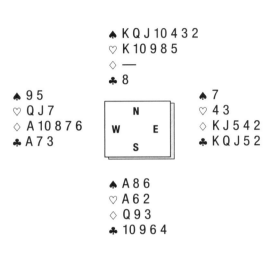

```
                    ♠ K Q J 10 4 3 2
                    ♡ K 10 9 8 5
                    ◇ —
                    ♣ 8
♠ 9 5                                    ♠ 7
♡ Q J 7              N                   ♡ 4 3
◇ A 10 8 7 6     W       E               ◇ K J 5 4 2
♣ A 7 3              S                   ♣ K Q J 5 2
                    ♠ A 8 6
                    ♡ A 6 2
                    ◇ Q 9 3
                    ♣ 10 9 6 4
```

West Meckstroth	North Bocchi	East Rodwell	South Duboin
			1NT
pass	4♠	all pass	

West Ferraro	North Nickell	East de Falco	South Freeman
			pass
pass	4♠	4NT	5♠
5NT	pass	6♣	pass
6◇	6♠	dbl	all pass

Meanwhile USA 1 had got a very lucky break on an early board in their match.

Italy scored 450 North-South which looked to be a good result, especially when Nickell-Freeman got too high. The slam had two sure losers, so it looked as if Italy were going to gain 11 IMPs. The defense took their club trick and declarer needed either a stiff heart honor in the East hand or QJ doubleton somewhere. He hopefully played the ♡A and another heart — and West followed with the queen and jack! He had not spotted the ♡7 in his hand! So Nickell scored up his slam for 13 lucky IMPs.

So after eighty of the ninety-six boards USA 1, the tournament favorites, led Italy by a mere 1.5 IMPs in an epic match and USA 2 led Poland by five. USA 2 had only gained points in one session, where the third pair, Wolfson and Silverman, had played a flawless set before giving some back in the next. The penultimate eight boards turned out to contain two sizable swing boards and one delicate play hand.

Meckwell bid effi-ciently to the top spot, while de Falco's strange 3NT bid with potential weak spots in three suits, result-ed in down one when Soloway led the ♠K and shifted to the ♡Q. Had declarer ducked this, Ham-man would have overtaken to lead a diamond, but de Falco won the heart and could only collect eight tricks: 10 IMPs for USA 1.

```
                ♠ 6 5
                ♡ K J 8 2
                ◇ K Q 7 5 2
                ♣ 10 2
♠ Q 8                        ♠ J 4 3
♡ A 7 6 5 4 3      N         ♡ 9
◇ 8            W       E     ◇ A 4 3
♣ J 9 8 6          S         ♣ A K Q 7 5 4
                ♠ A K 10 9 7 2
                ♡ Q 10
                ◇ J 10 9 6
                ♣ 3
```

West Ferraro	North Hamman	East de Falco	South Soloway
	pass	1◇	1♠
dbl	pass	3NT	all pass

Rodwell	Bocchi	Meckstroth	Duboin
	pass	2♣	2♠
3♡	pass	3♠	pass
4♣	pass	5♣	all pass

In the other match, Stansby-Mar-tel went astray in the auction on the same hand. Kwiecien jumped to 2♠ and made it slightly more awkward for East-West. However, West took a losing position by making a non-forc-ing bid without hav-ing shown his club support, so it was 10 IMPs to Poland.

Stansby	Pszczola	Martel	Kwiecien
		1♣	2♠
dbl	pass	3♣	pass
3♡	all pass		

Jassem	Rosenberg	Tuszynski	Zia
		1♣	1♠
2♡	pass	3♣	pass
4◇	pass	5♣	all pass

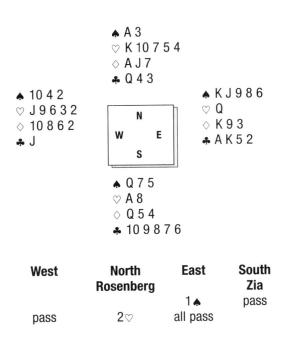

```
              ♠ A 3
              ♡ K 10 7 5 4
              ◇ A J 7
              ♣ Q 4 3
♠ 10 4 2                      ♠ K J 9 8 6
♡ J 9 6 3 2                   ♡ Q
◇ 10 8 6 2        N           ◇ K 9 3
♣ J          W        E       ♣ A K 5 2
                  S
              ♠ Q 7 5
              ♡ A 8
              ◇ Q 5 4
              ♣ 10 9 8 7 6
```

West	North Rosenberg	East	South Zia
		1♠	pass
pass	2♡	all pass	

On this deal, Michael Rosenberg declared 2♡ from the North hand on the lead of the ♣A. The low club continuation was ruffed by West, who continued with a spade, and at this point, declarer studied the position for some time. The VuGraph commentators suggested that he should win the ♠A and lead a spade to East's king. Now if East won, cashed his club and played another spade declarer would be able to win in dummy and play club winners through East, eliminating one of his losers. However when East wins the ♠K he can cash the ♣K and exit with his ♡K, reaching the position shown.

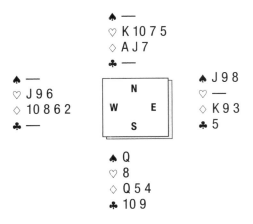

```
              ♠ —
              ♡ K 10 7 5
              ◇ A J 7
              ♣ —
♠ —                          ♠ J 9 8
♡ J 9 6          N           ♡ —
◇ 10 8 6 2   W        E       ◇ K 9 3
♣ —              S            ♣ 5
              ♠ Q
              ♡ 8
              ◇ Q 5 4
              ♣ 10 9
```

Now when declarer leads a black winner, West can ruff in and the defense will still come to a diamond and a heart. In the Closed Room, Martel and Stansby defended 2♡ in exactly this way to score down one. Taking a different line, Rosenberg won the spade switch, and led a heart to dummy before passing the ♡8. Now he was able to put East in with a club to leave this ending:

East cashed the ♠K and played a club and West was left facing an unpleasant choice — he could give up his trump trick or discard and lose the defensive diamond trick. So declarer could not be prevented from making his contract and as is so often the case, Rosenberg proved himself a better analyst than those who could see all four hands! This result was worth four very valuable IMPs to USA 2.

On Board 87, Meckstroth's gamble on 6◇ failed when dummy could not produce a cover for either his trump loser or his spade loser, and that was 12 IMPs to Italy. So now with only eight boards left to play, USA 1 trailed Italy by 1.5 points and USA 2 and Poland were back where they started — exactly even. The tension mounted as the teams began the last hour of play.

```
              ♠ 3
              ♡ K 10 7
              ♢ A J 7
              ♣ —
    ♠ 10            N          ♠ K J 9
    ♡ J 9       W       E      ♡ —
    ♢ 10 8 6 2      S          ♢ K 9 3
    ♣ —                        ♣ 5
              ♠ Q 7
              ♡ —
              ♢ Q 5 4
              ♣ 10 9
```

```
              ♠ J 10 9 7
              ♡ J 3 2
              ♢ J 4
              ♣ 8 6 3 2
    ♠ Q 8 6 5 4        N        ♠ A 2
    ♡ 10 9 7 5 4   W       E    ♡ —
    ♢ 8 2              S        ♢ A Q 10 9 7 6 5
    ♣ 4                         ♣ A K Q J
              ♠ K 3
              ♡ A K A 8 6
              ♢ K 3
              ♣ 10 9 7 5
```

West Ferraro	North Hamman	East de Falco	South Soloway
			1NT
pass	pass	5◇	all pass

Rodwell	Bocchi	Meckstroth	Duboin
			1♡
pass	pass	4NT	pass
5◇	pass	6◇	all pass

The VuGraph auditorium was packed with about a thousand spectators as news filtered through that both USA teams were in trouble and facing possible elimination. In order to have comparisons available from the Closed Room for the VuGraph audience as each hand was played, Boards 95 and 96 had been played first in the Open Room, and would be followed by Boards 81 through 94. The spectators knew at this stage, therefore, that Board 96 had been a flat board in both matches while Board 95 had been a possible partscore swing to both USA teams.

On Board 89, East played 3NT at all four tables. Both USA declarers, Meckstroth and Martel, ducked the first spade and won the second spade in order not to give South the chance to shift to a club. Both declarers now misguessed diamonds and, when the smoke cleared, Meckstroth was down two and Martel three. In the replays, Zia and Soloway were both allowed to hold the second spade. Now they could have defeated the contract if they had found a club shift, regardless of how declarer played the diamonds. However, both players continued spades and then both declarers guessed diamonds correctly. So Italy gained 13 IMPs to increase their lead to 14.5 IMPs and Poland gained 14 IMPs to take the lead over USA 2.

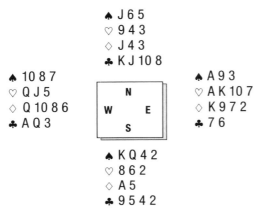

♠ J 6 5
♡ 9 4 3
◇ J 4 3
♣ K J 10 8

♠ 10 8 7
♡ Q J 5
◇ Q 10 8 6
♣ A Q 3

♠ A 9 3
♡ A K 10 7
◇ K 9 7 2
♣ 7 6

♠ K Q 4 2
♡ 8 6 2
◇ A 5
♣ 9 5 4 2

Board 90 was a partscore swing in both matches. The Italians played their 5-2 major fit instead of their 5-3 and lost 6 IMPs to USA 1, who were now down by only 8.5 IMPs. In the other match, playing weak notrumps, Rosenberg opened 1♡ and rebid 1NT showing 15-17. Zia held

♠ J 9 8 7 3   ♡ 8 4   ◇ A 8 2   ♣ 10 8 5

and chose to pass. It could have been the right decision, but not this time; Rosenberg went down two while nine tricks made in spades at the other table; six more to Poland who now led by a comfortable-looking 20 IMPs. At this stage the VuGraph commentators saw the distinct possibility of there being no USA team in the Bermuda Bowl semifinal and were trying to discover the last time this had happened.

Both matches were now very much on the line and the stage was set for the grand finale or as Hamman put it, 'the five o'clock lightning' — when the shadows come down on Yankee Stadium and both teams go out for the last inning with the game tied. These are the times that try men's souls...

On Board 91, Meckwell had an uninterrupted auction to reach the cold slam. At the other table, when Paul Soloway threw a wrench in by way of an opening three diamonds, Guido Ferraro took an overbid with his 3NT call, but despite this, his partner strangely could not find a bid. That was 11 IMPs to USA 1, who had regained the lead and were in front by 2.5 IMPs.

```
                    ♠ 10 9 7 5
                    ♡ A J 9
                    ◇ J 6
                    ♣ 10 8 5 3
♠ Q J 6 4                           ♠ A K 8 3 2
♡ 10 5              ┌─────────┐     ♡ K Q 7 3 2
◇ A 9 7 3          │    N    │     ◇ 5
♣ A K 7           │ W     E │     ♣ J 4
                   │    S    │
                    └─────────┘
                    ♠ —
                    ♡ 8 6 4
                    ◇ K Q 10 8 4 2
                    ♣ Q 9 6 2
```

West Rodwell	North Bocchi	East Meckstroth	South Duboin
			pass
1NT	pass	2♡	pass
3♠	pass	4NT	pass
5♠	pass	6♠	all pass

Ferraro	Hamman	de Falco	Soloway
			3◇
3NT	all pass		

This deal also produced more bad news for USA 2. Perhaps Martel should have made another try, but whoever was to blame, that was another 11-IMP swing to Poland. The Poles now led by 31 IMPs with only five comparisons left, one of which was known to be flat. It looked as if it was all over for USA 2.

West Jassem	North Rosenberg	East Tuszynski	South Zia
			2◇
dbl	3◇	4◇	pass
4♠	pass	4NT	pass
5♠	pass	6♠	all pass

Stansby	Pszczola	Martel	Kwiecien
			2♠[1]
dbl	pass	pass	redbl
pass	3♣	4♣	pass
4♠	all pass		

1. Minor-suit preempt.

```
              ♠ 10 9 8
              ♡ A K 10 7
              ◇ Q 10 6 2
              ♣ J 5
♠ 5 3                        ♠ J 6
♡ Q J 8          N           ♡ 9 6 2
◇ A K J 8 7 5  W   E         ◇ 9 4 3
♣ Q 4            S           ♣ 10 9 6 3 2
              ♠ A K Q 7 4 2
              ♡ 5 4 3
              ◇ —
              ♣ A K 8 7
```

West	North	East	South
Rodwell	Bocchi	Meckstroth	Duboin
1◇	pass	1♠	pass
2◇	pass	pass	3♠
pass	4♠	all pass	

Ferraro	Hamman	de Falco	Soloway
1NT	pass	2♣	dbl
all pass			

On Board 92, in the USA 1-Italy match, Meckstroth was facing a limited opening bid, so he knew there was at least a game on for the opponents and decided to steal their suit. Duboin came in with 3♠ and his partner should surely have found a stronger bid than a simple raise to four — either cuebidding a red suit or raising to 5♠ would seem to do the hand justice.

Meckstroth's tactical 1♠ call helped to save a slam swing against his team, since Hamman-Soloway also found the going difficult after their opponents had started with 1NT. However, at least 2♣ doubled was well defended: Soloway started with two top spades and shifted to a heart. Hamman won and played a club to the king, then the defense cashed two more hearts and played a third heart; when declarer ruffed, South discarded. South now ruffed the first diamond and played another spade and declarer could not avoid the loss of two more tricks: three more IMPs for USA 1 who had stretched their lead to 5.5 IMPs.

Giorgio Duboin

In the other match, on the same hand, we saw the weak 1NT opening by Stansby again making it difficult for North-South to bid constructively — in this case, meaning to get to their slam. On VuGraph, Zia started an improvisation by balancing with a

West	North	East	South
Stansby	**Pszczola**	**Martel**	**Kwiecien**
1NT	pass	pass	4♠
all pass			

West	North	East	South
Jassem	**Rosenberg**	**Tuszynski**	**Zia**
1◇	pass	pass	2◇
pass	3♣	pass	4♠
pass	5♠	pass	6♣
pass	6♡	pass	6♠
all pass			

Michaels 2◇ bid and when Rosenberg made a game try in hearts (3♣), he jumped to four spades showing a very good hand. Now Rosenberg, after a long, long pause, worked out that Zia must hold a game-going hand in spades, and that with the pseudo-Michaels start he had been trying to direct his partner's attention to hearts. Clearly, Michael had the right cards, and he raised to 5♠. Zia bid 6♣, which he meant as natural, and then signed off in 6♠.

The ◇A was led, which declarer ruffed. He decided to play to ruff only one club, and to make his twelfth trick either in hearts or via a double squeeze, and therefore started by playing a heart from hand at Trick 2 and inserting dummy's ♡10. This produced an unlooked-for bonus when it held the trick! Zia quickly scored up 1460 and won 13 IMPs, cutting the margin to eighteen. But surely this was too little, too late? After all, they were running out of boards.

Jacek Pszczola

```
              ♠ K 9
              ♡ Q J 10 9 5 4
              ◇ 9 7
              ♣ A 10 4
♠ Q 10 6 5                      ♠ A J 8 2
♡ A K 6 2        N              ♡ 8 7
◇ 8 3        W       E          ◇ A 10 2
♣ 7 6 3          S              ♣ K Q 8 5
              ♠ 7 4 3
              ♡ 3
              ◇ K Q J 6 5 4
              ♣ J 9 2
```

West	North	East	South
Stansby	Pszczola	Martel	Kwiecien
	1♡	dbl	2◇
2♠	pass	3♠	pass
4♠	all pass		

Jassem	Rosenberg	Tuszynski	Zia
	2♡	dbl	pass
2♠	all pass		

Martel did not like his game so far (with some justification) and on Board 93 essayed a delicate invitational raise which his partner jumped on with his maximum. Eleven tricks were made and when the thin game was avoided in the other room, it was another 11 IMPs to USA 2 who now trailed by only seven. In the other match, Italy stopped in partscore and made plus 200, but Meckwell had a bidding accident — after a Multi 2◇ opening from North, Meckstroth doubled and passed his partner's 2♡ bid. That contract went down a trick and Italy gained seven to retake the lead by 1.5 IMPs.

Now the VuGraph spectators heard the results of Boards 95 and 96, which we had seen played at the beginning of the set. As expected, the last board had been flat in both matches, but on Board 95 both USA teams had earned a partscore swing of 6 IMPs. So going into the very last board, Poland's seemingly invincible lead had been cut to 1 IMP, while once again in a seesaw match USA 1 had their heads in front of Italy by 4.5 IMPs.

On the last board (see top of next page), in USA 1-Italy, de Falco played in 3♣ (as East) on a low trump lead from Soloway. Declarer won and led the ◇J to Hamman's ace. Hamman played a second trump, won by declarer who ruffed his losing diamond before leading a heart from dummy to the king and Soloway's ace. Now a heart to the queen and a third heart promoted a trump trick for South and that was down one. In the replay, after a strong club opening Meckwell settled in 2♠. After the lead of the ♡Q and another heart to the king and ace, South now tried a low spade. Meckstroth put in the jack and then a diamond up secured the contract. USA 1 had gained a further 4 IMPs to win the match by 8.5 IMPs.

USA 2 and Poland, however, were destined to go right down to the wire.

It is hard to blame Pszczola for doubling 2♡, but as a result, his partner found the unfortunate lead of the ♡A which helped declarer along to his nine tricks and plus 110.

On VuGraph, East opened a strong club and Rosenberg was able to enter the auction with a heart overcall. If East had chosen to rebid 2♣ he had a chance to play a club partial, in which case nine tricks would win the match and eight would tie it. However, he decided to show his full values by rebidding 1NT. Now when Zia ventured 2♡, West felt

```
                ♠ 10 6
                ♡ Q J 9 8 5
                ◇ A 9 3 2
                ♣ J 5
♠ A J 7 5 4                      ♠ 8 3
♡ 6 4 3 2          N             ♡ K 10
◇ 8          W         E         ◇ K Q J 4
♣ 7 4 2           S             ♣ A K Q 8 6
                ♠ K Q 9 2
                ♡ A 7
                ◇ 10 7 6 5
                ♣ 10 9 3
```

West Stansby	North Pszczola	East Martel	South Kwiecien
		1♣	pass
1♠	pass	2◇	pass
2♡	dbl	pass	pass
3♣	all pass		

Jassem	Rosenberg	Tuszinski	Zia
		1♣	pass
1◇	1♡	1NT	2♡
3♠	all pass		

he had some catching up to do after his initial negative, and launched into 3♠ which was at least one too many. Making this contract would have won the match for Poland, but it was always hopeless. Declarer only managed seven tricks to give up 5 IMPs and USA 2 had scrambled home by four!

What a finish in both matches. Indeed, USA 1 had won the match by virtue of its 13.5-IMP carryover against Italy, so now you can see the significance of the two slam hands we looked at earlier from their match in the qualifying Round Robin. Had either slam hand gone the other way, the carryover would have been different, and maybe there would have been a different result. On the other hand, maybe USA 1 only picked Italy to play because of that carryover.

Players and spectators alike let out a collective metaphorical breath at this point, more or less emotionally drained. Did any of us have anything left for the rest of the championship?

The Last Act

As required by the rules, the two USA teams faced each other in one semifinal. USA 2 had a 3-IMP carryover in that match, while in the other, Brazil would start 1.3 IMPs ahead of Norway. The local oddsmakers had USA 1 and Norway each about 20-IMP favorites to meet in the final.

Even in a long match, it's important to get off to a good start. I watched Zia-Rosenberg play Nickell-Freeman in the first segment.

```
                  ♠ A 7 5
                  ♡ K Q
                  ◇ K 9 8 5 4
                  ♣ K 4 3
♠ K J 10                        ♠ Q 9 6 4 3 2
♡ 10 7 5 3 2       N            ♡ 6
◇ 3            W       E        ◇ Q 6 2
♣ Q 10 8 5         S            ♣ 9 7 2
                  ♠ 8
                  ♡ A J 9 8 4
                  ◇ A J 10 7
                  ♣ A J 6
```

West Zia	North Freeman	East Rosenberg	South Nickell
			1♡
pass	2◇	pass	3◇
pass	4♠[1]	pass	5♣[2]
pass	5◇	pass	6◇
all pass			

1. Key Card.
2. 1 or 4.

Sometimes it's surprising what you find out when you are actually at the table — things that the hand records will never tell you!

After the 5♣ bid, Zia asked Nick Nickell how many key cards it had shown. At that point, Nick realized he had misbid and raised to slam — no swing. Notice the huge advantage of playing behind screens — the question could be asked and answered without any possibility of unauthorized information for either pair. So no IMPs changed hand on this board after all. There *were* two slam swings in the first session, however, both of which depended on the opening lead.

Both East-West pairs arrived in 6◇ on this deal, which is a pretty reasonable contract. Freeman, however, led the ♣K and when declarer tried to dispose of his club loser quickly, he was able to ruff the third heart. Eventually West lost a club and the ◇K for down one. At the other

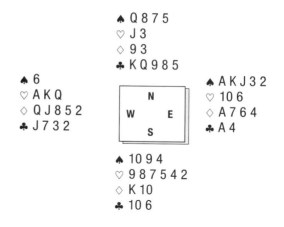

```
              ♠ Q 8 7 5
              ♡ J 3
              ◇ 9 3
              ♣ K Q 9 8 5
♠ 6                              ♠ A K J 3 2
♡ A K Q            N             ♡ 10 6
◇ Q J 8 5 2   W       E          ◇ A 7 6 4
♣ J 7 3 2          S             ♣ A 4
              ♠ 10 9 4
              ♡ 9 8 7 5 4 2
              ◇ K 10
              ♣ 10 6
```

table, Chip Martel led a trump, which allowed declarer to draw trumps before taking his club pitch, so USA 1 gained 14 IMPs. If Martel was unhappy with his lead on this board, unfortunately, worse was to follow.

This time, when a trump would have worked well, Martel made the unlucky choice of the ◇A as his opening lead, which gave declarer his slam. When Zia-Rosenberg sensibly played the hand in game, that was another 11 IMPs to USA 1. The rest of the set went to USA 2, however, and at the end of the session the score was 30–27 for USA 2. By contrast, the Brazil-Norway match was a low-scoring affair, the first sixteen boards ending 16-15 in favor of Norway.

```
              ♠ 7 4 3
              ♡ 4
              ◇ A 10 6 2
              ♣ K 9 7 6 2
♠ 9                              ♠ A K 10 6 5
♡ A K 8 7 5 3 2     N            ♡ Q 6
◇ —            W        E        ◇ K J 8 7 5 4
♣ A J 8 5 3         S            ♣ —
              ♠ Q J 8 2
              ♡ J 10 9
              ◇ Q 9 3
              ♣ Q 10 4
```

West Soloway	North Martel	East Hamman	South Stansby
		1♠	pass
2♡	pass	3◇	pass
3♡	pass	4♣	pass
6♣	pass	6◇	pass
6♡	all pass		

For the second session, USA 2 brought in their third pair, Wolfson-Silverman, who had an excellent set on VuGraph. This board was one of their successes.

```
                  ♠ K 8
                  ♡ J 10 9
                  ◇ A 7 5 2
                  ♣ 10 8 7 4
  ♠ 5                          ♠ A 2
  ♡ A K 4 3 2        N         ♡ Q 7 5
  ◇ K 10 6 4     W     E       ◇ Q J 9 8 3
  ♣ 9 5 3                      ♣ K 6 2
                     S
                  ♠ Q J 10 9 7 6 4 3
                  ♡ 8 6
                  ◇ —
                  ♣ A Q J
```

West	North	East	South
Wolfson	**Hamman**	**Silverman**	**Soloway**
pass	pass	2◇	4♠
5◇	5♠	all pass	

Silverman tried an offbeat 2◇ opening and Wolfson was able to compete to 5◇, setting Hamman a problem he did not need. In fact, 5◇ would only be set one trick but when Hamman tried 5♠, that had to go down a trick. Meckstroth opened the West hand 1♡ and was raised to 2NT by Rodwell. When South's 4♠ preempt came back to Rodwell he was unable to take any further action, and that was the final contract — 12 IMPs to USA 2 who won the set by 55-31 and had a 27-IMP lead. Meanwhile Brazil-Norway stayed tight, with Norway increasing its lead slightly to 42-35.

Could there be an upset in the making? The Nickell squad had looked vulnerable against Italy, while Zia's team was rolling. Would this be Zia's year to win a world title at last? The euphoria was short-lived. The third set proved to be a disaster for Wolfson-Silverman, who each went down in a vulnerable game they should have made, then missed a laydown slam and a good vulnerable game. This was one of their losses.

```
                  ♠ 9 6 3
                  ♡ A K 10 8 7 6
                  ◇ K 10 2
                  ♣ 5
  ♠ K 4                        ♠ Q J 10 2
  ♡ J 9 5 4         N          ♡ 3
  ◇ A 9          W     E       ◇ Q J 7 5 4
  ♣ J 10 8 6 2                 ♣ Q 4 3
                     S
                  ♠ A 8 7 5
                  ♡ Q 2
                  ◇ 8 6 3
                  ♣ A K 9 7
```

Rosenberg made it easy for Meckstroth when he led the ◇Q against North's 4♡; Zia won the ace and continued diamonds. The play was quickly over — ♡Q,

♡A, ♣A, ♣K, club ruff, ♠A, club ruff, claim. In the Brazil-Norway match, both declarers went down when they got the ♠Q lead, won the ace at Trick 1, and subsequently misguessed the play. Jeff Wolfson correctly ducked the spade lead and now the defense switched to diamonds. Declarer won the second diamond with the king and played the ♡Q and ♡A. Now he had reached the same position as Meckstroth and could have ruffed two clubs in hand before exiting a spade but instead he pitched his diamond loser on the ♣K and ruffed a diamond as West threw the ♠K. Now when he played a spade to the ace West could ruff in for down one.

In this session neither Meckwell nor Rosenberg-Zia gave much away but there was carnage at the other table; when the smoke cleared it was a total pickup of 53 IMPs to USA 1 who now led by 112-86. In contrast, little blood was shed in the Brazil-Norway match, Brazil picking up a mere 2 IMPs to trail by 3.7 IMPs at the halfway point.

Zia had an opening lead problem on the first board of the fourth session. Holding

♠ 10 9 8 7   ♡ A 8 3 2   ◇ 10 5   ♣ 10 8 7

he heard his partner open a weak notrump. He bid 2♣, it went 2◇ on his left, pass from partner, 2NT on his right, raised to 3NT on his left. What would you lead?

Zia chose the ♡2, so declarer knocked out the ◇A and wrapped up his game. Obviously, a spade would have been right on the hand — the defense would score three spades and two aces for down one. Rosenberg had passed over Meckstroth's 2◇ overall since he didn't feel that either his hand or his majors were good enough to intro-duce them opposite a

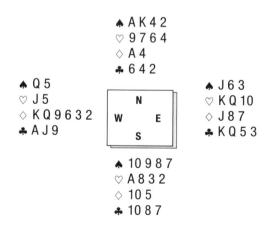

    ♠ A K 4 2
    ♡ 9 7 6 4
    ◇ A 4
    ♣ 6 4 2

♠ Q 5   ♠ J 6 3
♡ J 5   ♡ K Q 10
◇ K Q 9 6 3 2   ◇ J 8 7
♣ A J 9   ♣ K Q 5 3

    ♠ 10 9 8 7
    ♡ A 8 3 2
    ◇ 10 5
    ♣ 10 8 7

partner who might simply be scrambling to avoid a penalty (as he was!). He might have bid 2♠, but he didn't, and Zia might have led a spade, but he didn't. By such small differences are championships decided. This was an 8-IMP swing to USA 1 when Martel-Stansby played the hand in 3◇.

The ninth board of this set produced a swing in both matches.

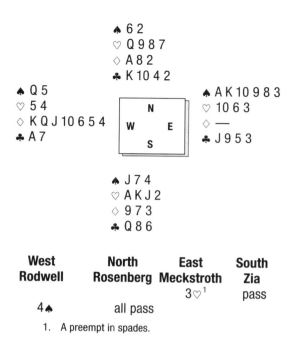

```
                      ♠ 6 2
                      ♡ Q 9 8 7
                      ◇ A 8 2
                      ♣ K 10 4 2
    ♠ Q 5                              ♠ A K 10 9 8 3
    ♡ 5 4            N                 ♡ 10 6 3
    ◇ K Q J 10 6 5 4  W   E            ◇ —
    ♣ A 7                 S            ♣ J 9 5 3
                      ♠ J 7 4
                      ♡ A K J 2
                      ◇ 9 7 3
                      ♣ Q 8 6
```

West Rodwell	North Rosenberg	East Meckstroth	South Zia
		3♡[1]	pass
4♠	all pass		

1. A preempt in spades.

Rosenberg led a low club to the nine, queen and ace. The ◇A was ruffed out, then declarer played the ♠A and a spade to his queen, cashed two diamonds pitching hearts, and led a club up for his tenth winner. Martel-Stansby bid 2♠-3♠ and lost 9 IMPs.

Taking a similar view, Helgemo passed his partner's opening 2♠ and also lost 9 IMPs to Brazil, who reached 4♠. The defense went ♡A, club to the king, ♡K and a second club. This seems the best defense but declarer now ruffed out the ◇A before ruffing a club, dropping the queen, and cashing the ♠Q; at this point he only needed to pitch one heart on a good diamond before ruffing a diamond back to hand to draw trumps and claim.

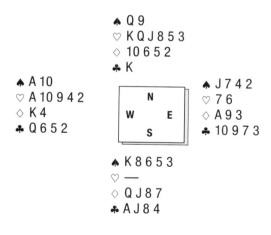

```
                      ♠ Q 9
                      ♡ K Q J 8 5 3
                      ◇ 10 6 5 2
                      ♣ K
    ♠ A 10                            ♠ J 7 4 2
    ♡ A 10 9 4 2     N                ♡ 7 6
    ◇ K 4           W   E             ◇ A 9 3
    ♣ Q 6 5 2           S             ♣ 10 9 7 3
                      ♠ K 8 6 5 3
                      ♡ —
                      ◇ Q J 8 7
                      ♣ A J 8 4
```

The second-last board of the set also caused a stir in the VuGraph theater.

When the hand appeared on the screen, it was obvious that there was potential for serious trouble East-West. Perhaps we would see an auction like this:

In fact, only one of the four tables produced this bidding. Helgemo was the unfortunate player who overcalled 2♡, and he managed to

West	North	East	South
			1♠
2♡	pass	pass	dbl
all pass			

escape for two down when he took three trump tricks along with his three side winners. This was a 9-IMP loss when Brogeland played the North-South cards in 2♠ on a club lead; he crossruffed the first seven tricks but could not manufacture an eighth. On VuGraph, Zia also played 2♠ on a club lead and nobody could help him find a way to make eight tricks either. There was a murmur of surprise when it was learned that in the Closed Room, Paul Soloway had actually made nine tricks in 3♠! Yes, it was Stansby's turn to lead an ace that got ruffed at Trick 1; after ruffing the ♡A, Soloway now had the timing to go back and forth for the first nine tricks and a 6-IMP swing.

In the battle of the Americas, USA 1 had picked up three more IMPs in the session, and now were ahead by 29 IMPs with thirty-two boards left to be played the following day. Meanwhile, Brazil had gained 24 IMPs to lead by 20.3. Both matches were still very much alive.

USA 2 came out punching the next morning and finally got a break on an opening lead.

After Hamman's double, Soloway led a heart and not the killing diamond, and the slam was home. As USA 1 stopped reasonably in 4♠, this was 11 IMPs to USA 2.

```
              ♠ A 9 8
              ♡ A 4 3
              ◇ 6 3
              ♣ K 10 9 8 3
♠ 6 3                        ♠ J 5
♡ Q 8 7 6          N         ♡ K J 9 5 2
◇ K 9 5 4 2    W       E     ◇ Q J 7
♣ 5 4              S         ♣ Q J 6
              ♠ K Q 10 7 4 2
              ♡ 10
              ◇ A 10 8
              ♣ A 7 2
```

West Soloway	North Rosenberg	East Hamman	South Zia
			1♠
pass	2♣	pass	2♠
pass	3♠	pass	4♣
pass	4♡	dbl	4NT
pass	5♡	pass	5NT
pass	6♣	pass	6♠
all pass			

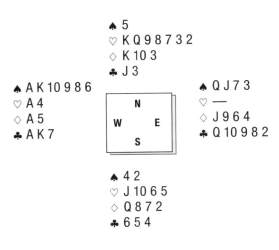

```
               ♠ 5
               ♡ K Q 9 8 7 3 2
               ◇ K 10 3
               ♣ J 3
♠ A K 10 9 8 6          ♠ Q J 7 3
♡ A 4                   ♡ —
◇ A 5                   ◇ J 9 6 4
♣ A K 7                 ♣ Q 10 9 8 2
               ♠ 4 2
               ♡ J 10 6 5
               ◇ Q 8 7 2
               ♣ 6 5 4
```

West	North	East	South
Soloway	**Rosenberg**	**Hamman**	**Zia**
1♣[1]	3♡	dbl	4♡
6♠	all pass		

1. Strong.

Martel	**Meckstroth**	**Stansby**	**Rodwell**
2♣	2♡	3♡	pass
3♠	pass	4♠	pass
4NT	pass	5♣	pass
5◇	pass	6♡	pass
6♠	all pass		

Then came another chance with this hand.

Faced with a barrage of hearts over the strong club, Soloway-Hamman were reduced to guesswork, and stopped at the six-level. Perhaps if Stansby had bid 5♠ showing the trump queen and Martel had followed up with 6♣, they might have reached the grand. As it was, it was another missed opportunity. The Norwegians started 2♣-2♡, 3♣-4♡ and now West just bid 7♣. When Brazil took the save in 7♡, they went down six for 1700. This would have been a gain for Brazil if their teammates had pushed on to the grand slam, but they too stopped in six so it was 6 IMPs to Norway.

Unfortunately for USA 2, on the very next board Martel-Stansby bid another slam which needed good breaks and a guess. The breaks were not good and they went down two along with the Brazilian pair who also tried the slam; both teams lost 11 IMPs.

Another chance for USA 2 went begging on this deal:

Michael Rosenberg and Zia

In the Closed Room, Stansby had an easy run in 3NT from the East hand on the lead of the ♡4; he won the ♡10 and led a club up to the ten, jack and king. In the replay, Zia found the best lead when he started with the ♠7. Hamman had no idea how the spades were because the lead could have been from length or second-highest from three small. He won the ♠9 and played the ◇9 to the queen and the ace. North played a second spade to the king and the ten. Now Hamman played a second

```
              ♠ 8 5 4 3 2
              ♡ 9 8 2
              ◇ A J 3
              ♣ Q 10
♠ A J 6                        ♠ K 9
♡ 10 6            N            ♡ A K Q 3
◇ Q 8 7 6 2   W     E         ◇ 9 4
♣ 7 4 2          S            ♣ A J 9 8 6
              ♠ Q 10 7
              ♡ J 7 5 4
              ◇ K 10 5
              ♣ K 5 3
```

West Soloway	North Rosenberg	East Hamman	South Zia
		1♣	pass
1◇	pass	1♡	pass
2♣	pass	2◇	pass
2♡	pass	2NT	pass
3NT	all pass		

diamond and Rosenberg had his first decision to make. If Zia had a guard in both hearts and clubs it would be safe to let him hold the trick; he would know to clear spades and ensure setting the hand. Not being certain of the position in the round suits however, he overtook Zia's ten with the jack. All he knew from the bidding was that the declarer had shown at least four hearts. Although there was the added inference that Zia might have led a club initially from a decent four-card holding, Rosenberg switched to the ♣10 and when Hamman covered with the jack he was home.

It was unlikely that Hamman held either a solid or a one-loser suit in hearts or clubs (he would surely have cashed the suit or played to set it up before leading his second diamond). Perhaps Hamman's strategy of playing on a suit which would take a lot of work to develop should have suggested that he was looking for some defensive assistance and probably had at least one potential loser in each suit. In that case, it would be reasonable to find the winning switch to a heart as partner could lead clubs safely from his side.

In what was perhaps the pivotal session, USA 2 had had their chances but had failed to get anything back. Indeed, the session score was 20-17 for USA 1, who now led by 32.2 IMPs. The tiny fraction was the result of a director's ruling — a 4NT bid had not been alerted as a spade cuebid, thus depriving Zia of the opportunity to double it for a spade lead. The players all accepted the ruling and the match continued to be played in the intense but friendly manner you would expect from these great players. USA 1 was now playing well, though, and would be hard to catch over the final few boards. Brazil, by contrast, had done little right on these hands, and lost the set by 34-4, giving Norway a lead of 10 IMPs going into the last set.

For the last sixteen boards, I watched Rosenberg-Zia play Meckstroth-Rodwell. On an early board Rosenberg–Zia stayed out of a vulnerable game which required either a two-way guess for a queen or a favorable lead. However, there was no other excitement until towards the end. Over the last six boards Meckwell stayed out of a poor game which happened to make on the lie of the cards, went down in a partscore that could have been made on a different line of play, bid a good slam but missed three other slams, all of which were biddable. In fact two of the slams were bid at both tables in the other match. This was the third, on Board 92.

	♠ 9 5	
	♡ K Q 8 6 3	
	◇ Q 3	
	♣ K 8 7 2	

♠ Q 10 8 7		♠ A K J 6 4 3 2
♡ J 7 4 2	N	♡ —
◇ 10 9 7 4	W E	◇ A J 5 2
♣ 5	S	♣ A 9

	♠ —	
	♡ A 10 9 5	
	◇ K 8 6	
	♣ Q J 10 6 4 3	

West	North	East	South
Rodwell	**Rosenberg**	**Meckstroth**	**Zia**
pass	pass	1♣[1]	2♣[2]
pass	3♡[3]	4♠	4NT
pass	5♣	dbl	5♡
pass	pass	5♠	6♡
pass	pass	dbl	all pass

1 Strong.
2. Alerted wrongly to Rodwell as two-way but really natural
3. Fit-showing jump.

Zia's 2♣ was explained by Rosenberg to Rodwell as natural but alerted by Zia to Meckstroth as showing either clubs or diamonds. Over Rosenberg's fit jump, Meckstroth bid what he thought he could make and Zia, knowing he needed a swing, bid 6♡ in the hope of a miracle make. Meckstroth made a disciplined double and led a top spade. Now Rosenberg was unable to avoid a trump loser as well as two aces and had to go down two for 500. However, this was a potential gain of 11 IMPs if Martel-Stansby could bid and make 6♠. Meckwell reserved their rights in case Rodwell had been affected in the bidding by the misexplanation.

Timing is everything — as in life, so in bridge. In the other room, with his partner unfortunately holding a classic Culbertson or Acol strong two-bid in spades, Stansby decided the time in

West	North	East	South
Stansby	**Hamman**	**Martel**	**Soloway**
1♠	pass	2NT¹	pass
pass	3♡	4♠	5♡
pass	pass	dbl	all pass

1. Jacoby.

the match had come to make his move and he psyched 1♠ first in hand. Since he could make 4♠ in his own hand, Martel was not too happy when Stansby passed out his forcing 2NT, but with the psyche exposed Hamman backed in with 3♡, and a relieved Martel bid 4♠. Now when Soloway bid 5♡ and this came back to him, Martel chose to double, but wild horses were not extracting another call from his partner.

Martel led the ♠A, which Hamman ruffed to lead the ♡10 to the king. Seeing the bad trump break, he now tried the ◇Q which went to the ace and the ten. Martel continued with a diamond, won in dummy with the king, and now a club to the king was ducked. Another club went to the ace and this was the last chance for the defense to promote a trump trick by playing a second spade. But Martel played a diamond at this point and Hamman could ruff and draw trumps for plus 850 to go with plus 500 in the other room or 16 IMPs. Effectively, 27 IMPs had swung on this one board (lose 16 instead of winning 11), and there was now no way back for USA 2. Even if Stansby-Martel had had perfect results for the rest of the session, they could no longer win the match. In fact they had two further slam disasters, which served to inflate the final margin of defeat to 92 IMPs.

Chip Martel

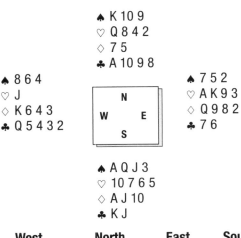

```
                    ♠ K 10 9
                    ♡ Q 8 4 2
                    ◇ 7 5
                    ♣ A 10 9 8
   ♠ 8 6 4                        ♠ 7 5 2
   ♡ J                            ♡ A K 9 3
   ◇ K 6 4 3                      ◇ Q 9 8 2
   ♣ Q 5 4 3 2                    ♣ 7 6
                    ♠ A Q J 3
                    ♡ 10 7 6 5
                    ◇ A J 10
                    ♣ K J
```

West	North	East	South
Rodwell	**Rosenberg**	**Meckstroth**	**Zia**
pass	pass	pass	1♣
pass	1♡	pass	1NT
pass	3NT	all pass	

Stansby	**Hamman**	**Martel**	**Soloway**
pass	pass	pass	1NT
pass	2♣	pass	2♡
pass	3♡	pass	3♠
pass	4♡	dbl	all pass

Looking back, Michael Rosenberg felt the match finally turned against his team on this hand, the fourth board of the last set.

Zia did well to suppress his heart support, and the best contract was reached; on a club lead he made a quiet ten tricks for plus 630. In the other room, Soloway was not happy with the texture of his hearts and hoped Hamman could bid 3NT, but he in turn was worried about diamonds. Martel took a piece of 4♡ and Stansby led a club. Soloway could not have been thrilled at his prospects but won the jack and played three rounds of spades, the ♣K, and a fourth spade, throwing a diamond when Stansby ruffed. Stansby switched to a diamond but Soloway won the ace and led back the ◇J, which was covered by the king, and ruffed in dummy. Now he led the ♣A and the defense was helpless. Martel pitched his diamond as did Soloway. Declarer now simply ruffed a club in hand and led a heart to the queen, making his ten tricks for a very fortunate plus 790 and a 4-IMP gain instead of a 13-IMP loss had it gone down. Stansby-Martel clearly felt some obligation to try to get this result back, and this may explain some of what happened later.

Meanwhile, in the other match, Norway picked up a 6-IMP swing on Board 92 by bidding and making 6♠ while Brazil was doubled in 5♠ making six. But Brazil had also been presented with a gift 11-IMP swing when Helgemo and Austberg had a strange system blip and missed an easy vulnerable game. With Norway ahead by 2 IMPs, this hand was to decide the match:

Against Branco's notrump game, Furunes made the unfortunate choice of the ♡K as his opening lead. Branco won in dummy, played the ♣K which was ducked, and continued with a second club which went to the ace. Helness returned a low spade. Worried that West would win this to clear hearts, Branco rose with the ace to play a low diamond. When West played low he could either cash his club winners and exit a diamond or just take one more club winner and play a diamond, whichever he pleased, to score up his game. Plus 400

```
                  ♠ 10 9 5 2
                  ♡ A
                  ◇ J 6
                  ♣ K Q J 9 8 6
♠ 3                            ♠ K Q J 8 7 6
♡ K J 10 9 6 4     N           ♡ 8
◇ A 9 7         W     E        ◇ 5 4 3
♣ 5 3 2            S           ♣ A 10 4
                  ♠ A 4
                  ♡ Q 7 5 3 2
                  ◇ K Q 10 8 2
                  ♣ 7
```

West Furunes	North Chagas	East Helness	South Branco
2♡	3♣	pass	3◇
pass	3♠	pass	3NT
all pass			

Campos	Austberg	Villas Boas	Helgemo
2♡	dbl	pass	3♡
pass	3NT	dbl	4◇
dbl	all pass		

was a huge result for Brazil, since West could have defeated the game by rising with the ace on the first round of diamonds and playing a second round; this would have broken declarer's communications after the clubs were cashed.

When North reached 3NT in the replay, Villas Boas doubled for Brazil. On the lead of the ♠K, the play in this contract would have been interesting. If declarer wins the ♠A and leads a club, East can win, cash his two spade winners and play a heart to set up the fifth defensive trick. If declarer leads a diamond at Trick 2 the defense must duck, take the first club, cash one high spade and play a heart. Now when declarer runs the clubs, his own hand gets squeezed in hearts and diamonds. But it was all academic because Helgemo ran to 4◇ and went for 500 when Brazil found the double. So Brazil gained 14 IMPs on this board — and their final margin of victory was twelve.

So after almost two weeks of preliminaries, we were down to the last two teams. The final would be contested by USA 1, the pre-tournament favorites, and Brazil. After all the excitement of the quarterfinals and the semifinals, there was a danger that the final might prove to be an anticlimax, especially if USA 1 got off to a quick start. As a result of their Round Robin match against Brazil, they were already sporting a 24-IMP carryover.

In fact, the first two sets were close, with USA 1 gaining only 13 IMPs, but they began to pull away with another 25 IMPs in the third. There followed seventeen in the fourth, a huge eighty-seven in the fifth, and fifty-eight more in the sixth. If this had been a boxing match, the referee would have stopped the contest by this point — with sixty-four boards left to play, USA 1 led by a staggering 224 IMPs. Although the match was long gone for Brazil, they went through the motions of playing out the last four sets, managing to reduce the margin by 6 IMPs.

What happened? Perhaps fatigue, perhaps just a let-down after a nerve-racking semifinal against Norway? Who knows? After all, the USA team had also survived two tough matches to reach the final, and they showed no signs of faltering. Firing on all cylinders, the Nickell team did everything right, while unfortunately Brazil seemed to go wrong whenever they had a decision to make. At one stage, Chagas, arguably one of the world's best players, went down in a routine contract any club player would have made — surely the result of fatigue, lack of concentration, or both. The Brazilians also had a bidding misunderstanding on the deal shown.

	North	
	♠ 6 5 2 ♡ 10 8 7 2 ◇ 10 6 4 2 ♣ 10 2	
West ♠ A ♡ 5 ◇ K Q J 9 8 7 3 ♣ A J 7 5	N / W E / S	**East** ♠ K J 3 ♡ K J 6 4 3 ◇ A 5 ♣ Q 9 4
	♠ Q 10 9 8 7 4 ♡ A Q 9 ◇ — ♣ K 8 6 3	

West	North	East	South
Campos	**Meckstroth**	**Villas Boas**	**Rodwell**
		1♡	2♠
3◇	pass	3NT	pass
4◇	all pass		

Soloway	**Chagas**	**Hamman**	**Branco**
		1NT	2♠
6◇	pass	pass	dbl
all pass			

In the Open Room Villas Boas passed his partner's forcing 4◇ bid and when Meckstroth led the ♣10, that was twelve tricks.

In the Closed Room, rather than get involved in a tortuous auction, Soloway took a shot at what he thought he could make

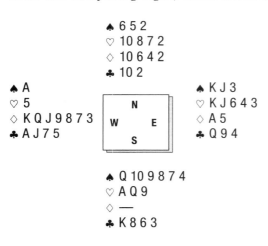

Eric Rodwell

and Branco doubled for a non-spade lead. Chagas led the ♡2 and Branco won the queen. With no attractive return, Branco tried to cash the ♡A, giving Soloway his contract with the aid of the club finesse. However, it is unlikely that this play made any difference. Had Branco returned a spade to Soloway's blank ace, Paul would have discovered how the diamonds lay and taken a club pitch on the ♠K. Now he would have guessed that the club length lay with South and run the ♣Q — so with the ♣10 falling doubleton he would have scored up his doubled slam anyway.

Eric Rodwell had an opportunity for a brilliancy on this next hand:

Here you see another example of Meckwell's aggressive bidding style in the game zone. Branco led the ♣K which declarer ruffed to lead a diamond to dummy and a spade to his queen, which held. He played a second spade to East's jack, and the club return was ruffed. Rodwell played a spade to Branco's ace and, when Branco played a diamond, he rose with the ace dropping the queen, crossed back to the ◇8 and led a heart towards dummy. Now

	♠ 5 4	
	♡ 10 6 3	
	◇ A K 7 2	
	♣ 10 7 6 5	

♠ A 10 3		♠ J 7
♡ J 9 8 4		♡ Q 5
◇ 6 5 4 3		◇ Q 9
♣ K 3		♣ A Q J 9 8 4 2

	♠ K Q 9 8 6 2	
	♡ A K 7 2	
	◇ J 10 8	
	♣ —	

West	North	East	South
Branco	Meckstroth	Chagas	Rodwell
pass	pass	1♣	1♠
dbl	pass	2♣	2♠
3♣	3♠	pass	4♠
all pass			

if West had held the ♡QJ or if the hearts had been 3-3 (although this was unlikely on the bidding) he would have made the hand. As it was, the defense came to their two heart tricks for down one.

However, Rodwell could have cashed the ◇A before playing the third trump, then returned to his ◇8. This would have been the position:

When South exits with a trump, West cannot lead a diamond to the good ♢7 in dummy, so he has to get out with the ♡9 to the ten, queen and king. Now South can lead a low heart towards the six, and when West wins he is endplayed. All very pretty, but Chagas could have thwarted this very stylish line of play by play

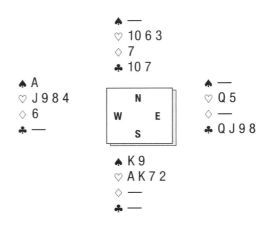

```
            ♠ —
            ♡ 10 6 3
            ♢ 7
            ♣ 10 7
♠ A                      ♠ —
♡ J 9 8 4      N         ♡ Q 5
♢ 6         W     E      ♢ —
♣ —              S       ♣ Q J 9 8
            ♠ K 9
            ♡ A K 7 2
            ♢ —
            ♣ —
```

ing the ♠J on the first round of trumps. Branco would have been able to take both the ♠A and ♠10 before getting out a diamond. Meanwhile Chagas' ♠7 stops declarer both from taking the three diamonds before exiting in trumps (as Chagas can ruff) and from trying to ruff a heart in dummy as the ♠7 beats dummy's spots. As an aside, it is often right on defense to play your jack from a holding like Jx even if you don't see why it's going to help at the time.

Although they had a big fright in the quarterfinal against Italy and were perhaps lucky to survive, nobody could deny that the Nickell team were the best team at Bermuda 2000. With two World Championships and a silver medal in the last three years, they have substantially augmented their reputation as being not only the best team in the USA but the best in the world. If they can sometime add the Olympiad title as well, there will be few to argue their ranking.

The win in the final was the largest winning margin in the history of the Bermuda Bowl — a result which contrasted dramatically with the Venice Cup, where the Dutch women edged out USA by one half of an IMP. In that match, if USA had scored one more trick, as they could have done on a number of hands in the last session, it would have changed the result. In addition, they surely regretted taking a slow play penalty, which proved to be the difference between winning and losing.

Afterword

At the top of the world, there is so little to choose among the very best players and teams that the tiniest slip can mean victory or defeat; and inevitably, Lady Luck has her part to play as well. In the long run, the best teams will win, most of the time; but on any given day — who knows? Perhaps in the end that's what keeps us all coming back to the table — even the best in the world can be beaten, and maybe next time will be our turn to do it. Bridge is not an exact science; luck, skill, judgement all play their part, and to some extent that's what makes it the fascinating game that it is. There are very few sports where you can take on a world champion, and just occasionally, come out on top.

In this book, by recounting some of my own experiences as a player and a bridge journalist, I've tried to put you at the table with the best players of our time, and give you a taste of what the game can be like at the highest levels. I hope you've enjoyed the experience, and will be inspired to get out there and compete with the best, because on any given day, you never know.

See you at the table!

More Bridge Titles from Master Point Press

Around the World in 80 Hands by Zia Mahmood with David Burn
256pp., PB Can $22.95 US $16.95

A Study in Silver *A second collection of bridge stories* by David Silver
128pp., PB Can $12.95 US$ 9.95

Bridge the Silver Way by David Silver and Tim Bourke
192pp., PB Can $19.95 US $14.95

Bridge: 25 Ways to Compete in the Bidding
by Barbara Seagram and Marc Smith (Available October 2000)
192pp., PB Can $1995 US $15.95

Bridge, Zia... and me by Michael Rosenberg (foreword by Zia Mahmood)
192pp., PB Can $19.95 US $15.95

Classic Kantar *A collection of bridge humor* by Eddie Kantar
192pp., PB Can $19.95 US $14.95

Competitive Bidding in the 21st Century by Marshall Miles
254pp.,PB Can. $22.95 US. $16.95

Countdown to Winning Bridge by Tim Bourke and Marc Smith
92pp., PB Can $19.95 US $14.95

Easier Done Than Said *Brilliancy at the Bridge Table*
by Prakash K. Paranjape
128pp., PB Can $15.95 US $12.95

For Love or Money *The Life of a Bridge Journalist*
by Mark Horton and Brian Senior (Foreword by Omar Sharif)
189pp., PB Can $22.95 US $16.95

I Shot my Bridge Partner by Matthew Granovetter
384pp., PB Can $19.95 US $14.95

Murder at the Bridge Table by Matthew Granovetter
320pp., PB Can $19.95 US $14.95

Partnership Bidding *A Workbook* by Mary Paul
96pp., PB Can $9.95 US $7.95

Playing With The Bridge Legends by Barnet Shenkin
(foreword by Zia and Michael Rosenberg) **available October, 2000**
192pp., PB Can $22.95 US $16.95

Saints and Sinners: *The St. Titus Bridge Challenge*
by David Bird & Tim Bourke
192pp., PB Can $19.95 US $14.95

Tales out of School *'Bridge 101' and other stories* by David Silver
(foreword by Dorothy Hayden Truscott)
128pp., PB   Can $ 12.95   US $9.95

The Bridge Player's Bedside Book edited by Tony Forrester
256pp., HC   Can $27.95   US $19.95

The Complete Book of BOLS Bridge Tips edited by Sally Brock
176pp., PB (photographs) Can $24.95   US$17.95

There Must Be A Way*... 52 challenging bridge hands*
by Andrew Diosy (foreword by Eddie Kantar)
96pp., PB $9.95 US & Can.

You Have to See This*... 52 more challenging bridge problems*
by Andrew Diosy and Linda Lee
96pp., PB   Can $12.95   US $9.95

World Class — *Conversations with the Bridge Masters* by Marc Smith
288pp., PB (photographs)   Can $24.95   US $17.95

For more information
visit our Web site at
www.masterpointpress.com
or call
(416) 781-0351